The Complete Guide to Role-Playing Games

The Complete Guide to

Role-Playing Games

RICK SWAN

St. Martin's Press • New York

Design by Judy Dannecker

Library of Congress Cataloging-in-Publication Data

Swan, Rick.
    The complete guide to role-playing games / Rick Swan.
      p.   cm.
    ISBN 0-312-05060-7
    1. Fantasy games.   I. Title.
    GV1469.6.S93 1990
    793.93—dc20   90-37270
                                                    CIP

First Edition: November 1990

10 9 8 7 6 5 4 3 2 1

Contents
. . . .

The Complete Guide to Role-Playing Games

Introduction

....

It used to be easy.

Back in the dark ages of role-playing, there was only one choice. The year was 1974, and the game, of course, was Dungeons and Dragons. Originally intended as a fantasy supplement for a medieval wargame, D&D immediately attracted large numbers of curious players and soon exploded into a full-fledged phenomenon, selling thousands of copies within its first few years to fans around the world.

The rise of Dungeons and Dragons wasn't lost on the rest of the game industry. No longer a specialty item, role-playing quickly became an established hobby, and it remains so today. Millions of people regularly play the games, role-playing conventions held throughout the country attract legions of rabid fans, and the market continues to be flooded with new products.

But as the hobby continues to grow, so does confusion for the consumer. Dozens and dozens of role-playing games have been published in the wake of Dungeons and Dragons, along with hundreds of supplements, accessories, and expansion sets. Veteran players now face a baffling variety of products—how do they separate the good from the bad? And where do newcomers begin?

You hold the answer in your hands. *The Complete Guide to Role-Playing Games* is intended to serve as both a buyer's guide for the novice and a critical reference for the experienced player. It includes reviews of virtually every role-playing game available as of spring 1990, rating them for complexity and overall value and examining their best and worst features. It tells which supplements are recommended and which ones you can live without. For beginners, there are tips on how to get started, how to navigate complicated rules, and suggestions for preparing adventures. For experienced players, there's plenty of information to help with your next purchase.

Whether you've yet to invest in your first game or you're a role-playing veteran from the early days of D&D, I hope this book helps you make some informed choices. The good, the bad, and the awful—it's all here. Welcome to the world's most fascinating hobby.

Part I
How Many Pages of Rules Was That?

Want to drive a role-player crazy? Ask him to describe his game. Ask him why there's no board. Ask him why there are so many rules and why it's so hard to learn, and why it takes forever to finish, and why there aren't any winners. Just watch him stammer.

Over the years I've done a fair amount of stammering myself trying to explain this stuff. It finally dawned on me that it's impossible to define role-playing in terms of conventional games, because role-playing games aren't really games at all. A game is competitive; role-playing has no winners or losers. A game has strict rules; role-playing rules exist only as general guidelines. A game has a rigid structure, a definite beginning and a definite ending; a role-playing game can continue indefinitely.

Actually, role-playing has a lot more in common with novels than it does with games. Just as a good novel takes readers to places they've never imagined and enables them to experience incredible adventures and live the lives of colorful heroes, so does a good role-playing game. A role-playing game is, in fact, an improvised novel in which all the participants serve as authors. The results can be as vivid and memorable as those of the best books in anyone's library.

Of course, learning a role-playing game is hardly as easy as reading a novel. Most game designers are former hobbyists, and they tend to be better players than writers. They're fond of long-winded, excruciatingly detailed explanations of situations that might occur once in a decade of play, and they love jargon—why call them "dice" when you can call them "random number generators"?

A glossary at the end of this book translates some of the most commonly used role-playing terms into regular English; readers are invited to peruse them at their leisure. But before we go any further, let's define a few of them here:

First, the *referee*. The referee serves as the impartial judge of a role-playing game, the person who allegedly has read all of the rules and is responsible for adjudicating the results of all those random number generators. More important, he's the person who controls the events of the story. Most games use a different name for the referee—he's called the Keeper in Call of Cthulhu and the Dungeon Master in Dungeons and Dragons—but for consistency's sake, he's called the referee throughout this book.

Next, the *players*. These are all the participants in a role-playing game other than the referee. Players usually work as a team. Their only job is to control their *player-characters*. The referee does everything else.

Player-characters, also referred to as *PCs*, are the imaginary characters controlled by the players. Don't confuse players with PCs—a PC exists only on paper and in the player's head; the player is the person sitting in the chair.

Finally, the *adventure*. This is the story in which the PCs are participating and that they are creating with the guidance of the referee. Role-players sometimes refer to adventures as *scenarios*; a series of linked adventures is called a *campaign*.

Now let's look at how a typical role-playing session actually works.

Rick, Amy, Lindsey, and Allison have gathered for a game of Dungeons and Dragons. Rick is the referee—he knows the rules and has prepared an adventure involving the quest for a magic jewel in a haunted castle. He's worked out the general details of the plot and even has prepared a rough map showing all of the rooms of the castle and what's inside each one.

Amy, Lindsey, and Allison are the players. They'll be working together as a team. Since the game hasn't yet begun, they have no idea what the adventure is about. Each has chosen a player-character; Amy's PC is a wizard named Blackskull, Lindsey's is an elf named Spud, and Allison has chosen a dwarf PC named Zelda Pinwheel. Each has a piece of paper describing her character's Strength, Intelligence, Dexterity, and various other attributes. All attributes have a numerical rating: the higher the rating, the better the attribute. For instance, Spud's strength is rated at 6, while Zelda Pinwheel's strength is 10; therefore, we know that Zelda is considerably stronger than Spud. Rick will use these ratings during the game to help decide what the PCs can and cannot do.

Rick begins by telling the players that all of their characters have been ordered by the king to investigate an abandoned castle on the outskirts of their village. Their mission: to retrieve a magic jewel hidden somewhere inside. Rick asks the players what they want their characters to do. Amy, Allison, and Lindsey briefly discuss their options, then announce that their characters will walk to the castle after the sun has set.

Rick tells them their trip to the castle is uneventful, then describes the castle in detail—crumbling stone walls, boarded-up windows, a heavy front door, a bat circling overhead. Rick asks them what their characters are doing now. Allison, getting into the spirit of the game, says that Zelda Pinwheel is nervous and refuses to go forward. Amy, speaking for Blackskull, warns Zelda that if they don't fulfill the quest, the king might throw them in prison.

Lindsey says that Spud is listening at the door, and asks Rick if she hears anything. Rick says she hears nothing. (As the referee, Rick knows every detail of the castle. He knows, for instance, that the bat circling overhead is really a vampire. If any of the PCs had disturbed the bat, Rick would've had the vampire attack them. But because they didn't, Rick decides that the bat will stay out of sight for the time being.)

Lindsey says that Spud will attempt to pry open the front door. Rick decides that because the door is heavy, Spud's attempt won't succeed automatically. He tells Lindsey that if she can roll Spud's strength rating or less on a single toss of a twenty-sided die, the door will open. Lindsey throws the die, the result is 4. Because Spud's strength rating is 6, Rick declares that the door creaks open.

Rick says that the interior of the castle is musty and dark—what will the PCs do now? Lindsey says that Spud will light a torch and go in first. Amy and Allison announce that Blackskull and Zelda are right behind Spud. Rick says that the bat follows them in, then vanishes in the shadows. Lindsey, Amy, and Allison are beginning to get nervous.

And on it goes. The PCs will continue to explore the castle, and Rick will continue to tell the players what their characters see and hear. Depending on the decisions of the players, the PCs may or may not encounter the vampire. They may or may not find the jewel that Rick knows is guarded by an ailing dragon deep beneath the castle. (Rick also knows that if they find the secret cure hidden in the upstairs bedroom and give it to the dragon, the grateful beast will present them with the jewel they're seeking.)

Now let's see if we can answer all those annoying questions that begin, "If this is supposed to be a game . . .

". . . *why isn't there a board?*" Because role-playing is mostly verbal. In the preceding example, Zelda, Blackskull, and Spud exist only in the players' minds, as do the castle, the creaking door, and the bat.

". . . *why aren't there any winners?*" Because just as with a novel, the fun of role-playing is seeing how the story develops and what happens to the characters. If a PC dies (the vampire eats Spud), the player simply uses another one (Lindsey brings in Bernie, Spud's uncle). Because the players function as a team, they all win or lose together (if the PCs find the jewel, the king gives them a fortune in gold; if they fail to find the jewel, the king throws them in jail, and the players will have to use new PCs next time out).

". . . *why does it take so long to play?*" It doesn't, necessarily. Some adventures are like short stories and can be completed in a single session. Others are like soap operas; they can continue indefinitely, with the same PCs—or their successors—participating in an endless series of episodes.

"*. . . why are there so many rules?*" Because game designers try to include rules for every conceivable action a PC might attempt. If a PC wants to swim, there may be rules to tell him how long he can swim, how much weight he can carry, and how fast he can go. If he wants to fly, there may be a lengthy section describing magical flying spells. If he wants to throw a rock at a dragon, there may be rules to calculate his precise chance of hitting it. Depending on the fanaticism of the designer, game rules can be mercifully brief (". . . throw a six-sided die, and on a result of 5, the PC hits the dragon.") or excruciatingly detailed (". . . calculate the distance between the PC and the dragon in meters, add the weight of the rock, and divide the result by the PC's rating for rock-hurling . . .").

"*. . . why is it so hard to learn?*" For the players, it isn't. If a newcomer joins an ongoing role-playing group, he should be able to pick up the basics in a few minutes. For the referee, it's admittedly a different story, but it's still easier than it looks.

WHAT THE REFEREE NEEDS TO KNOW
....

A typical role-playing rulebook is as thick as a telephone directory and contains as many charts as the tax code. There are pages upon pages of dense text, convoluted formulas, and confusing terminology. It doesn't look like a game—it looks like a college text. Does the referee really have to learn it all?

Absolutely, unequivocally, no way. It isn't necessary for the referee to memorize the rules—he doesn't even have to read them all. Role-playing, remember, is not about competition, and if competition isn't important, then exact adjudication of the players' actions isn't either. The referee's primary responsibility is to provide his players with an entertaining, exciting adventure, and to that end, the elements of good storytelling far outweigh the importance of knowing all the rules.

In fact, there are only two rules that count—call them the Golden Rules of Role-Playing:

- Rule Number One: *The referee can make up anything he wants.*

• Rule Number Two: *The referee's word is law.*

Unlike the judge of a regular game, a role-playing referee is not bound by written rules. The rulebook should be considered a collection of suggestions; the referee can use the ones he likes, simplify the ones he thinks are too complicated, and eliminate the ones he thinks are stupid. Though fair play obligates the referee to inform the players of any radical departures from a game's accepted conventions—for instance, if he's using a different combat system or has decided that magic spells work only during a full moon—the referee enjoys unlimited freedom to improvise once the game begins. So long as he's consistent and impartial and adheres to the spirit of the game, players are obligated to accept his decisions without question.

It's fair to ask, then, why game designers go to the trouble of including all those meticulously detailed rules if referees are going to ignore them anyway. The reason is simple: Role-playing games are designed to accommodate vastly different styles of play. Beginning referees who feel uncomfortable with improvisation can take comfort in having all decisions made for them somewhere in the rules; as they gain confidence, they'll rely less on the written rules and more on their own imaginations. There are some referees—and many players—who enjoy playing strictly by the book, and take pride in knowing how to calculate the velocity of a spear thrown on the moon to the last decimal point. And then there are people like me, who can barely remember the title of the game we're playing, let alone how to calculate spear velocity to any decimal point—we tend to rely entirely on improvisation.

A few years ago I judged a championship Advanced Dungeons and Dragons tournament at a major game convention. These were hardcore players—the decimal-point variety—who played for blood. When I showed up, I discovered I'd forgotten all my rulebooks and notes in my hotel room. Also, the batteries were dead in the electronic gadget I use instead of dice to generate random numbers. For the entire tournament, I made everything up as I went along, including the results of my "dice rolls." If people knew I was improvising, they didn't say anything, because they were all having a good time; the adventure was exciting, and I was fair and impartial throughout. I don't recommend this approach for first-time referees, but with practice, anybody can do it.

Until they reach the point where they can abandon the rulebook altogether, referees are advised to forget about memorizing the details and instead to concentrate on three areas: setting, characters, and combat.

First and foremost, a referee needs to become thoroughly familiar with the genre of the game and the specific *setting* in which the adventure takes place. The cultural, technological, historical, and ecological details of a role-playing environment are the actual "rules" of the game that neither the referee nor the players should be allowed to violate. If it's a science-fiction world, the referee needs to know how space travel operates, the relationship between humans and aliens, and which planets have been colonized. If it's fantasy world, he needs to know how magic works, if elves exist, what dragons are like, and where the king lives. How does the government function? The economy? How hard is it to buy a horse, build a robot, find a library? Most of the necessary background information should be included in the rulebook. Ambitious referees can supplement this information with history texts, encyclopedias, and role-playing sourcebooks. Lazy referees can pick a movie or a novel with a similar setting and use it as a reference.

The referee needs to understand how to create *player-characters*. Specifically, he needs to know how to determine ratings for their attributes and skills, and how the ratings function in the context of the game. Usually the referee leads his players through the character-creation rules at the beginning of a game so everyone can learn them together, but it's a good idea for the referee to look them over in advance, possibly creating a practice character of his own to see how everything works.

Combat situations typically involve the game's most difficult rules. But though it's necessary for the referee to understand how to resolve combat, it isn't necessary for him to digest all the details. Combat follows a strict sequence of steps; look for this section in the rulebook, and read it until you understand what the authors are talking about. It's standard for a combat routine to comprise a series of rounds; at the beginning of each round, the referee describes the current situation (the dragon is baring its fangs at the PCs), then the players declare what their PCs are attempting to do (Spud will lunge at the dragon with her sword, Blackskull will cast a fireball spell, and Zelda will hide behind a tree). Players whose PCs are attacking then roll dice to see if the attacks are successful. It's up to the referee to interpret the dice-rolls, determine the actions of the PCs' opponents, assess the damage, and describe the results. There are usually pages and pages of rules to help him accomplish all this.

But as long as the results are reasonable and fair, the referee doesn't necessarily have to worry about the fine points of the combat rules. For instance, let's assume that in the previous example, it's a general rule that the higher the attack roll, the more likely the attack will succeed. Spud's roll is a measly 2, Blackskull's is an outstanding 19. It seems reasonable that Spud's lunge misses completely and that Blackskull's fireball scores a direct hit. The referee can fine-tune the results as much as he likes; the rules may state that because the dragon was fifty yards away, Blackskull's attack roll should be reduced by 10, meaning that the fireball merely singed the top of the dragon's head. Or maybe it didn't. Remember the Golden Rules: the referee's word is law, and he can make up anything he wants.

I don't advocate ignoring the combat rules entirely. But I'll point out that the referee computes his results in private, and his methodology really isn't any of the players' concern. As long as his rulings are fair and consistent, and the encounters are exciting, it's unlikely that players will complain too much.

If the referee thoroughly understands the game setting and has a handle on the character-creation and combat rules, he need only concern himself with where to find everything else in the rulebook. He doesn't have to read it all—he just needs to know how to use the contents page and the index. Then when Amy wonders how Blackskull's empty stomach affects his chance of casting a fireball, the referee can look it up. Or, of course, he can make it up.

HOW TO PREPARE AN ADVENTURE
....

The hardest part of the referee's job isn't digesting the rulebook, it's preparing an adventure. A role-playing adventure should be as richly textured and solidly plotted as a novel. Not surprisingly, good adventures are just as rare as good novels, but there are steps a referee can take to maximize the odds of preparing an enjoyable adventure.

First, the referee must decide whether to use a published adventure or write one of his own. Writing role-playing material is an art form in itself, and even the pros tend to miss a lot more than they hit. Most referees are better off sticking with published adventures, at least until they get the hang of what goes into a good one.

It's difficult to run a published adventure without preparing it first. For experienced referees, a cursory reading of the adventure may be preparation enough, but beginners might want to dig a little deeper. Here's a six-step approach you might find helpful.

Step 1: Determine the Goal

Read through the entire adventure as you would a story or novel, ignoring all game statistics, rules, and other technical information. Make sure you have a clear understanding of the plot line, and pay particular attention to the goal the PCs must achieve or the main problem they're supposed to solve. Read the climax carefully—what must the PCs do to complete their goal or solve the problem successfully?

Step 2: Determine the Core Encounters

Like a movie, a role-playing adventure is arranged as a series of discrete scenes. In role-playing games, these scenes are called *encounters*. An encounter usually takes place in a single setting and requires the PCs to solve a minor problem, explore a new area, or resolve a confrontation with a monster or another character. Examples of encounters:

- The PCs approach a river and must figure out a way to cross it.

- The PCs enter a cave and come face to face with a dragon.
- The PCs enter a previously unexplored room of a castle and must search it for clues or treasure.
- The PCs meet a hungry man who begs them for food. (The man, incidentally, is called a *non-player character*, or NPC for short. NPCs are imaginary characters controlled by the referee. A published adventure usually supplies game statistics and background information on all significant NPCs.)

Most published adventures are pretty good about explaining where one encounter ends and the next one begins, but if they're not clearly indicated as such, look for numbered or boldface headings and use the above examples as guidelines. An encounter may be as short as a few sentences or as long as several pages, but they're usually a few paragraphs. A short adventure may include fewer than a dozen encounters, while a long adventure—particularly one with a lot of buildings or geography to explore—may include hundreds of them. The PCs probably won't experience all of the encounters in a long adventure, or even most of them. For instance, if a castle has fifty rooms and each is a separate encounter, the PCs will only experience the encounters keyed to the rooms they actually enter.

The referee should read the adventure a second time, looking for all encounters that relate directly to the PCs' goal. These "Core Encounters" are ones the PCs need to experience and resolve in order to achieve the adventure goal. In short adventures, every encounter is probably a Core Encounter, but in longer adventures, there are likely to be a lot of incidental encounters that don't relate directly to the adventure goal. Make a mark beside all of the Core Encounters; if you're not sure if a particular encounter is a Core Encounter, assume that it is and mark it anyway. When you've marked all of the Core Encounters, read them one after the other; if the PCs experience and resolve all of the encounters you've marked, then they should be able to complete the adventure goal.

Here's an example. Assume we have a short adventure with ten encounters. We've read the adventure once and know that the goal is to recover a ring at the bottom of a lake. The encounters are as follows:

1. A messenger meets the PCs at an inn and tells them that the king's wife dropped her wedding ring in the bottom of Lake Risvold. If the PCs recover it by sundown, he'll give them each a bar of gold.

2. On their way out of town, the PCs see an adorable child, sobbing uncontrollably. If they talk to the child, he tells them he's lost. If the PCs spend an hour asking around, they find someone who'll take him home.

3. Leaving town, the PCs come to a fork in the road. The left route leads through the woods, the right route leads through a meadow.

4. If the PCs take the left route, the road leads them through the woods and ends at a bottomless chasm that can't be crossed. They'll have to go back and take the right route.

5. If they take the right route, the road leads them through the meadow and directly to Lake Risvold. The meadow is full of pollen, and all of the PCs sneeze incessantly unless they cover their noses.

6. A fisherman waves at them from the opposite side of the lake. If the PCs approach him, he asks if they'd like to trade one of his fish for one of their horses. If they agree, he takes a horse, gives them a fish, and leaves. If they decline, he calls them a bunch of cheapskates and leaves. He also knows about the snake in the lake (see encounter 8); he'll tell them about it if they treat him nicely.

7. There is a boat on the bank of the lake. It appears to be poorly constructed. If the PCs attempt to use it, it will fall apart.

8. The lake is about ten feet deep. There's a giant water snake living on the bottom. As soon as a PC enters the water, the snake attacks. The snake will continue to attack until the PCs leave or they wound it, at which time it slithers away, never to be seen again. If the PCs defeat the snake, they can retrieve the ring.

9. When the sun sets, the PCs must return to the king's messenger. If they bring him the ring, he gives them the gold.

If they don't, he calls them incompetent failures, and they
slink away in shame.

In this adventure, the Core Encounters are numbers 1, 3, 5,
8, and 9; in order to achieve the goal, the PCs must learn about
the mission (encounter 1), take the right path (3), walk through
the meadow to the lake (5), defeat the snake to get the ring (8),
and return to the king's messenger (9). Numbers 2, 4, 6, and 7
are incidental and could be eliminated without affecting the adventure: the PCs don't have to meet the child (2), take the path
into the forest (4), meet the fisherman (6), or use the boat (7) to
achieve their goal.

Step 3: Customize the Adventure

Take another look at all of the incidental encounters (the
non–Core Encounters) of the adventure. If they sound boring,
silly, or you don't like them for any other reason, cross them
out; in your version of the adventure, these encounters no
longer exist. In the preceding example, the encounter with the
boat (7) sounds boring to me, so I'll get rid of it. The fisherman
encounter (6) isn't necessary either, but it looks like fun, so I'll
keep it in. However, I think I'll eliminate the left route through
the forest (3)—I don't want the PCs wasting time taking the
wrong direction, and besides, this encounter doesn't strike me
as particularly interesting. In my revised version of the adventure, the path leads directly to the lake (it doesn't fork), and
there's no boat in the lake.

You're also free to tinker with any of the remaining encounters to make them more fun. For instance, instead of having an
adorable child in encounter 3, you could make him obnoxious
(he kicks the PCs when they approach him) or mute (he can't
talk—the PCs will have to figure out another way to find out
where he lives). You can also modify the Core Encounters, so
long as you don't modify them out of existence; if you eliminate
Core Encounters, the PCs won't be able to reach their goal. To
make life difficult for the PCs and the game more of a challenge
for the players, I'll put two giant snakes at the bottom of the
lake (encounter 8) instead of just one.

Step 4: Study the NPCs and Monsters

One of the referee's most important functions is controlling the NPCs and monsters (for our purposes here, we'll define "monster" as an unintelligent animal or creature). To control them effectively, it's necessary to be familiar with their personalities, motivations, and combat routines. Sometimes this information is clearly explained in the encounter description, but often it's up to the referee to work out the details.

Look through the adventure and find the NPCs and monsters for every encounter. In each case, you'll need to know all of the information listed below. Underline relevant key words or phrases in the encounter descriptions, or jot down notes in the margin or on a separate sheet of paper.

For an NPC, you need to know four things:

His general personality. Is he pleasant or hostile? Honest or deceitful? Cheerful or morose? Bright or stupid? How will he interact with the PCs? In most cases, one or two descriptive words will tell you everything you need to know to run him effectively. For instance, in the sample adventure just given, we could describe the child in encounter 2 as "frightened" and "trusting." The fisherman in encounter 6 is "amiable" and "dumb" (he could just as well be "distrustful" and "hostile," but "amiable" and "dumb" sounds like more fun). Now we know that when the PCs approach the "frightened" child, he'll tremble and cower, but because he's also "trusting," he'll let the PCs help him. When the PCs approach the "amiable" fisherman, he'll smile and wave, but since he's also "dumb," he won't understand why they refuse his offer to swap a fish for a horse.

His motivation. What's the NPC's function in the encounter? Is he an innocent bystander? Is he guarding the way? Does he have an interest in helping or hindering the PCs? (The lost boy's goal is to find his way home. The fisherman's goal is to get a horse.)

His information. Does the NPC have any information that might be helpful to the PCs? Make sure you're clear about what he knows and what he doesn't (the encounter description should tell you what the NPC knows, but as always, you're free to modify it). Note that an NPC shouldn't offer his information unless the PCs ask the right questions. (It's unlikely the fisherman will tell the PCs about the snake in the lake if they insult him by flatly rejecting his offer to trade.)

His combat routine. Just in case violence ensues, you need to be familiar with the NPC's combat statistics, his weapons and special powers, and his fighting style. Will he fight to the death? Retreat at the earliest opportunity? Call for reinforcements? (If the PCs give him trouble, the fisherman will punch the closest PC in the mouth, then fall to his knees and beg for mercy if they fight back.)

For a monster, you need to know three things:

Its personality. A monster's personality isn't as sophisticated as an NPC's, but you still need to know how it reacts to strangers. Again, one or two words of description will suffice. For instance, our snake in the lake is "vicious."

Its motivation. Simpler than an NPC's, but no less important. What's the monster's purpose in the encounter? Is it looking for food? Curious about the strangers? (The snake is guarding its home.)

Its combat routine. Monsters in role-playing games tend to have all types of special powers. Make sure you know how they work. Will the monster fight to the death, or retreat as soon as it can? (The snake will fight to the death to protect its territory.)

Step 5: Prepare the Maps and Props

Take an inventory of all the maps you'll be using in the adventure and make sure you understand them. If you've customized the adventure, you may have to adjust the maps as well. If the players need a map, make a sketch or a photocopy. Some published adventures come with letters, documents, clues, and other props that are distributed to the players at various points in the adventure (for instance, when a PC discovers an ancient document in a treasure chest, the referee hands the player the prop document). Make copies as necessary of all props included with the adventure, or devise your own if you like.

Step 6: To Steer or Not to Steer

Players are unpredictable, and no amount of adventure preparation can ensure that they'll follow the Core Encounters and successfully achieve their goal. For many referees, that's fine; part of the fun is watching the players stumble down one blind alley after another, and if they never figure out where to go or what they're supposed to do, too bad for them.

More compassionate referees, however, might want to consider some techniques for steering hopelessly lost PCs in the right direction. The trick is to steer them without their realizing it. Rather than fumbling with on-the-spot improvisations, it's better to plan in advance. Here are some suggestions:

1. Make up a new NPC, such as a scholar, explorer, or similarly knowledgeable character. Have him cross paths with the PCs and offer his guidance or assistance (in exchange, perhaps, for a favor or modest fee).

2. Have the PCs discover a diary or letter in a treasure chest, desk drawer, or clump of weeds. The document reveals pertinent information about the adventure (the document's author might be a deceased hero or scholar who had pursued the adventure goal prior to the PCs' involvement).

3. A ghost of a PC's ancestor visits him in a dream with an important clue. (Obviously, this idea makes more sense in fantasy and horror games.)

In writing original adventures, the criteria are the same as for any type of fiction. It's beyond the scope of this book to discuss effective fiction technique; suffice it to say that a good role-playing adventure should include all of the following:

- an intriguing introduction that provides the PCs with a clear goal
- a strong plot that unfolds and develops as the PCs move further into the adventure
- vivid NPCs (avoid stereotypes and characters lifted from other adventures)
- a variety of encounters, including violent confrontations, nonviolent interactions with interesting NPCs, and situations that require problem-solving

- a dramatic climax where the PCs achieve their goal and earn a meaningful reward, or fail and suffer serious consequences

To exercise your writing skills, start by incorporating original encounters into published adventures. Then try several short scenarios, consisting of no more than a dozen or so encounters, and see how they go over with your players before attempting a long adventure.

WHAT PLAYERS NEED TO KNOW
....

Compared to the referee, the players have it made. Basically, all they have to do is show up and cooperate. In theory, it's the referee's responsibility to adjust his style to accommodate players of all skill levels, explaining the rules as necessary. In practice, it's to everyone's advantage if a new player educates himself on the fundamentals of the rules. Specifically, he should be familiar with the game environment, the character-creation process, and the basics of combat resolution. It isn't necessary or even desirable for a player to read all of the rules; the best way to learn the nuts and bolts of the game is to sit down with a group and learn as you go.

To make the game enjoyable for all, it's important that everyone participate. Novices often feel too inhibited to take active roles, but they shouldn't. You can't really make mistakes in role-playing games—there are no rigid rules and no winners or losers. In fact, a really inept player can often add to the fun—he's essentially playing an inept PC, which tends to make a role-playing adventure a lot more like real life.

Above all, players need to keep the Golden Rules in mind (the referee can make up anything he wants; his word is law). Even if you're absolutely, positively certain that the referee is misinterpreting a rule, don't be a pest; as long as the game's fun, who cares? If you feel compelled to bring an error to the referee's attention, do it after the game or during a break, then accept whatever explanation he offers. If you think you can do a better job at refereeing, you'll undoubtedly get your chance.

A NOTE ABOUT EQUIPMENT
....

As with any hobby where there's money to be made, the role-playing industry has produced a variety of products to complement their games. None are essential, but a lot of them add to the fun. Here's a quick rundown:

Supplements. These include rules expansions, sourcebooks, and adventures. Supplements are covered in detail in the game reviews in Part II.

Dice. Unless you're playing Prince Valiant, the only role-playing game I can think of where dice aren't necessary, you've got to have some of these. In the old days, it was common for publishers to include dice as part of the game package. This trend is fading fast, as fewer games are published as boxed sets and more are published as paperback or hardback books. A good basic collection, suitable for virtually any role-playing system, consists of three or four six-sided dice, one eight-sided die, one twenty-sided die, and two ten-sided dice. They're available at any hobby shop.

Referee Screens. These are cardboard sheets folded into the shape of a screen, usually consisting of three or four panels. The referee stands the screen on the table in front of him, presumably to shield his notes and dice-rolls from the players. Pertinent tables, charts, and other technical data fill the inside panels for easy reference. Though screens are helpful, it obviously doesn't take much effort to make your own. Lazy referees like me prefer to buy them.

Character Sheets. Players can use these forms to record their PCs' ratings, equipment, history, and other key information. In many games, there's a page somewhere in the rulebook to photocopy for use as a character sheet. For other games, you can buy pads of printed sheets. As with referee screens, it's not too hard to make your own. Whether you make them, copy them, or buy them, character sheets are quite helpful, particularly for complicated games that require players to keep track of a lot of statistical information.

Miniatures. These are little figures resembling toy soldiers, usually made from lead or plastic. The idea is for each player to use a figure to represent his character, and then display the figures on a table to indicate their relative proximity to one another as they march through the forest or skulk down a corridor. When a vampire leaps out of the shadows, the referee places a figure of a vampire on the table next to the PC it's about to attack. When a combat round begins, the player moves his figure on the table to show if he's moving closer to the vampire or running away.

I'm not a big fan of miniatures. I think they're awkward, and they interfere with the players' mental images of the characters they're supposed to represent. It's disconcerting for a referee to describe the most ferocious, awesome, terrifying dragon that's ever walked the earth, then plunk down a dinky little dragon statue for the players to gawk at. That said, I'll confess to owning about a thousand of them. Even though I never use them, they're still fun to collect.

Part II
The Good, the Bad, and the Awful

....

The bulk of this book features more than a hundred and fifty reviews of a wide variety of role-playing games (or RPGs) released over the past fifteen years, including a few generic products that can be adapted to a variety of role-playing systems. The opinions expressed reflect my own impressions; you can compare your standards with mine by examining my lists of favorites in the Recommendations appendix.

Not every role-playing game is included. Games published outside the United States are underrepresented, as are games published prior to 1980 and those from small publishers that receive limited distribution. But my criterion for inclusion was simple: If I found it for sale as of spring 1990 in a hobby shop or a dealer's booth at a game convention, it's reviewed here.

You'll find a lot of games that are technically out of print. Role-playing games are like zombies; they don't know when their time has come to lie down and die. Long after their publishers have lost interest, a surprising number of out-of-print games enjoy continuing popularity from a core of devoted fans. Theoretically, an out-of-print game can be played forever, so long as a referee remains willing to invent new adventures. For that reason, I have also included all such games that are still reasonably easy to locate.

HOW TO USE THE REVIEWS
....

In addition to a game's subject matter, rules highlights, and its best and worst features, each review includes the following information:

Publisher and Date of Release. The publisher is self-explanatory—this is the game's manufacturer. Generally, the release date is based on the copyright date, but exceptions abound. Some games may debut at a summer game convention and not hit the stores until the following year. A few receive regional release, taking a year or more to reach players in the outlands. The proliferation of updates and revised editions adds more confusion. As a rule of thumb, the listed date indicates when the game generally became available, accurate within a year or two, and refers to the edition discussed in the review. The release dates of any significant earlier editions are also indicated.

Ratings. The games are given an overall rating of one to four stars. Four-star and three-star games are all recommended. Four-star ratings indicate state-of-the-art, top-of-the-line masterpieces of game design. Three-star ratings designate first-rate, highly entertaining games, certain to satisfy fans interested in the game's subject. Two-star ratings point out flawed games; enjoyment of a two-star game requires a special interest in its subject or a willingness to overlook its problems. One-star games alert buyers to failed experiments, ill-conceived ideas, and miscellaneous junk, recommended for collectors and the insatiably curious.

Ratings tend to be fairly lenient, because I'm less interested in the specific rules of a game than its overall approach. For reference, here's what I look for:

- Presentation. This counts a lot. Role-playing games are hard enough to learn without having to endure ambiguous rules, scrambled syntax, endless misspellings, poor organization, and amateurish graphics. Good writing is rare in RPGs, good editing is rarer still.
- Completeness. All the information needed to play the game should be included in the rules. This doesn't necessarily mean that a game must have detailed rules for

every conceivable action, but there should be suggestions for handling the most likely game situations or reasonable explanations of why the game doesn't need them.

- Characters. Are the PCs fun to play? The character-creation rules should generate interesting, three-dimensional PCs that players can't wait to use.
- Game Environment. The game world should be vividly described, original in conception, and filled with potential for exciting adventures.
- Internal Logic. Players who squawk about inaccurate combat resolution or violation of physical laws miss the point of these games—RPGs are supposed to approximate reality, not slavishly duplicate it. Still, a game's rules should be consistent with its intent. If an RPG portrays a nonviolent fantasy society where citizens resolve conflicts through peaceful negotiation, then we shouldn't have to suffer through fifty pages of combat rules. On the other hand, if an RPG claims to portray battlefield action in World War II accurately, then combat resolution had better involve more than a coin flip.
- Playability. Is play relatively smooth, or does every minor action require endless number juggling and dice-rolls? If the game is complex, do the extra rules pay off in a richer experience? Simply put, is the game any fun?

Complexity. Complexity is relative. There's no such thing as a "simple" role-playing game, though some are clearly easier than others. In a sense, a game's complexity level is more relevant to a potential player than its quality rating; for a beginner, tackling a four-star RPG of high complexity is like attempting calculus before mastering arithmetic.

There are three complexity levels used in the reviews: Low, Medium, and High. Low complexity indicates beginners' games; though experienced players will enjoy them too, newcomers should definitely stick with these. Medium complexity refers to moderately difficult games, recommended for those who aren't totally unfamiliar with role-playing concepts. Ideally, a referee attempting to run a Medium game has experienced it as a player first. High complexity designates games for experienced players and seasoned referees.

Buyer's Notes. This section indicates the physical format of the game. If more than one format is available, the Buyer's Notes explains the differences and makes a recommendation. Most role-playing games are published as boxed sets, hardback books, or trade paperbacks (used here as a generic term indicating all softcover books larger than the 4 × 7 mass-market paperbacks).

Suggested Supplements. This section recommends the game's best expansions (advanced rules), sourcebooks (books of background material pertaining to a particular game setting or genre; typical subjects include animals, personalities, cultures, and locations), and published adventures. If a review omits this section, it's safe to assume that there are no supplements worth recommending (or none that are better than those you can dream up yourself), or there simply aren't any available.

SHOPPING TIPS
....

Your best source of role-playing products is your local game store. Bookstores and comic-book shops—the better ones, anyway—also stock RPGs and supplements. For hard-to-find products, try mail-order houses (many advertise in hobby magazines) or look for them in the dealer's booths and auctions at game conventions (check the hobby magazines for dates and locations). If all else fails, try writing directly to the publishers; see the Addresses appendix for a list of addresses. Also included in the appendix sections of this book are recommended RPGs for beginners, along with an index of all the games covered in this book, arranged by subject.

Part III
The Games

....

Advanced Dungeons and Dragons****

....

Complexity: Medium
TSR Inc., First Edition: 1979; Second Edition: 1989

Advanced Dungeons and Dragons is the *Citizen Kane* of role-playing, the classic against which all others are measured. For many, the game has become synonymous with the hobby itself, which is understandable, since no RPG has been more visible or has attracted more fans. Emphasizing ease of play over nitpicking detail, AD&D is easily the most fun of all the fantasy RPGs.

AD&D began as an expansion of Dungeons and Dragons, but they are, in fact, two distinct games, though they share the same basic concepts. In both games, players choose character classes to define their PCs' lots in life, and roll dice to determine their characters' beginning attributes (Strength, Dexterity, Constitution, Intelligence, Wisdom, and Charisma). Both games are set in fantasy worlds vaguely based on medieval Europe, both use simple combat rules that match an attacker's "to hit" number (his prowess rating) against the defender's Armor Class (his protection rating), and both use an experience system that elevates PCs to increasingly higher levels of skill.

Initially, the mechanical differences between the two games may be apparent only to students of the rulebooks. For instance, D&D has fewer alignments and spells; elves and dwarves are treated as character classes in D&D and as races in AD&D; and D&D characters tend to advance in level more quickly but are slightly less powerful than their AD&D counterparts. Overall, D&D has significantly fewer rules than AD&D and is much less structured. AD&D provides specific rules or general guidelines for every conceivable game situation, and is therefore more difficult to master; newcomers might want to warm up with a session or two of D&D before tackling AD&D.

The biggest RPG event of 1989 was the long-awaited second edition AD&D game, a meticulous overhaul intended to update and streamline the original rulebooks. It was an unprecedented undertaking that made a lot of old-timers nervous; for many, this was comparable to retouching the *Mona Lisa*. But the results were impressive. Thanks to the skillful touch of designer David Cook (with development assistance from Steve Winter and Jon Pickens), second edition AD&D is a model of organization, clarity, and imagination.

The second edition cleans up the proliferation of character classes in the original rules, now confining them to four distinct categories. The Warrior category includes Fighters, Paladins (who resemble knights), and Rangers (noble woodsmen, sort of like Robin Hood). The Priest class features Clerics (holy men and women who can cast spells) and Druids (guardians of nature). Thieves and Bards (loosely based on Celtic poets and storytellers) compose the Rogue class. The Wizard class received the most radical reorganization; it now includes specialists of eight different schools, among them Conjurers, Illusionists, and Necromancers, each with his own talents and restrictions. Revised AD&D adds proficiency rules (comparable to the skill systems of other games) to give characters specialized talents ranging from Animal Lore and Blind-fighting for Warriors to Spellcraft and Astrology for Wizards. The broadened experience rules now reward cooperation and heroism as well as monster bashing and treasure snatching. With dozens of new optional rules covering such fine points as terrain effects, infravision, and aerial combat, referees can add as much detail to their games as they wish.

Purists may balk at AD&D's stubborn insistence on playability over realism, grumbling that the hit point system doesn't accurately portray wounds, that the character classes are too rigid, and that the Armor Class rules are inadequate for measuring defense. So what? Even though AD&D is designed for players, not for rules lawyers, fussy referees are free to substitute systems from other games if they like, or they can make up their own; AD&D is flexible enough to handle just about anything.

Advanced Dungeons and Dragons is a sprawling, versatile system of unlimited scope, beautifully presented and elegantly designed. A role-player who's never experienced AD&D is like a board-gamer who's never tried Monopoly or a kid who's never played baseball. In a well-run session, it's just about impossible not to have a good time.

Buyer's Notes: Both the *Player's Handbook* and the *Dungeon Master's Guide* hardbacks are necessary for play. Stick with the second edition versions, which are improvements in every way over the now-obsolete first edition rules. The Monstrous Compendium Volume One boxed set includes statistics, combat routines, and ecological details about the monsters most common to the AD&D game; it's essential for serious players.

Suggested Supplements: There are several official settings for the AD&D game world. All use the same rules, but all have their own sourcebooks and adventures. Here's a rundown.

The Forgotten Realms is a broad campaign setting encompassing the majority of AD&D adventures. Though the Forgotten Realms weren't officially designated until 1987, it's safe to assume that most AD&D adventures and supplements published prior to that date also fit somewhere in the Forgotten Realms universe. Equally suited to both single-session adventures and extended campaigns, *The Forgotten Realms* remains the setting of

choice for experienced players and is also a good place for
novices to begin. Best adventures for new players: *Under Illefarn*
(a crack in the earth reveals a lost kingdom) and *Treasure Hunt*
(shipwrecked sailors on the isle of the Sea King). For experienced players: *Ravenloft* (vampiric activity in a haunted house),
Desert of Desolation (a long campaign set in a desert wasteland; it
includes revised material from the *Pharaoh*, *Oasis of the White
Palm*, and *Lost Tomb of Martek* adventures), *Moonshae* (a strange
island of magicians, dragons, and druids), and the three-volume
Shadowdale/Tantras/Waterdeep series.

Developed from an early campaign of Gary Gygax, the father
of Dungeons and Dragons, Greyhawk was the first official
AD&D game world. It's somewhat more entrenched in the traditions of fantasy literature than other AD&D settings, and is
therefore not as open-ended, but players interested in the gene-
sis of AD&D might enjoy checking it out. The *Greyhawk Adventures* hardback details spells, personalities, and monsters
exclusive to the world of Greyhawk; though not essential, it's a
useful reference for referees interested in adding authenticity to
their Greyhawk adventures. *Forgotten Temple of Tharizdon* (a
stronghold of an evil deity) is a good introductory adventure,
while *Temple of Elemental Evil* (featuring revised material from
Village of Hommlet) and its sequel, *Scourge of the Slavelords*,
(which includes revised material from the *Slave Pits of the Under-
city*, *Secret of the Slave Stockade*, *Assault on the Aeire of Slave Lords*,
and *Dungeon of the Slave Lords* adventures) form the basis of an
action-filled Greyhawk campaign.

Set on the world of Krynn, *Dragonlance* focuses on rich characters, vivid locales, and a detailed story line supported by a
successful series of novels. Dragons play a fundamental role in
the *Dragonlance* mythos, as does a centuries-long struggle between the good people of Krynn and the evil Takhisis, Queen
of Darkness. It's as charming as a fairytale, and a bit more structured than the sprawling *Forgotten Realms*. The *Dragonlance Adventures* hardback includes a wealth of information about
Krynn's history and personalities, along with a few rule modifications; it's a must for hardcore *Dragonlance* fans, as is the impressive *Atlas of the Dragonlance World*, a beautiful book of

Krynn maps. The fourteen-volume Dragonlance Saga series is among the most ambitious and satisfying campaign epics ever published, comprising (in order) *Dragons of Despair, Dragons of Flame, Dragons of Hope, Dragons of Desolation, Dragons of Mystery, Dragons of Ice, Dragons of Light, Dragons of War, Dragons of Deceit, Dragons of Dreams, Dragons of Glory, Dragons of Faith, Dragons of Truth,* and *Dragons of Triumph.* Players on a budget can omit *Dragons of Mystery,* a sourcebook pertaining to the first four adventures, and *Dragons of Glory,* a board game simulation of the War of the Lance. A revision of the first four adventures, collected into a single book entitled *Dragonlance Classics, Volume One,* is scheduled for release in 1990. Also recommended is *The World of Krynn,* a collection of short adventures, and *Time of the Dragon,* a boxed set detailing the lands of Taladas, located on the far side of Krynn.

Spelljammer takes AD&D into outer space via starships powered by the magic of wizards and priests. It's a whimsical, exciting premise full of strange twists—wait till you get a load of the interstellar orcs—yet is presented as a logical extension of the AD&D universe. The *Wildspace* adventure pits the PCs against a spacefaring race of savage beholders (gigantic floating eyeballs)—exciting and bizarre.

Oriental Adventures is an Eastern-based spin-off of AD&D. Though the lands of Kara-Tur are considered part of *The Forgotten Realms,* the character classes, magic spells, and other fundamentals differ significantly from AD&D conventions, essentially making it a separate game. (For more about Oriental Adventures see the entry on page 147.)

There are a number of AD&D supplements adaptable to all of the above settings. The *Complete Fighter* sourcebook considerably expands the options of Warrior characters; the companion volumes—*Complete Thief, Complete Wizard,* and *Complete Priest*—do the same for the other major classes. There are several additional Monstrous Compendium volumes available, each containing dozens of detailed monster descriptions, perfect for enlivening adventures of all types. The *Manual of the Planes* (a superb treatment of alternate planes of existence), *Dungeoneer's Survival Guide* (rules for subterranean adventures),

and *Wilderness Survival Guide* (rules for outdoor adventures) are
hardback expansions that predate the second edition rules;
they're useful for players wanting more detail, but the referee
will have to do some work to adapt them to the second edition
material. It's also possible to convert Dungeons and Dragons
supplements to the AD&D system, providing the players are
willing to accept some rules compromises and the referee is familiar enough with both games to switch from one to the
other.

Aftermath**

Complexity: High
Fantasy Games Unlimited Inc., 1981

Aftermath takes place in the not-too-distant future, when the
Earth has been demolished by some unnamed catastrophe,
leaving behind a handful of intrepid survivalists to struggle in
an exceedingly hostile environment. It's an interesting premise,
but somewhere along the way, the game lost its focus. Instead
of exploring the rich possibilities of a postapocalyptic setting,
Aftermath bogs down in a mire of rules, resulting in a game so
complicated that it's nearly unplayable.

There's an uncomfortable preoccupation with violence in Aftermath, with virtually every facet of combat rendered in excruciating detail. Characters aren't merely wounded, they suffer
damage in one of thirty different body locations. The effects of
acid—to pick just one of the dozens of assault techniques described in the basic book—get nearly a full page of rules, including an Acid Special Effects Table that randomly determines
whether a character is blinded in one eye, both eyes, or is
merely scarred. Combat resolution is absurdly complex, requiring as many as two dozen steps to complete a single action, and
that's assuming I'm reading the two-page Combat Procedure
Flow Chart correctly. Not even dogs are spared—they can be
wounded in the nose, two different parts of the tail, or twenty-
seven other distinct areas of the body.

Character creation involves the allocation of a fixed number of Attribute Points to several basic characteristics (including Strength, Speed, and Health), deciding an area of specialization (such as Communicative or Scientific), then adding a host of personal details (Age, Clothing, Equipment, and so on). Trouble is, though the characters are well rounded, they're not particularly robust, which is a big drawback in a game as violence-prone as Aftermath. A well-placed shot from a sniper or a bite from a poison cookie can instantly wipe out a character that it took a couple of hours to create.

Though its drawbacks are many, Aftermath is paradise for players who thrive on detail or for those who want to wring every last drop of blood out of combat encounters. But for those more interested in role-playing than in staging detailed fights, wading through the two-hundred-plus pages of Aftermath rules is hardly worth the effort.

Buyer's Note: Boxed set.

Suggested Supplements: Sydney, the Wilderness Campaign, an adventure set in a ruined university laboratory in Australia, features an interesting setting, and because it's focused and streamlined, it's more enjoyable than the original game. *Into the Ruins* stresses violent encounters, a perfect adventure for players who've thoroughly digested the combat rules.

Albedo***

Complexity: Medium
Thoughts and Images, 1988

Based on the comic book of the same name (or more accurately, on the Erma Felna EDF feature story), Albedo is a science-fiction game set on a war-torn, high-tech world populated by anthropomorphic animals. These aren't the adorable fuzzy-wuzzies of Saturday morning cartoons, but sophisticated, grim, and violent creatures engaged in life-or-death struggles for political control of a society in chaos. It's an intriguing concept, entertainingly explained by designer Paul Kidd, with editorial and artistic input from the comic's author, Steven Gallacci.

Albedo attempts to stress interpersonal relationships among the characters instead of combat encounters, and though that's an admirable goal, the game mechanics don't quite pull it off. Instead of ideas to encourage role-playing, the game substitutes formulas, numbers, and charts for elements that are better left up to the improvisational skills of the players. For instance, in addition to the standard Strength, Stamina, and Dexterity attributes, characters are also rated for psychological characteristics such as Drive (a measure of willpower and determination), Stability (how easily a character changes his emotional reactions), and Disposition (his general approach to life). Though it's helpful for players to have general guidelines for their PCs' attitudes, Albedo goes way too far. Requiring players to check Disposition or Stability scores to determine a reaction sabotages role-playing's fundamental appeal—namely, allowing players to improvise the responses of their imaginary characters. The system reduces role-playing to a series of dice-rolls and stretches credibility to the limit; a world populated by talking dogs and cats is easier to accept than personality factors determined by formulas and tables.

The rest of the rules are equally clunky. Combat, which is supposedly de-emphasized, requires players to struggle with Impact Distribution, Penetration Resistance, and other difficult concepts that give realistic but unnecessarily detailed results (there's a separate table just to determine the location of head wounds). Skill resolution involves a convoluted system of Skill Governors, Task Difficulty, and Training Levels. The rulebooks are poorly organized—there's no table of contents, combat rules are scattered all over the place, and the character-generation flow chart is hidden away on the last page of the last book.

Though the rules may be a mess, the background material is superb. The history, culture, and technology of the game world is richly detailed and always fascinating, even for those who've never heard of the comic book. As a sourcebook of interesting ideas, Albedo is first rate. But as a game, it needs some work. *Buyer's Note:* Boxed set.

Arcanum***

Complexity: Medium
Bard Games, 1985

Arcanum is the first of three volumes of Bard Games' Atlantean trilogy, and it's a winner. The book can be used as a stand-alone game set in the lost continents of Atlantis, Hyperboria, and Lemuria, or as a supplement for any other fantasy RPG that emphasizes magic. As a game, it's adequate, but nothing special. As a supplement, Arcanum is unsurpassed, easily one of the best treatments of magic ever published, thanks to the wealth of detail supplied by designers Stephen Michael Sechi and Vernie Taylor.

Attributes, saving throws, experience points, and other basic concepts of character creation will be familiar to anyone who's ever played Dungeons and Dragons. The combat rules and skill systems are also routine, but they're sensible and easy to learn. In addition to the standard elven, dwarven, and human races, several unusual character types are available, among them the leonine Adaman, the skyfaring Zephyr, and the goblinlike Nethermen. Players can choose from over thirty professions, including a number of interesting wizard variants such as Shaman, Witchdoctor, and Thaumaturge.

Where Arcanum really shines is in its exhaustive magic section, nearly eighty pages of fascinating material covering nine different fields of study (including Astrology, Divine Magic, Mysticism, and Sorcery) and hundreds of spells. The exceptional section on alchemy includes clever suggestions for researching magical items, creating herbal elixirs and alchemical dusts, and transcribing mystical inscriptions. A section on advanced operations adds rules for necromantic rituals, golems, and magical constructs, all carefully described and easily adaptable to other games.

To stage an Atlantean campaign, referees will need the two companion volumes of the trilogy—there isn't enough background material in Arcanum alone to do the job. For those interested in expanding the magic systems of other fantasy RPGs, Arcanum serves as an excellent source of ideas.

Buyer's Note: Trade paperback.

Suggested Supplements: Lexicon, the second volume of the Atlantean trilogy, features historical notes and detailed maps of Stonehenge, Hyperboria, and other legendary locales. *Bestiary,* the third book, is an encyclopedia of mythical creatures and nonhuman races. Both are fun to read and filled with interesting material, adaptable to virtually any fantasy RPG.

Arduin Adventure**½

Complexity: Low/Medium
Grimoire Games, 1980

Among the earliest fantasy RPGs, Arduin Adventure was intended as both an introductory game for newcomers and an alternative to Dungeons and Dragons for veteran players. Though it falls short on both counts, the game boasts a fair number of appealing innovations, thanks to the skewed approach taken by designer David Hargrave.

The fundamentals are nothing out of the ordinary. Players choose their character types from a routine selection of races (Elf, Dwarf, Human, etc.) and professions (Warrior, Mage, Thief, etc.), and randomly determine the usual attributes (Dexterity, Strength, Intelligence, etc.). Hit points, experience levels, and other standard concepts will be familiar to anyone who's ever cracked a D&D rulebook.

But once the basics are out of the way, Arduin introduces a number of unusual twists. For instance, characters gain new experience levels based on the number of adventures in which they've participated instead of their accumulated experience points. Whereas D&D characters acquire hit points in leaps and bounds as they ascend to new levels, Arduin characters earn only a few extra hit points, enabling low-level characters to fight on more or less equal footing with their higher-level companions. Weapons don't have hit-point ranges; instead, each inflicts a fixed amount of damage. Though the magic system requires Mages and Priests to memorize spells, Priests must perform a prayer ritual before a spell can be cast.

Ambiguous rules, an unnecessarily complicated combat system, and insufficient instructions for staging adventures ultimately makes Arduin Adventures too difficult for beginning players and too frustrating for experienced ones. There are a lot of good ideas here, however, and an enterprising referee might be able to adapt some of them to a different game.

Buyer's Note: Boxed set.

Suggested Supplement: The Lost Grimoire is an interesting compilation of essays about magical devices, monsters, and a variety of other topics that can be used as adventure springboards for Arduin Adventures as well as other fantasy games.

Ars Magica***½

Complexity: Medium/High
Lion Rampant, 1989

You want magic? You've got it in Ars Magica, an inspired fantasy RPG that focuses exclusively on wizards and spellcasting. It's a delightfully original treatment of a familiar topic, a beautiful job by designers Jonathan Tweet and Mark Rein Hagen.

Each player creates not only a Magus (wizard) but also a nonwizardly Companion to assist the Magus, along with a few mercenary soldiers called Grogs to serve as bodyguards and cannon fodder. A player rates his Magus for Intelligence, Perception, Quickness, and five other basic attributes, then determines descriptive adjectives for him based on his attribute ratings. Positive ratings receive favorable descriptions, negative ratings receive unfavorable ones; for instance, a PC with an Intelligence rating of +1 might be Quick-Witted or Creative while a Magus with an Intelligence of −3 might be Addled or just plain Stupid. Characters also acquire Virtues (such as Prestigious Family, Clear Thinking, and Keen Vision), Flaws (Bad Reputation, Criminal Brand, Missing Eye), Talents (Alertness, Direction, Sense, Read Lips), Skills (Survival, Storytelling, Diplomacy), and Knowledge (Magic Theory, Occult Lore, Medicine). Though the procedure takes a while, the resulting PCs are vivid, charming, and perfectly suited to a supernatural life-style—these are state-of-the-art wizards.

The magic system features two distinct spell styles. Formulaic spells are those that can be cast dependably, but their effects are narrow and specific. Spontaneous spells are not as reliable as their formulaic counterparts but have a variety of applications. Each spell combines one Technique, its active component, and one Form, which is the object of the Technique. For instance, Creo (which means "I create") is a Technique, and Aquam (water) and Auram (air) are both Forms; therefore, Creo Aquam is a spell for creating water, while Creo Auram is a spell for creating air. Advanced rules explain the manipulation of Divine, Infernal, and Faerie powers, along with laboratory techniques for arcane research and spell invention.

The game's biggest flaw is its combat system, which is far too complicated for an RPG that downplays physical encounters. And though the magic rules are fascinating, they're probably too sophisticated for newcomers. But for experienced players, Ars Magica is one terrific product; this is wizardly role-playing at its finest.

Buyer's Note: Trade paperback.

Suggested Supplements: Stormrider is an excellent introductory adventure, perfect for easing new players into the game system. Advanced players should investigate the *Broken Covenant of Calebais* adventure, a hair-raising mystery set in the Covenant of Calebais.

Batman***

....

Complexity: Medium
Mayfair Games Inc., 1989

It was inevitable that a role-playing game would be included among the avalanche of products accompanying the release of the 1989 movie. Surprise—it's a good one. Essentially a stripped-down version of Mayfair's outstanding DC Heroes game, Batman is both a nice introduction to role-playing and a competent simulation of the Caped Crusader's adventures, ideal for those too cheap to buy the entire DC Heroes set.

All of the elements that make DC Heroes so much fun remain intact in Batman albeit on a more modest scale. Every unit of measurement is expressed in Attribute Points (APs), and each additional AP doubles the amount measured by the previous AP. For instance, 1 AP of distance equals 20 feet, while 2 APs of distance equal 40 feet. A character with 2 APs of Strength can lift 200 pounds, a character with 3 APs of Strength can lift 400 pounds. What's more, AP values are interchangeable, making the system a snap to use; a villain whose rocket sled has a speed of 5 APs can fly 5 APs worth of distance per phase (about 100 yards in 4 seconds). All actions are resolved on an Action Table by cross referencing a die-roll with the appropriate Acting Value (say, Batman's batarang) with its Opposing Value (the Joker's skull).

Batman emphasizes quick play and intense action, though realism takes a beating; the bat-guy featured in this game can easily lift a half ton of weight, and that's not how I remember him from the comic books. The game includes some helpful tips for staging encounters, a nice selection of bat gadgets, all of the supporting cast members, and a good introductory adventure starring the Joker. What it doesn't have are all of the powers and skills, the dozens of superheroes, the lavish play aids, and the extensive background material featured in the DC Heroes game. In fact, since DC Heroes essentially contains everything in the Batman game, I can't think of a single reason anyone shouldn't skip this and go directly to DC Heroes, with the exception of collectors who need to own every last product with a bat emblem on it.

Buyer's Note: Trade paperback.

Suggested Supplements: DC Heroes supplements featuring Batman and company include the *Night in Gotham* adventure, the *Batman Sourcebook*, and the solitaire scenario *Wheel of Destruction*, all of it first-rate material.

Behind Enemy Lines*½

Complexity: Medium
FASA Corp., 1982

Behind Enemy Lines is a military RPG focusing on World War II. The game mechanics are adequate, but bland, with soldiers rated for Strength, Endurance, Weapons Handling, Agility, and Stamina, and assigned various skills necessary for front-line survival, such as Demolitions, First Aid, and Rifle Use. A few dice-rolls resolve most skill attempts, and while large combat encounters bog down in a swamp of formulas, tables, and modifiers, they're reasonably exciting, if not exactly realistic. Purists will be appalled at the liberties taken with the weapon descriptions, as well as the game's narrow focus; apparently, only the Western front exists in the world of Behind Enemy Lines. Students of the era might be able to do something with this, but casual players won't find much to like, since playing a WW II private isn't nearly as interesting as playing a wizard or superhero.

Time has not been kind to Behind Enemy Lines, as more sophisticated military RPGs such as Phoenix Command and Merc have left it in the dust. Neither good history nor interesting fantasy, Behind Enemy Lines is best forgotten.

Buyer's Note: Boxed set.

Suggested Supplement: The Guns of Navarone is a moderately entertaining adventure inspired more by war movies than history books. With its interesting NPCs and melodramatic encounters, this is as good as Behind Enemy Lines gets.

Beyond the Supernatural***

Complexity: Medium/High
Palladium Books, 1988

A contemporary horror RPG, Beyond the Supernatural stakes out a territory somewhere between the literary nightmares of Call of Cthulhu and the comic fantasies of Ghostbusters. Though the cover illustration of a fanged monstrosity groping a helpless explorer leads one to believe that this is pretty grim stuff, the inclusion of laser guns, UFOs, and other lightweight science-fiction conventions betrays the game's spiritual pedigree of Saturday matinee B-movies.

As with Teenage Mutant Ninja Turtles, Ninjas and Superspies, and other Palladium products, the game mechanics of Beyond the Supernatural derive from the Palladium Role-Playing Game. That's both good news and bad: good, in that fans of the other Palladium games won't have to start from scratch; bad, in that new players will have to navigate some tedious character-generation rules (too many random dice-rolls; it's totally up to fate whether you're a rich man or a pauper, a Ph.D. or a high school graduate), a combat system that requires players to keep track of two kinds of damage (Hit Points, which measures personal health, and Structural Damage Capacity, which measures damage absorbed by armor), and other difficult concepts that Palladium stubbornly insists on hauling from game to game, regardless of whether they're appropriate to a particular genre.

Players take the roles of regular humans who specialize in Psychic Healing, Parapsychology, and other paranormal occupations. Some PC types, such as the Physical Psychic, are blessed with special mental powers, while others, such as the Archanist/Mage, have an exceptional aptitude for magic. Most PCs have access to a variety of exotic weaponry, ranging from submachine guns and rocket launchers to flamethrowers and laser pistols. With their psionics, spells, and lasers, the PCs are a little too powerful for the game's own good; the stronger the characters, the less threatening the menaces. Consequently, Beyond the Supernatural lacks the edge that makes Call of Cthulhu genuinely scary.

The game shines in its treatment of magic, monsters, and other supernatural elements. With its complicated system of invocations and rituals, the magic rules radiate creepiness, while the monster menagerie includes some of the wildest creatures this side of H. P. Lovecraft, such as the Mind Slug, the Scarlet Hunter, and slime-dripping Goqua. Best of all are the scholarly discussions of supernatural phenomena. The significance of power triads, the vernal equinox, Stonehenge, and the globe-spanning Ley Lines (a matrix of psychic energy) are examined in detail and neatly linked with the game system.

Thanks to the enthusiasm of designers Randy McCall and Kevin Siembieda, the text sparkles and is a delight to read. With the inclusion of some excellent introductory scenarios and lucid staging tips for the referee, Beyond the Supernatural stands as a solid, entertaining horror RPG. It's no classic, but if a subsequent edition dumps the goofy science-fiction elements, it might be someday.

Buyer's Note: Trade paperback.

Suggested Supplements: There are no supplements specifically intended for this game yet. However, supplements for other Palladium games are compatible with Beyond the Supernatural with Teenage Mutant Ninja Turtles adventures the best bet for creative referees.

Book of Mars**½

Complexity: Medium/High
Image Game Co., 1981

Though only a fair role-playing game, the out-of-print Book of Mars features a superb combat system that can be grafted onto any fantasy RPG without too much trouble. The system strikes an elegant balance between detail and playability, producing realistic results with a minimum of dice-rolling and chart-checking. The rules cover combat encounters of all eras, from tribesmen tossing rocks at each other circa 4000 B.C. to spacemen exchanging laser fire in the far future. There are endless tables of statistics for every conceivable weapon and streamlined, realistic combat routines for all types of melee, missile, and troop attacks.

As for the role-playing elements, they don't involve much more than a rudimentary character-generation system and some bland background information. Ignore the game, but keep the combat rules; they're as satisfying as those of RuneQuest, nearly as comprehensive as Aftermath, and not much more difficult than Advanced Dungeons and Dragons.

Buyer's Note: Trade paperback.

Boot Hill***

Complexity: Medium
TSR Inc., 1979

Boot Hill earns a qualified recommendation. As a tactical simulation of Western gunfights, it's unsurpassed. As a role-playing game, there's not really enough here to put together a meaningful campaign, apparently an intentional decision by designers Brian Blume and Gary Gygax, since combat rules comprise the bulk of the rulebook.

Characters are rated for Speed, Gun Accuracy, Throwing Accuracy, Strength, and Bravery, all of which directly affect their combat effectiveness. For instance, a PC's likelihood of getting off the first shot in a gunfight depends on his Bravery and Speed, while his Strength indicates the amount of damage he can take before biting the dust. Combat is detailed but reasonably smooth, following a strict sequence of movement, fire order determination, fire resolution, and wound assessment. Because combat tends to be bloody, fire order is crucial; slowpokes don't last long in Boot Hill. Survivors earn experience points to raise their attributes. Opponents who run out of ammunition can resolve their differences with the brawling rules, which allow for haymakers, elbow smashes, bear hugs, and nearly every other type of punch or grapple imaginable.

Advanced rules add simultaneous movement (requiring players to write down orders for their characters), sharpshooting, intoxication, stray bullets, and misfires. There are some general suggestions for campaigns, but Boot Hill works best as a board game, where players rough out a city map on a tabletop or floor, then use miniature figures to stage showdowns. Two scenarios included in the rulebook, "Gunfight at the O.K. Corral" and "Battle of Coffeyville," show just how to do it.

Buyer's Notes: Boxed set. Watch for a Boot Hill revision sometime toward the end of 1990, planned as a trade paperback.

Suggested Supplements: Lost Conquistador Mine, featuring a quest for a secret gold mine, is not only the best of the Boot Hill supplements, it's also the best Western adventure ever published. Also recommended is *Burned Bush Wells*, a classic Western scenario set in the dead of winter.

Bullwinkle and Rocky***

Complexity: Low
TSR Inc., 1988

I've never met a kid who wasn't fascinated by the concept of role-playing, but getting him to sit still long enough to learn a game is another story. More often than not, the rules are too dense, there's too much math, and it takes too much time. Over the years, game designers have made numerous attempts at child-friendly RPGs, but none have matched the success of Dave Cook's remarkable Bullwinkle and Rocky, a game that's as enjoyable for grade-schoolers as it is for adults.

Of its two versions, the Narration Game is the simplest. Each player receives a hand of cards describing items (such as Exploding Mooseberries), events (Inherit Something Valuable), and personalities (King Amos Bushwick the Thirty-Third). One player chooses a plot from the Stories Book, which gives only the story's beginning and ending. In turn, players add to the story by supplying narrative details based on their cards, twisting the story in all kinds of unexpected and hilarious directions. When the cards have all been played and the story wheezes to an end, awards (in the form of photocopiable "diplomas" supplied with the game) are presented for the best pun, best ending, or whatever else seems appropriate to the players.

In the Everybody Can Do Something Game, players assume the personas of specific characters from the cartoon series, such as Dudley Do-Right, Mr. Peabody, or even Rocky himself. Each receives a spinner, a character card, and a plastic hand puppet of his character. As in the Narration Game, a plot is selected from the Stories Book, with the object being to bring the story to a successful conclusion. However, in this version, story details are generated not only from card play, but also from each character's special powers, detailed on the back of the character cards. Rocky, for instance, can Fly and is Nimble and Quick, while the evil Natasha has the power to Drive Men and Mooses Wild and can use a Pretty Good Disguise. The spinners determine if a power is used successfully. As for the hand puppets, they serve no specific function other than adding to the general chaos.

Bullwinkle and Rocky may be too trivial for serious-minded players, and its lack of formal structure may intimidate those used to games with rigid rules. However, as a painless introduction to role-playing, it's without peer—cleverly designed, beautifully produced, and irresistibly fun.

Buyer's Note: Boxed set.

Bushido***

Complexity: High
Fantasy Games Unlimited Inc., 1981

Bushido is one of the earliest and most successful fantasy RPGs with an Oriental setting, thoroughly grounded in medieval Japanese history. Designers Paul Hume and Bob Charette took their subject seriously and opted for a dense, highly detailed treatment. It's not an easy game to learn—the rules more closely resemble those of a military simulation than a conventional RPG—but experienced players with an interest in the era should find a lot to enjoy.

As is appropriate to the era, a PC's lot in life is largely dependent on his social class, which suggests his choice of profession and his most likely skills. Of the two general categories of skills, combat skills encompass various aspects of hand-to-hand fighting and weapon prowess, while knowledge skills include broad categories of artistic, professional, and practical abilities. Though somewhat convoluted—there are a lot of dice-rolls and calculations required—the character system does a good job of generating well-rounded samurai, yakuza, and the like.

There are two types of spellcasters in Bushido: the magician/scientist Shugenja, whose powers are a product of research and study, and the holy man/spiritualist Gaskusho, whose magical abilities are bestowed by the gods. Shugenja learn their spells from the Five Elements (whose spell categories include soil, air, fire, water, and wood), while Gaskusho learn theirs from the Five Yogas (destiny, knowledge, body, balance, and breath). In spite of the difference in orientation, both types cast spells in pretty much the same way and both have access to most of the spells from their respective Yogas or Elements. Spellcasters expand their abilities by accumulating Knowledge Points that can be exchanged for increasingly powerful spells. It's a good, workable system, which could have been even better if clearer distinctions existed between the Shugenja and the Gaskusho.

Resolving most actions, including combat, involves computing a character's BCS (Base Chance of Success) for the task in question, which can be modified by skill levels, magic resistance, terrain, and a host of other variables. A roll on a twenty-sided die determines success or failure. Actions requiring longer time periods to complete, such as manufacturing a weapon or learning a new spell, involve a series of dice-rolls in order to accumulate Effect Numbers. When the Effect Numbers exceed the action's Task Number, the action is completed. Though versatile and simple, the system can also become tedious, particularly in detailed combat encounters that can take dozens of dice-rolls to resolve.

Literate discussions of Oriental religions, social customs, and governments add to the game's depth, while the background of Nippon—the mythological country where Bushido takes place—is drawn so vividly that it could've been ripped from the pages of a history book. Its systems may creak a bit, but for experienced players with an interest in the Orient, Bushido's scholarship far outweighs its flaws.

Buyer's Notes: Boxed set. Bushido was originally published in 1980 by Phoenix Games; their version consisted of two booklets packaged in a plastic bag. The Fantasy Games Unlimited version cleaned up the original and is superior in every way; skip the bag and stick with the box.

Suggested Supplements: Valley of the Mists is an outstanding collection of three interlocked adventures that begins with a search for a stolen puzzle box and ends with an exciting confrontation in an enchanted valley. It's also an excellent springboard for a Bushido campaign.

Call of Cthulhu****

Complexity: Medium
Chaosium Inc., First Edition: 1981; Fourth Edition: 1989

Call of Cthulhu is a masterpiece, easily the best horror RPG ever published and possibly the best RPG, period. Based on the writings of H. P. Lovecraft, Call of Cthulhu vividly portrays the gruesome universe of the Cthulhu Mythos and brings to life the mind-bending horrors described in the *Necronomicon*, Lovecraft's imaginary bible of nightmares. Designed by Sandy Petersen, Call of Cthulhu boasts an ingenious system, an exciting setting, and a beautiful presentation—they don't get any better than this.

The game is set in the 1920s, approximately the same era in which the Lovecraft stories take place. Players assume the roles of regular people—professors, journalists, authors, lawyers— who are perhaps a bit smarter than average and definitely less skeptical, because most of them have firsthand experience with supernatural phenomena. Character creation, as well as the game's other systems, derives from the rules common to Rune-Quest, Stormbringer, and other Chaosium games. Players roll dice to randomly determine their PCs' Strength, Dexterity, Intelligence, Size, Power, Appearance, and Education. Then each receives a fixed number of Skill Points to distribute among a list of talents appropriate to his profession; a journalist, for instance, has an exceptional aptitude for Oratory, Psychology, and Speaking Other Languages, while a lawyer's skills include Accounting, Library Use, and Reading Latin.

Those familiar with the source material may recall that when a Lovecraft hero encounters a supernatural phenomenon, he typically responds by fainting. To simulate the intense horrors of the Cthulhu Mythos and the weak knees of the protagonists, all PCs have a Sanity rating to measure their mental fragility. Sanity scores fluctuate between 1 and 100; a high score indicates a strong mind, a low score means it's time for the straitjacket. The creatures of the Cthulhu Mythos are so terrifying that merely laying eyes on them may cause permanent damage to one's mental health. When a PC confronts a Mythos creature, or if he reads a disturbing passage from the *Necronomicon* or other Mythos tome, he must make a Sanity check by rolling percentile dice and comparing the result to his current Sanity score. If the roll exceeds his score, he loses a few Sanity points and becomes temporarily insane, which may last anywhere from a few minutes to several months. The precise effects of temporary insanity are up to the referee, but they typically include catatonia, amnesia, and various phobias. If a PC suffers an excessive loss of Sanity, he becomes permanently insane and is confined to a mental hospital for an indefinite period, effectively removing him from the game. The catch, of course, is that the PCs can't learn about their adversaries without reading the Mythos books, and they can't get rid of the creatures without looking at them; hence, their Sanity is constantly at risk. It's an ingenious system, adding immeasurably to the excitement and tension of the game.

There are simple, elegant rules for combat and magic, but because physical confrontations with the Mythos minions inevitably result in the death of the PCs (a Cthulhu spawn could vaporize a platoon without lifting a tentacle), the game rewards intelligence, caution, and planning. Familiarity with the Lovecraft stories isn't necessary; in fact, half of the fun of Call of Cthulhu is unraveling the terrifying secrets behind the Deep Ones (a race of Lesser Servitors), Shub-Niggurath (the Black Goat of the Woods with a Thousand Young), Nyarlathotep (the Crawling Chaos), and the mighty Cthulhu himself. Call of Cthulhu is breathtaking in scope and as richly textured as a fine novel. All role-players owe it to themselves to experience this truly remarkable game.

Buyer's Notes: The various editions are packaged as boxed sets, hardback books, and trade paperbacks. The trade paperback fourth edition (clearly labeled as such on the cover) is the best buy; it includes all of the material from the previous editions, along with material from the *Cthulhu Companion* and *Fragments of Fear* sourcebooks.

Suggested Supplements: All of the Chaosium supplements are enthusiastically recommended. The best: *Dreamlands* (background material and ready-to-play adventures set in the world of dreams; lighter in tone than the Mythos-based material, but just as engaging), *Great Old Ones* (six adventures, each featuring a different Cthulhu horror; a good place to begin for first-time players), *Cthulhu Classics* (a collection of early adventures, another good introductory supplement), *Terror Australis* (Mythos adventures in Australia), *Cthulhu by Gaslight* (Mythos adventures in Victorian London), and *Masks of Nyarlathotep* (a brilliant, ambitious globe-spanning campaign; perhaps the best role-playing adventure ever published, and the all-time favorite of the author of this book). Supplements produced by Theatre of the Mind Enterprises (*Death in Dunwich*, *Whispers from the Abyss*) and Games Workshop (*Green and Pleasant Land*, *Statue of the Sorcerer*, *Trail of the Loathsome Slime*) are also good, but they don't quite have the flair of the Chaosium books. Owners of the earlier editions of the game should investigate the *Cthulhu Companion* and *Fragments of Fear* sourcebooks, which include new rules, extra creatures, and helpful referee tips.

Champions***½

Complexity: Medium/High
Hero Games/Iron Crown Enterprises, First Edition: 1981;
Fourth Edition: 1989

In addition to being one of the oldest superhero RPGs, Champions is easily the biggest and arguably the best. It's been squeezed, expanded, modified, and amended for nearly ten years, finally emerging in 1989 as a massive 300-plus-page hardback that's as complete as a comic-book game can be. Befitting its scope, Champions boasts a formidable list of designers, among them George MacDonald, Steve Peterson, Rob Bell, Aaron Allston, Jim Dorethy, Dennis Mallonee, Steve Maurer, Greg Porter, David Rogers, Mike Stackpole, Tom Steubing, Doug Tabb, Duane Tremaine, and Scott Bennie.

Character creation is the heart of any RPG, but it's really what superhero games are all about. Champions has a terrific system that gives players near-total freedom in assembling the superheroes of their dreams. Each player receives a fixed number of Character Points, which he spends to improve his PC's basic attributes (Strength, Dexterity, Intelligence, etc.) and buy skills, talents, superpowers, and equipment. Within modest restrictions, any combination of skills, talents, and powers is allowable, and there are dozens to choose from. Skills include Acrobatics, Computer Programming, Seduction, and Electronics. Talents range from Ambidexterity and Perfect Pitch to Danger Sense and Speed Reading, while powers include Telekinesis, Energy Blast, Invisibility, and Missile Deflection. Players can also buy a Power Advantage to increase the effect of a power, or accept a Power Limitation to weaken a power and reduce its cost. If a player runs out of Character Points, he can acquire more of them by accepting one or more Disadvantages, such as a special vulnerability (comparable to Superman's weakness to kryptonite) or a secret identity (which he must protect at all costs). It's a flexible, comprehensive system, but with over one hundred pages of rules, it can also become tedious; Champions is not for the impatient.

The combat system is the game's weakest feature, a seemingly endless parade of numbers, formulas, and tables that's all but certain to discourage first-timers. For instance, to determine a PC's Offensive Combat Value (one of the variables necessary to compute an attack attempt), a player must (1) determine his base OCV by dividing his Dexterity by 3, (2) add the applicable skill levels, (3) apply the relevant weapon and armor modifiers, (4) check for Combat Maneuver modifiers, (5) apply any combat modifiers, and (6) factor in the range modifiers. In the game's defense, combat receives no more emphasis here than it does in the comic books, but be forewarned that a simple fistfight can take an hour or more to resolve.

The rest of the game is terrific. There's a long section explaining the fine points of superhero campaigns, complete with adventure design sheets, combat record sheets, and adventure recap sheets to record your hero's greatest triumphs. The Campaign Book section provides a ready-made superhero group called—what else?—the Champions, an assortment of gaudy supervillains such as the Tombstone Kid and the Stalker, and two brief but engaging introductory adventures. Even with the clunky combat rules, Champions successfully captures the peculiar ambiance of a comic book in all its melodramatic splendor. Of all the superhero RPGs, Champions remains the connoisseur's choice.

Buyer's Notes: Hardback book. The earlier trade paperback editions are now obsolete.

Suggested Supplements: The following adventures were published in conjunction with earlier editions of Champions, but can be converted to fourth edition rules with a minimum of effort (suggestions are included in the fourth edition): *V.O.I.C.E. of Doom* (death sentence for the Freedom Squad), *Wrath of the Seven Horsemen* (search for evil artifacts), and *To Serve and Protect* (renegade superheroes). Keep an eye out for *Classic Enemies* (compilation of adversaries), *Mindgames* (parapsychological adventures), and *Challenges for Champions* (several short scenarios and more new villains), all designed with the fourth edition rules in mind. Champions is also compatible with other games using the "Hero System" rules, most notably Justice Inc., Star Hero, and Danger International.

Chill**

Complexity: Low
Pacesetter Ltd., 1984

A horror game for the easily frightened. As members of S.A.V.E. (the Societas Albae Viae Eternitata, also known as the Eternal Society of the White Way), players attempt to flush out the forces of darkness and banish them from our besieged planet. While most of Chill's vampires, werewolves, and other B-movie refugees wouldn't scare a ten-year-old, they're appropriate to the modest ambitions of the game.

The game systems stress action and simplicity, not unlike the rules for Pacesetter's other RPGs, Timemaster and Star Ace, from which they derive. Character creation involves the usual random dice-rolls to determine the usual attributes (Strength, Dexterity, Agility, etc.); exceptional characters have access to the Art, a form of user-friendly magic, which enables them to scare off the bad guys. Though the simple rules are fitting for novice players, requiring that all PCs belong to this dumb S.A.V.E. organization is too restrictive, and the Art stuff is just plain silly. A single table resolves all game actions, but it's a mixed blessing—the results are so vague that the referee might as well make them up himself. The fear rules are puzzling (PCs get brave awfully fast and for no apparent reason), the combat rules are stiff (one side moves and attacks, then the other side moves and attacks), and the economic system is ridiculous (everybody seems to have an unlimited bank account).

Though it's been out of print for years, Chill remains as popular as ever on the convention circuit. I'm not sure why—maybe because its flexibility lends itself to short, convention-length adventures, or maybe because it's easy to learn and run. Whatever the reason, Chill is too shallow for extended campaigns, and lacks the depth to please anyone but the most undemanding players. For beginners only.

Buyer's Notes: Boxed set. A completely revised hardback edition is scheduled for publication toward the end of 1990 by Mayfair Games.

Suggested Supplements: Though well written and fun to read, the Chill supplements also tend to be underdeveloped and dull to play. *Vampires* is the best of the lot, a sourcebook detailing several different varieties of bloodsuckers. Acceptable adventures: *Death on Tour* (rock-and-roll vampires), *Isle of the Dead* (haunted amusement park), and *Village of Twilight* (deadly Mexican jungle).

Chivalry and Sorcery**½

Complexity: High
Fantasy Games Unlimited Inc., 1983

In the wake of the stunning success of Dungeons and Dragons, it didn't take long before everyone with a typewriter and a copy of *Lord of the Rings* was publishing fantasy RPGs. Designers Ed

Simbalist and Wilf Backhaus took a different approach from their competitors, stressing the realistic elements and minimizing the whimsy. The result was Chivalry and Sorcery, a meticulously detailed simulation of life in medieval Europe, where characters were more likely to face the challenge of a taxpayer's revolt than a fire-breathing dragon. However, the game's unparalleled complexity discouraged all but the most determined players, and Chivalry and Sorcery seemed fated for oblivion.

In 1983, Fantasy Games Unlimited released a revised edition of Chivalry and Sorcery that eliminated much of the original's superfluous material, such as the mass combat rules, and streamlined the systems to make them more palatable for players who weren't interested in making C&S a lifetime project. While it's certainly more manageable than the original, it's still among the most complex RPGs ever published.

The game systems aren't particularly innovative—the basics of character creation, combat, and encounters will be familiar to anyone who's played D&D—but they're stupefyingly convoluted. Nowhere is this more evident than in the magic system, which gets off to an uneasy start by warning players to think twice before choosing mages as characters. It's a warning worth taking seriously: the C&S magic system involves a mind-numbing collection of tables, formulas, and rules that could serve as a grad school text in wizardry. There are well over a dozen different fields of study for would-be wizards, each of which has distinct rules for acquiring spells and how to use them in combat. Learning a spell is more than just making a few dice-rolls; it involves tracking the time spent studying a new procedure, determining the influence of all applicable skills, and factoring in the magnitude of the spell itself. The system works, but not without a considerable investment of time and effort from both the players and the referee.

The rest of the game is equally tough, and the skimpy examples of play, poor organization, and confusing charts don't help. Still, the discussions of medieval history and the sections on campaign design are superb; it's almost worth the purchase price just to get this material. For players with insatiable appetites for detail, there are few better choices than Chivalry and

Sorcery. The less obsessive will find C&S more valuable as a source of ideas.

Buyer's Notes: Boxed set. Avoid the sloppy original edition, published as a trade paperback.

Suggested Supplements: The *Swords and Sorcerers* sourcebook contains detailed information on Viking, Celtic, and Mongol cultures; not only is the material useful for expanding the scope of Chivalry and Sorcery, it's easily adaptable to other fantasy RPGs. The *C&S Sourcebook* includes new rules for monsters, commerce, and mass combat; essential for referees planning an extended campaign.

City State of the Invincible Overlord***

Complexity: Medium
Mayfair Games Inc., 1987

This is not a self-contained game, but a supplement that can be adapted to Dungeons and Dragons, RuneQuest, Rolemaster, or any other fantasy RPG. City State portrays a fantasy city in lavish detail, complete with descriptions of over two dozen neighborhoods, a history of the Briarwood area, and loads of important personalities. Special touches abound; there's a parchment player's map, a transparent grid overlay to facilitate movement, and a surplus of adventure ideas. A truly beautiful product.

The problems with City State are common to all generic supplements; namely, it takes a fair amount of work from the referee to adapt the material to a specific game system, and there are some obvious continuity problems when abruptly dropping a setting this detailed into an existing campaign world. But for referees in the market for this type of generic material, City State of the Invincible Overlord is a great buy.

Buyer's Note: Boxed set.

Suggested Supplements: Those reluctant to invest in the complete boxed set might want to sample it first by looking at one of the numerous City State supplements. Try *Wraith of Derric's*

Deep (haunted coal mines), *Betrayal at Bogwater* (dwarven domains), and *The Haunt* (vampires and magic); all include interesting sourcebook information and adventures. The Mayfair City State series adapts material previously published by the Judges' Guild organization. A lot of the Judges' Guild material is still around, but though it's all well done, the Mayfair editions are much classier products.

Conan***

Complexity: Low
TSR Inc., 1985

Who's better suited for a fantasy RPG than literature's most famous barbarian? Designer Dave Cook brought the big lug to life in a game that's simple to play and remains true to the spirit of the Robert E. Howard stories. As in TSR's Marvel Super Heroes game, all actions in Conan are resolved on a single table, color-coded for easy reference. It works like this: A player rolls a die against his PC's rating for an applicable talent (say, his attack talent), then cross references the roll on the table; a White result means that the action was unsuccessful (the victim suffers no damage), a Green result means the action was modestly successful (the victim suffers one point of damage), and so on through five color ranges, peaking with the Red result (maximum damage, possibly fatal). It's versatile, easy to use, and produces reasonably accurate results.

Conan sidesteps the traditional attribute system—randomly determined ratings for physical and mental characteristics aren't used—opting instead to define PCs by their talents. A player chooses his character's country of origin, then buys talents by spending an allotment of thirty-five points; no more than five points can be spent on any single talent, and at least one talent must be taken from each of several talent groups. At the end of a successful adventure, surviving PCs earn additional points that can be spent to improve old talents or purchase new ones.

Though clearly not as sophisticated as, say, Advanced Dungeons and Dragons, the game's streamlined rules and clearly defined characters make it an excellent introduction to fantasy role-playing. That Conan remains true to its source material is both a strong point and a weakness. Fans of the Howard stories will feel right at home, but others may feel frustrated by the narrow focus; magic, for instance, is downplayed here, as it is in the stories. As for solving the game's biggest problem—namely, which player gets to play Conan—the referee is on his own.

Buyer's Note: Boxed set.

Suggested Supplements: The *Conan Unchained* adventure evokes the Hyborian world with style; it's an exciting introduction to the game.

Crimefighter***½

Complexity: Medium
Task Force Games, 1988

Released a few years ago without much fanfare, Crimefighter is a sleeper of a game that most role-players missed. A superb simulation of television cop shows along the lines of "Dragnet" and "Adam 12," Crimefighter features a slick, clever design by Aaron Allston that perfectly captures the campy tone of its source material.

The simple character-generation system uses basic attributes as skill modifiers; that is, Strength, Dexterity, Constitution, Intelligence, Willpower, and Charisma are expressed as positive and negative ratings, each of which affects particular skills. For instance, a Dexterity rating of +2 acts as a positive modifier to the Gymnastics and Firearms skills, while an Intelligence rating of −3 worsens the Chemistry and Medicine skills. All game mechanics revolve around Success Rolls, where players roll three six-sided dice and compare the result against the applicable skill level, modified by the difficulty of the task; rolls of 11 or more are automatically successful. For example, assume that a PC cop wants to shoot at a fleeing criminal. The referee decides that the situation calls for a difficulty rating of −3 (reflecting the difficulty of hitting a moving target). The PC has a Dexterity rating of +2, which results in a cumulative modifier of −1. He rolls a 12, subtracts the penalty, and with a final score of 11, he successfully shoots the bad guy. It's a great system: elegant, flexible, and as easy for the referee as it is for the players.

Combat is more complicated, involving grid maps, counters, and tactical rules more befitting a board game than an RPG. It's comparable to the combat system of Gangbusters, not quite as streamlined but nearly as much fun. A comprehensive sourcebook section details police procedures, weapons and equipment, and the American legal system, including rules that generate random sentencing for convicted criminals. Two brief but entertaining scenarios round out the rulebook. Fresh, imaginative, and fun, Crimefighter is the best game of its type.

Buyer's Note: Boxed set.

Critter Commandos***

Complexity: Low
Crunchy Frog Enterprises, 1989

Designed by Paul Arden Lidberg, Critter Commandos is a simple tactical wargame using cartoon animals for soldiers. The critters, represented by counters supplied with the game or by metal miniatures supplied by the players, are rated for Strength, Accuracy, Mind, Movement, and Holes (a measurement of damage), assigned to troops, then deployed on a tabletop battlefield. Combat follows a sequence of movement, target selection, fire resolution, hand-to-hand (or paw-to-paw) attacks, and morale checks (scaredey cats always retreat). With a minimum of charts and dice-rolls, the game moves quickly and is a snap to learn, even for those unfamiliar with miniatures games.

What makes Critter Commandos so much fun are its cartoon elements. The critters don't die, they fill up with "holes" and disappear. There are special rules for four-legged movement, along with combat bonuses for Mice (who scare their opponents), Turtles (whose shells make them hard to hit), and Kangaroos (who can hop up mountains). Weapons choices include

Rubber Mallets, Cream Pies, Sneezing Bombs, and the deadly Giant Banana Peel. Role-playing takes a backseat to combat, which is too bad because there's an intriguing section at the end of the book describing a cartoon universe where the F.R.O.G. Federation, the Ratzi Empire, and the Zen-Toadies compete for control. The material is far too underdeveloped to be of much use for role-playing adventures, though ambitious referees might be able to do something with it.

Buyer's Note: Trade paperback.

Cyberpunk***

Complexity: Medium
R. Talsorian Games, 1988

Spearheaded by science-fiction novelists William Gibson and Bruce Sterling, the cyberpunk movement depicts a nightmare future of sprawling corporations, crumbling governments, and high-tech killers enhanced with cybernetic implants. Role-playing designers have been quick to jump on the bandwagon, with Cyberpunk, Cyberspace, and Shadowrun being the most prominent examples. Cyberpunk, designed by Mike Pondsmith, remains the purist's choice, the RPG most successfully capturing the genre's grim atmosphere.

Set a few years after the turn of the twenty-first century, players take the roles of shadowy vigilantes struggling for survival in a world beset by food blights, drug plagues, and rampant corruption. There are a number of colorful character types from which to choose, including Rockerboys (rock-and-roll revolutionaries), Nomads (homeless road warriors), Solos (corporate hit men), and Netrunners (renegade computer hackers). Each character has a unique ability; Solos, for instance, excel in combat, while Netrunners can penetrate protected computer networks. Players buy attributes for their PCs with a random number of character points, then run them through a Lifepath system to generate skills, personal histories, and educational levels. Finally, PCs acquire cybernetic abilities via artificial limbs and implanted computer circuits. Such enhancements border on the superhuman, and they're not without risk: increased cybernetics make a character more machinelike, and a surplus of them can displace his humanity altogether, transforming him into a mindless NPC controlled by the referee. It's a fascinating, sophisticated character-generation system, and the game's best feature.

Combat is chart-heavy but playable, and extremely dangerous for PCs; one well-placed shot is usually all it takes to wipe out a careless Nomad. Courageous PCs can enter the Net, a bizarre telecommunications network of linked computers that stores protected programs and secret information. Various interfaces defend the Net from intruders, and PCs may find themselves facing a startling array of computer-generated opponents, some resembling magical monsters, others resembling Prohibition-era gangsters. Still other Net defenses can wipe an intruder's brain clean or freeze his heart. It's a chilling, evocative setting, endlessly adaptable.

Cyberpunk's gritty realism may not be everyone's idea of a good time; characters tend to lead short, intense lives, flashy heroics are in short supply, and cynicism abounds. A terrific game for pessimists.

Buyer's Note: Boxed set.

Suggested Supplements: Hardwired is an excellent source of background material, personalities, and adventure ideas. Slickly presented and tersely written, it's a great place to start a Cyberpunk campaign.

Cyberspace***

....

Complexity: High
Iron Crown Enterprises, 1989

Cyberspace is another excellent cyberpunk RPG, replete with cybernetic misfits, maniacal corporate giants, and a vast assortment of futuristic nightmares, but this one is recommended with reservations. Packed with tables, numbers, and formulas, Cyberspace is clearly intended for sophisticated players who don't mind thumbing through a thick rulebook to dig out the string of modifiers necessary to resolve combat or create characters. Not surprisingly, it's a close cousin of Iron Crown's equally demanding Space Master game.

Rules aside, Cyberspace features the most thoroughly developed background of any cyberpunk RPG, including in-depth history of a world enslaved by the powerful MegaCorps, a fascinating glossary of high-tech street slang ("on ice" refers to comrades in cryogenic suspension, "wormtech" is black market technology), and a meticulously detailed listing of cybernetic enhancements, such as microprocessors implanted in the heart to analyze and filter chemicals, and a synthetic fiber called Neo-Muscle used to replace normal body tissue. Computer technology receives the best treatment I've ever seen in an RPG, a scholarly discussion of processor cores, operating systems, and machine languages that also includes ingenious rules for designing computers and their programs.

Players can take the roles of Sleazes, Net Junkies, Tech Rats, and other colorful types, but creating them involves a tedious amount of number-juggling and chart-checking. Combat is likewise cumbersome, though it produces realistic if somewhat fussy results (the Personal Maneuver Chart, for instance, has nine action categories and twenty-four possible results for each). As a game, Cyberspace is playable for those determined enough to untangle the rules. As a sourcebook, it's an essential purchase for anyone planning a cyberpunk campaign, regardless of the game system they're using.

Buyer's Note: Trade paperback.

Suggested Supplements: Edge-On is an excellent introductory adventure; tense, colorful, and challenging. Cyberspace can also be adapted to Space Master material; the Cyberspace rules explain how to do it.

Cyborg Commando***½

Complexity: High
New Infinities Productions, Inc., 1987

Cyborg Commando was easily the most anticipated role-playing release of 1987; it was the first design by Gary Gygax following his departure from TSR Inc., the company built on his groundbreaking Dungeons and Dragons. Equally impressive was the inclusion of co-authors Kim Mohan and Frank Mentzer, two superstar designers who were instrumental in guiding D&D through its glory days in the late 1970s and early 1980s. With heavyweights like these in charge, it was no surprise that Cyborg Commando was a first-rate design—innovative, compelling, and startling in its uncompromising approach to science-fiction gaming. Unfortunately, its difficult rules and narrow scope severely limited its appeal, and Cyborg Commando has been languishing ever since.

The game takes place in the year 2035, when Earth is being overrun by the hostile Xenoborgs, bent on adding our planet to their roster of slave colonies. Naturally, conventional forces have no chance against the Xenoborgs, so the fate of the Earth is in the hands of the Commandos, a formidable squad of cybernetic supersoldiers controlled by the players. To create a Commando, a player first designs a normal human character, then transplants the brain into a mechanical body (the human body spends the rest of the game in cryogenic storage). The resulting Commando can do just about anything the player likes—it can blast holes through buildings with its forearm lasers, smash opponents with its martial arts abilities, and even straighten up the house with its domestic skills. The possibilities are endless, and role-playing a Commando is as much fun as it sounds.

Though the rules are straightforward and clearly explained, they're also quite complicated. The section on the biology of the Xenoborgs is as detailed as a medical book and just as intimidating. Combat resolution is spread over two Activity Cycles, which are divided into five Phases; various actions are assigned to particular phases depending on their speeds; it works, but it's a headache to learn. Computing movement in outer space requires an understanding of basic calculus, along with tackling mind-bending concepts, such as "the Schwarzchild solution for the metric tensor outside a static spherically symmetrical mass distribution." For players used to dealing with dragons and magic wands, this is mighty heady stuff.

Though Cyborg Commando is not intended for beginners,

the no-nonsense approach and sheer volume of detail can overwhelm even the most experienced player. There are few guidelines for adventures, and the game's strict insistence on authenticity (fire-breathing space monsters and time-traveling aliens are strictly forbidden) make the referee's job all the more difficult. But for those up to the challenge, it's definitely worth checking out—Cyborg Commando is hardcore role-playing at its best.

Buyer's Note: Boxed set.

Suggested Supplements: Tacky artwork notwithstanding, all of the Cyborg Commando supplements are worth a look. Especially good are *Operation Bifrost*, featuring new rules for underground exploration and combat, *Film at Eleven*, a rousing adventure set in the Xenoborg-occupied Midwest, and *San Francisco Knights*, a three-chapter adventure involving the establishment of a Commando base near Big Sur, California.

Danger International***

Complexity: Medium
Hero Games, 1985

Danger International is essentially an updating and expansion of Hero Games' Espionage RPG. While Espionage focuses on secret agents, Danger International adds private eyes, mercenaries, and antiterrorists who operate in any era, ranging from the mid-1940s all the way into the twenty-first century. Obviously, this is a more frivolous game than the dead-serious Espionage. Thanks to the entertaining approach taken by designers L. Douglas Garrett, George Mac Donald, and Steve Peterson, it's also more fun.

The rules are similar to those of Champions, Justice Inc., and other Hero games, with players building characters from scratch by buying attributes and skills with a fixed number of character points, or by choosing "package deal" templates such as Police

Detective or Secret Agent for ready-to-play PCs. Skills are heavily combat-oriented, and the weapon list looks like the Pentagon's Christmas catalog, but then violence is basically what Danger International is all about. The combat system involves some tricky mechanics; vehicles, for instance, have eight distinct combat ratings along with separate procedures for ranged combat, ramming and forcing, and collisions. It's all clearly explained, though the detail is likely to intimidate casual players.

The sourcebook material is the game's best feature, especially the informative sections for adapting Danger International to various role-playing genres, including Crime Fighting, Martial Arts, Modern Military, and even Horror and Science Fiction. Though no single genre is covered in depth, there's enough here to give creative referees a solid foundation for designing their own scenarios. To show how it's done, the book concludes with two interesting introductory adventures, one featuring martial arts, the other dealing with antiterrorist operations. Because Danger International sprawls in so many directions, it's not as good as the more focused Top Secret/S.I. or James Bond games, although it's clearly superior to the turgid Espionage.

Buyer's Note: Trade paperback.

Suggested Supplements: All Espionage supplements are compatible with Danger International, as are supplements for other Hero Game RPGs; Champions and Justice Inc. material works especially well. Danger International also includes conversion notes to adapt the rules to the Twilight: 2000 game.

Daredevils***

....

Complexity: Medium
Fantasy Games Unlimited Inc., 1982

Set in the era of pulp heroes, circa 1930, Daredevils allows players to take the roles of swashbuckling soldiers of fortune along the lines of Indiana Jones and Doc Savage. Designed by Bob

Charette and Paul Hume, the game systems derive from the team's Aftermath game, but Daredevils is a vast improvement, avoiding Aftermath's cumbersome mechanics with simpler rules and clearer organization.

Along with workmanlike rules for character generation, combat, and skills, there's an interesting section detailing the use of luck (to save the PCs' hides at last minute, in the pulp tradition) and a detailed description of the world of the 1930s, complete with profiles of key personalities, a time line of historical events, and other informative material. The problems with the game are mostly minor. Supernatural pulp heroes like the Shadow notwithstanding, the inclusion of invisibility, hypnosis, and other extraordinary powers jars with the game's gritty realism. A few of the concepts, such as acquiring skills and handling NPCs, are a little fuzzy. And though a vast improvement over Aftermath the combat system is still a little awkward. But overall, Daredevils successfully captures the flavor of the era and sets the stage for challenging pulp hero adventures.

Buyer's Note: Boxed set.

Suggested Supplements: All of the *Daredevil Adventures* anthologies feature exciting scenarios and interesting sourcebook material. Especially recommended are *No. 2: The Menace Beneath the Sea* (adventures in the South Pacific, including a showdown with the nefarious Dr. Ling and the Society of the Blue Dragon) and *No. 3: Supernatural Thrillers* (three entertaining excursions into the occult).

Darksword Adventures**½

Complexity: Medium/High
Bantam Spectra Books, 1988

I imagine a lot of people picked this up thinking it was the fourth installment of the Darksword novel series. Surprise— it's a role-playing game in the guise of a mass market paper-

back. Though they're now firmly established in the novel
business, authors Margaret Weis and Tracy Hickman have
solid roots in the role-playing industry, having written the
groundbreaking Dragonlance novel trilogy for TSR Inc. Hickman
also designed some of the all-time best Advanced Dungeons and
Dragons adventures, including *Ravenloft* and the *Desert of Desolation* series.

I don't know what they were thinking of when they came up
with "Phantasia," the role-playing system featured in
Darksword Adventures. The rules are tied so closely to the novels (*Forging the Darksword, Doom of the Darksword,* and *Triumph
of the Darksword*) that adapting the material to other systems,
such as AD&D or RuneQuest, is all but impossible. Worse,
they're so detailed and jargon-heavy that role-playing novices
won't know where to begin.

I've never encountered a game so determined to speak its
own language. For instance, the term "mystery" is used to
designate some kind of character class, distances are measured
in "decimetra" (equal to 1.5 meters), and the results table is
called a Comparative Probability Standard chart. Movement
rates are given in "mila" per hour; a "mila" is about the same
as a mile, so why the new word? There's a special form of
combat called Possessional Combat, used when two characters
are struggling over an object; most other games would resolve
this with one die-toss—why does it require its own special section in "Phantasia"? Even the term "Life" is used in a context
guaranteed to baffle anyone unfamiliar with the Darksword
novels.

What's aggravating is that when all the verbiage is cleared
away, "Phantasia" is a pretty good little RPG, similar in tone to
Advanced Dungeons and Dragons and featuring an especially
nice magic system. Clearly, the authors intend Darksword Adventures to enhance the enjoyment of the novel trilogy, not
vice versa, but in doing so, they've limited the game's appeal to
a very narrow group; namely, advanced role-players who've
thoroughly digested all three of the novels and are willing to
learn a difficult game system that's essentially useless in any
setting other than the Darksword universe.

Buyer's Notes: Mass market paperback. All three of the Darksword novels are required to fully appreciate Darksword Adventures.

DC Heroes***½

Complexity: Medium
Mayfair Games Inc., First Edition: 1985; Second Edition: 1989

For more than half a century, DC Comics has published thousands of stories featuring Superman, Batman, Wonder Woman, and dozens of other legendary superheroes, creating a mythos so complex that only the most dedicated fan can keep it all straight. Designer Greg Gordon performed a remarkable job shaping it all into the stylish, innovative DC Heroes game. Ray Winninger and Thomas Cook, responsible for the classy second edition, didn't do too badly either.

A game alleging to cover the entire DC universe must account for a lot of characters with wildly divergent abilities, ranging from the relatively powerless Lois Lane to the nearly omnipotent Superman. DC Heroes addresses the problems with the Attribute Point, a generic unit used to measure time, distance, weight, volume, and any other concept that can be expressed as a quantity. The system has a base value of zero, equivalent to the lowest quantity of any measured unit; in the game, an AP of zero equals 4 seconds, 50 pounds, or 10 feet. Each additional AP doubles the value of the previous amount; therefore, an AP of 2 equals 8 seconds, 100 pounds, and 20 feet, while an AP of 3 equals 16 seconds, 200 pounds and 40 feet. A hero with an intelligence of 4 APs is twice as smart as a character with 3 APs.

All characters have fixed ratings in their Physical, Mental, and Mystical abilities, each of which is divided into Action, Resistance, and Effect components for a total of nine basic attributes, all expressed in APs. AP units are interchangeable, meaning that Hawkman, with a strength of 6 APs, can lift 6 APs of weight (about 1.5 tons). Captain Marvel, with a flying speed of 14, can fly a distance of 14 APs per phase (about 16 miles in 4 seconds). Each character has a number of Hero Points that can be spent to boost his abilities temporarily, usually by one or two APs, allowing him to perform extraordinary feats in times of crisis.

It's a brilliant system, simple to use and adaptable to any situation, though at first it's hard to get used to the rapid growth rate of APs. For instance, the difference between 1 AP and 2 APs of time is only 4 seconds, but the difference between 18 and 19 APs is a full week. Higher-level APs are increasingly imprecise; a hero who can lift 1.5 tons and another who can lift 2.9 tons both have a Strength of AP 6. The power boosts provided by Hero Point expenditures might also raise some eyebrows; it's possible for a human character like Green Arrow or Batman to juggle cars if he gets the right dice-rolls.

Action resolution, including combat, is as simple as the AP system, but it's likewise imprecise. Every action has an Acting Value (such as the Flash's fist) and an Opposing Value (such as Captain Cold's jaw), which are cross-indexed with a die-roll on the Action Table. Success on the Action Table leads to a second roll on the Result Table. These are the only two tables needed for play, which is good news. The bad news is that it's up to the referee to interpret the results (exactly what happens when the fist connects with the jaw).

Both the first and second editions of DC Heroes feature identical game mechanics, though the second edition clarifies some of the fuzzier rules from the first, especially those pertaining to equipment, money, and the costs of powers and skills. The second edition also adds a wealth of additional background material, including new characters, new powers, and informative commentary by DC Comics writers and artists (Roy Thomas discusses Golden Age Heroes, Jack Kirby writes about the New Gods, and Robert Kahniger explains his approach to DC's war comics). In a hobby where bargains are scarce, DC Heroes contains an exceptionally generous number of components, including a seventy-two-page Rules Manual, a sixty-four-page Character Handbook, a ninety-six-page Roster Book, an Action Wheel used to resolve game actions, a thirty-two-page introductory adventure starring the Justice League International, a three-panel referee's screen, and seventy-five color character cards.

Buyer's Notes: Boxed set. Stick with the second edition (the black box with Superman, Batman, and the yellow DC logo on the front).

Suggested Supplements: All of the adventures star specific characters from the DC universe. The best: *Countdown to Armageddon* (Superman), *Pawns of Time* (Legion of Super Heroes; this is an extended adventure continued in the *Knight to Planet 3*, *Mad Rook's Gambit*, and *King for All Time* supplements), *Eternity, Inc.* (Infinity Inc.), *City of Fear* (Flash), *Operation: Atlantis* (Suicide Squad), and *Wheel of Destruction* (solitaire adventure for Batman). Mayfair also publishes a series of sourcebooks detailing the casts, backgrounds, and locales pertinent to various DC titles; they're all excellent, as enjoyable for comic fans as they are for role-players. The best: *Superman Sourcebook*, *Legion of Super Heroes* (both volumes), *Batman Sourcebook*, and *Green Lantern Corps*.

Deepsleep**

Complexity: Low
Godiva Productions, 1988

A game with some clever ideas and a good attitude. Instead of assuming the roles of imaginary characters, Deepsleep players essentially play themselves as visitors to a secret government research installation. While they're there, World War III abruptly breaks out. To maximize their chances of survival, the players hide out in suspended animation tubes. The game begins when they wake up and find themselves in the headquarters of a crime-busting superhero, in an Amazon slave pit, on the moon, or in any other setting of the referee's choice. From there, the referee more or less makes up the rest of the adventure as he goes along. Other quirky rules enable dead PCs to continue the game as ghosts and allow Demigod Class PCs to take control of the game from the referee and direct the adventure themselves. Anarchy at its finest.

Unfortunately, the anarchic approach extends to the writing and editing as well, where it's not nearly as charming. The rulebook is haphazardly organized; inexplicably, the first section after "Starting the Game" is "Non-Magical Combat," and "Anti-Matter Magic" precedes the general discussion of how magic is supposed to work. Some sections, such as the rules for spellcasting, are woefully underdeveloped, while in others the explanations are so casual that it's nearly impossible to tell what the designer is getting at. The scenarios are very sketchy, and staging advice is all but nonexistent. With a thorough rewrite and a merciless editor, Deepsleep could someday emerge as a major system. For now, it's primarily a collection of intriguing ideas.

Buyer's Note: Trade paperback.

Delta Force**½

Complexity: Medium/High
Task Force Games, 1986

In Delta Force, the PCs are part of an elite U.S. commando unit charged with defending the world against terrorist activities. Character creation, skill use, and other basic systems are fairly routine, with the exception of PC damage; players are kept in the dark about their character's actual number of hit points, meaning that they're never quite sure when their PCs are about to bite the dust. It's a nice touch, even if it means more work for the referee, who has to track the PCs' health in addition to all of his other duties. Combat is detailed and realistic, involving a staggering number of weapons, equipment, and vehicle statistics.

Actually, Delta Force has a lot less to do with role-playing than it does with tactical wargames. The characters have no personalities to speak of, and the adventures involve little more than completing military missions, not unlike the search-and-destroy and hostage rescue scenarios featured in Sniper, Squad Leader, and other wargames. Delta Force works as a reasonably challenging tactical exercise, but it misses the mark as an RPG.

Buyer's Note: Boxed set.

Suggested Supplement: The *Delta Force Companion* sourcebook adds meat to the bones of the original game; essential for serious players. The best adventure: the challenging *Terror at Sea*.

Doctor Who**½

Complexity: Medium
FASA Corp., 1985

Games derived from television shows, movies, or books had better deliver the goods to the fans, or they'll soon be gathering dust in the publisher's warehouse. Doctor Who strives mightily to capture the flavor of the long-running British TV series, but though it gets all the details right, it misses the essence. *Doctor Who*—the series—is witty and fun. Doctor Who—the game—is dry and dull.

The game mechanics are adequate but unimpressive, reminiscent of FASA's superb Star Trek game. Players roll for Strength, Endurance, and other standard attributes, then add special abilities (such as Enhanced Endurance and Telepathy) and skills (such as Artistic Expression and Engineering). Both humans and the alien Gallifreyans are available as PCs; it's also possible to recruit the Doctor himself as a PC. Oddly, though players have a certain amount of freedom in deciding their PCs' skills and attributes, their appearance, age, and personality traits are determined at random, which can result in Indecisive Homely Old Adults or Squeamish Adolescent Midgets—except for extremely flexible players, this isn't a very satisfying system. The combat rules derive from tactical board games and apparently require grid maps and counters, which is okay, except that there are no grid maps or counters included with the game.

What saves the day for Doctor Who is its superb sourcebook material, page after page of detailed essays discussing the Tardis, the Temporal Marauders, Gallifreyan history, and other Who-ish minutiae, recommended for all fans of the TV series, whether they're role-players or not. As for the game itself, *Doctor Who* loyalists are likely to enjoy it, but players who've never heard of the Doctor will probably wonder what the fuss is all about.

Buyer's Note: Boxed set.

Suggested Supplements: Both *Harlewick Horror* and *Legions of Death* are good introductory adventures that capture the ambiance of the TV show reasonably well.

Domination**½

· ·

Complexity: Medium
Star Childe Publications, 1989

It's the last decade of the twentieth century, and the Earth is being overrun by a race of alien warriors called the Kalotions and their evil allies. It's up to a group of noble heroes—like the PCs—to rally and save the planet. That's about all there is to Domination, a straightforward science-fiction military simulation that works better as a supplement to the Sabot and Laser miniatures game (see under *Suggested Supplements*) than as a stand-alone RPG.

Rated for five basic attributes (Strength, Aptitude, Agility, Fortitude, and Presence) and assigned to various paramilitary careers (such as Freedom Fighter, Infantry Soldier, and Armored Vehicle Specialist), the characters are long on numbers and short on personality. Though the character-generation rules are brief and uncomplicated, the resulting PCs don't always make sense. As each basic attribute can range anywhere from 1 to 100, it's possible for a beginning character to have an IQ of 50 (based on an Aptitude of 15 or less) while his friend has an IQ of 130 or more (based on an Aptitude of 100); the first PC might be able to lift only 40 kilograms (20 or less in Strength), while his friend could lift over 400 (a Strength score of 130 or more, including bonuses).

The combat system is quick and easy, involving a three-step procedure of Initiation (who shoots first), Contact (which shots hit), and Results (how much damage). The game intends to focus on armed engagements, but there's little help for the referee on setting up an adventure. Though designer Blaine Pardoe includes a lengthy background section describing the history and ramifications of the Kalotion invasion, it's hard to tell how it all fits in with the role-playing rules.

Buyer's Note: Trade paperback.

Suggested Supplements: Sabot and Laser features board-gaming rules based on the concepts introduced in Domination. Designed for 1:285–1:300 scale micro-size armored vehicles, it's not unlike the military simulations familiar to wargamers. The game is simple and clever, featuring an especially nice set of rules for jet aircraft that uses a standard mapboard and a special Aircraft Tracking Map. The board-game rules of Sabot and Laser are superior to the role-playing rules of Domination, so I'd go with Sabot if I were only buying one.

DragonQuest***

Complexity: Medium/High
Simulations Publications Inc., First Edition: 1980; TSR Inc., Revised Edition: 1989

In the 1970s, Simulations Publications Inc. of New York cranked out wargames at an unprecedented rate, including such now-classic titles as War in Europe, Terrible Swift Sword, and Campaign for North Africa. These weren't games for casual players, but meticulously detailed simulations intended for an audience of hardcore historians. Recognizing the skyrocketing popularity of role-playing, SPI took the plunge with a fantasy RPG of their own and, with great fanfare, released Dragon-Quest in 1980.

To no one's surprise, DragonQuest was an impressive product, assembled by a crack team of designers, including Eric Goldberg, Gerald Klug, David James Ritchie, Edward Woods, and Redmond Simonsen. The lavish package included three rulebooks, a color map, and over one hundred die-cut counters. Though the basic concepts didn't dramatically depart from Dungeons and Dragons, the game did include a number of interesting twists. In addition to standard fantasy occupations such as alchemists and thieves, characters could also pursue such unusual careers as military scientist, troubadour, and mechanician. The innovative magic system was based on three "branches" of magical energy—Thaumaturgies, Elementals, and Entities—each divided into a number of specialized colleges to give magic-wielding characters a startling variety of options.

But though the systems were as thorough as any of SPI's historical simulations, closer inspection revealed a lot of annoying rules, some of them awkward (a tediously complicated combat system), some underdeveloped (a dull selection of monsters), and some just plain silly (if a male player wants to use a female character, he has to roll the dice for permission). Whether the designers would be able to iron it all out in supplements, errata, and new editions became a moot point, as SPI went down the tubes in the early 1980s and DragonQuest was added to the list of Great Games That Never Were.

But this story has a happy ending. TSR Inc., publisher of Dungeons and Dragons, revived the game in 1989, with an impressive clean-up courtesy of Jon Pickens and original designer Gerald Klug. All of the game's deficiencies were neatly addressed, including a thorough revamping of the clunky combat rules. The result: a polished and sophisticated fantasy RPG with one of gaming's best-ever magic systems. The game's wargaming roots are still in evidence—the combat system is obviously derived from tactical wargames, and the formal writing style tends to be a little stiff—and it desperately needs a more colorful setting. But for now, the future looks bright for DragonQuest.

Buyer's Notes: The TSR trade paperback is the one to buy; it also includes a reprint of one of the game's original supplements, "The Camp of Alla-Akabar," a short but engaging introductory adventure.

Suggested Supplements: The adventure *Shattered Stone/*

Enchanted Wood is a nice introduction to the game, with the added bonus of some AD&D material if the DragonQuest rules aren't to your liking. If you can find it, the now-defunct Judges Guild published an excellent DragonQuest adventure in 1982 called *The Magebird Quest*, featuring a journey through the mysterious Rookeries in search of the rare azure-tipped sea falcon.

Dungeons and Dragons***½

Complexity: Low
TSR Inc., First Edition: 1974; Revised Edition: 1983

This, of course, is where it all started. Dungeons and Dragons is the oldest role-playing game and easily the best known. It began in the early 1970s as a fantasy supplement for a miniatures wargame called Chainmail. In 1974 designers Gary Gygax and Dave Arneson published the first official Dungeons and Dragons rules as a set of three booklets, which eventually were revised and refined into the first of the "basic" sets published in 1977. The rules received another polish in 1983, resulting in the Dungeons and Dragons Basic Rules boxed set, the definitive incarnation—for now, anyway—of the hobby's most enduring game.

Virtually all role-playing concepts now accepted as standard conventions began with Dungeons and Dragons. D&D introduced the idea of using player-characters as alter egos for the game's participants, as well as the concept of an independent referee (the Dungeon Master) to act as an impartial rules judge. Players determine random ratings for six basic attributes—Strength, Intelligence, Wisdom, Dexterity, Constitution, and Charisma—by rolling three six-sided dice for each, then choose character classes from seven general templates, including Cleric, Fighter, Thief, Elf, Dwarf, Halfling, and Magic-User. Each class has its own special abilities: Clerics and Magic-Users can cast spells, Elves can see in the dark and find secret doors, Thieves can pick pockets and open tricky locks.

Characters conduct attacks by comparing a die-roll against an opponent's Armor Class, which is a number representing his defensive capacity. Successful attacks result in a loss of hit points; when a character is reduced to zero, he's dead. PCs who survive an adventure acquire experience points that can be exchanged for higher ability levels. Each successive level gives PCs additional hit points, improved skills, and for Clerics and Magic-Users, more spells. D&D adventures tend to be very simple, typically involving a search for treasure to loot and monsters to battle in an underground labyrinth or an abandoned castle.

Purists grumble that D&D isn't just simple, but simple-minded. The rigid character classes give players little freedom in customizing their PCs, and advancement by levels is arbitrary and unrealistic. The magic system and combat rules are illogical, Armor Classes represent the chance of being hit rather than offering protection from damage, experience points are meaningless and abstract, the adventures are juvenile . . . you get the idea.

These grouches completely miss the point. Complaining that Dungeons and Dragons is an unrealistic RPG is like saying that chess is an inaccurate wargame. We're not talking about delving into the social structure of medieval Europe here, we're talking about tossing fireballs at lizard men and swiping gold pieces from ogres. Dungeons and Dragons provides a streamlined, easily mastered set of rules that emphasizes action and adventure. And as a bonus, it's an excellent introduction to the entire hobby.

Dungeons and Dragons also serves as as bridge to the more detailed Advanced Dungeons and Dragons. Though the games share the same concepts, they don't share the same rules. However, it's possible for experienced referees to adapt D&D supplements to the AD&D system and vice versa, as long as the players are willing to accept a few compromises here and there. Generally, D&D is the best choice for beginning players, as well as for experienced players who prefer its more improvisational approach. AD&D has rules and guidelines for nearly every conceivable game situation; it's the game of choice for sophisticated players comfortable with a higher level of detail.

Buyer's Note: Boxed set.

Suggested Supplements: Dungeons and Dragons is a modular game; that is, each successive expansion adds more rules, allowing players to run characters of increasingly higher levels. There are five D&D boxed sets in all, each with their own supplements.

Set 1: Basic Rules covers character levels 1 to 3. This is where to begin. The best basic supplement is *In Search of Adventure*, a thick anthology of related scenarios filled with monsters, treasures, and magic. It's a perfect introduction to D&D (note that this book collects material originally presented in the following supplements: *Castle Caldwell and Beyond, Journey to the Rock, The Keep on the Borderlands, Palace of the Silver Princess, Horror on the Hill, Rahasia, The Lost City*, and *The Veiled Society).*

Set 2: Expert Rules, for levels 4 to 14, provides rules necessary for outdoor scenarios. Best adventures: *Curse of Xanathon* (a mad duke's reign of terror) as well as *Master of the Desert Nomads* and its sequel, *Temple of Death* (an exciting desert quest in search of the mysterious Master).

Set 3: Companion Rules, for levels 15 to 20, features advanced rules for building and maintaining kingdoms. Best adventures: *Tree of Life* (all about elves; great fun), *Test of the Warlords* (deadly games for prizes and glory), and *Endless Stair* (investigating a wizard's death).

Set 4: Master Rules is for levels 21 to 25. By this stage, PCs are powerful enough to take on the gods; recommended for experienced players only. Best adventures: *Into the Maelstrom* (confrontations with the Immortals), *Five Coins for a Kingdom* (the secret of a vanishing city), and *Twilight Calling* (exploring the deadly Realm of Nightmares).

Set 5: Immortals Rules is for levels 26 and beyond. Here, the PCs become godlike entities. Creating challenges for characters this powerful is extremely difficult, but the set is worth investigating for ambitious referees. Best adventures: *Immortal Storm* (featuring the bizarre Spheres of Power) and *Wrath of Olympus* (a showdown with the Lords of Olympus).

Also recommended: the *Gazetteer* sourcebooks (a series of guides to the various D&D lands, each including elaborate histories and personality profiles, along with new rules and adventure suggestions) and the *Book of Wondrous Inventions* (a collection of goofy devices, such as the Inflatable Scare Dragon and the Thermoaerohydrometeorological Precipitation Generator, none of which may have many practical applications in a D&D campaign but all of which are a lot of fun to read about).

Element Masters***

· ·

Complexity: Medium/High
Escape Ventures, 1984

Element Masters combines science fiction and fantasy elements to produce an appealingly original game. The setting is the planet Vinya, one of many worlds created by a pantheon of anonymous gods upon which magic and technology flourish side by side. To encourage interaction with alien cultures, the rulers of Vinya created teleportation gates capable of instantaneous transportation. Unfortunately, hostile invaders used the gates to swarm over Vinya and have reduced the planet to a wasteland.

Luckily, the PCs are here to save the day. Elves, dwarves, and other familiar fantasy races are represented, along with the not-so-familiar half-trons, a rare cross between humans and some double-spined aliens. The game covers character creation in great detail; in addition to such standard attributes as Strength, Intelligence, and Appearance, there are also tables to determine a character's Materialism (is he altruistic, acquisitive, or avaricious?), Handedness (left, right, or ambidextrous), and even his Drinking Capacity (which can be modified by various Beverage Values). Though designers Kenneth Burridge, Robert Finkbeiner, Kevin Nelson, and Brian Pettitt have a lot of fun with this—Beverage Values?—they have a tendency to go overboard. For instance, there's an Ingenious Idea ability that allows the PC to come up with a perfect solution to a problem automatically. But problem-solving shouldn't be handled by dice-rolls—players should have to come up with solutions themselves.

The combat and magic systems are detailed but not overly complicated. There's an imaginative assortment of spells, such as Ghost Arrow and Mana Search, and some strikingly original monsters, including an animated sludge puddle called the Bolsh and a lemur/praying mantis combination named the Mip. High-level PCs eventually get the chance to become element masters, powerful characters with total mastery of an elemental force. Element Masters suffers from crude graphics and occasionally clumsy writing, but overall, it's an inventive, entertaining RPG, an excellent alternative to conventional fantasy games.

Buyer's Note: Trade paperback.

Elfquest**½

Complexity: Medium
Chaosium Inc., 1984

From a modest beginning as a homemade comic book by Wendy and Richard Pini, Elfquest soon blossomed into a genuine phenomenon, spawning books, magazines, a planned feature film, and, inevitably, a fantasy RPG. Like the comics, the game is an engaging blend of high adventure and whimsy, with players taking the roles of Cutter, Skywise, Redlance, or elves of their own design for adventures in the mystical World of Two Moons. Those unfamiliar with the comic books will be at a disadvantage, but imagine a cross between Conan the Barbarian and the Smurfs and you'll have a good idea of what Elfquest is all about.

The game is easy to learn, thanks to the clear rules by Steve Perrin, liberally illustrated with excerpts from the original comics. Experienced role-players will find themselves on familiar ground, as the nuts and bolts of the rules are similar to those of RuneQuest, Call of Cthulhu, and other games originating from Chaosium. Players randomly determine Strength, Dexterity, and other basic attributes, then choose from a brief selection of skills, including Troll Lore, Wolf Riding, and other elven specialties. It's all straightforward and uncluttered, with the puzzling exception of the combat rules. Why nearly twenty pages of combat rules are necessary is anybody's guess, especially since the rulebook says that combat is "contrary to the spirit of the story."

There aren't many opportunities for combat anyway. Most of the game is spent interacting with the good characters, avoiding the bad ones, and learning to survive in an environment distinctly hostile to elvenkind. Monsters are scarce, and magic barely exists, very disappointing in a fantasy game and not particularly exciting. Without the comics as a reference, players may find themselves at a loss for what to do next. The rulebooks aren't much help, offering only sketchy adventure situations that do little more than illustrate specific portions of the rules.

The problems with Elfquest have more to do with the limits set by the comic books than with the game itself. Fans of the comics will have a ball replaying their favorite sequences. Others should check out the comics first.

Buyer's Notes: The original boxed set has been repackaged as a trade paperback. The paperback includes material from the *Elfquest Companion* and is a better buy.

Suggested Supplements: Not much to recommend. The *Elfquest Companion* is a collection of essays, character descriptions, and four skimpy adventures; interesting reading, but nothing special. *The Sea Elves* sourcebook describes a new tribe of sea-dwelling characters; again, fun to read but nonessential. *Elf Wars* is the best of the lot, a long adventure about warring elf factions that includes a much-needed simplification of the combat rules.

Empire of the Petal Throne***

Complexity: Medium/High
Different Worlds Publications, 1987

Created by Professor M. A. R. Barker in the mid-1970s, Empire of the Petal Throne began as science fiction, evolved into fantasy, was published by TSR Inc. in 1975 as a fantasy role-playing game, spawned a host of sourcebooks and expansions, faded into obscurity, reemerged as a Gamescience series in 1983, faded again, and was finally revived in 1987 as a single-volume RPG published by Different Worlds. While Empire of the Petal Throne may not be the most memorable RPG, it's certainly been one of the most durable.

Actually, Empire has less value as a game than as a sourcebook. With its character levels, armor classes, and experience points, the mechanics are quite similar to those of Dungeons and Dragons, though the rules lack the elegance and simplicity of D&D. But as a generic fantasy setting, Empire is without peer, a richly developed, exhaustively detailed treatment of a truly alien setting. Barker avoids medieval European fantasy clichés, instead combining elements of Aztec, Egyptian, Mayan, and other ancient cultures to create a world of startling originality. Instead of elves and dwarves, Empire offers the multi-armed Ahoggya ("the Knobbed Ones"), the sticklike Pe Choi ("the Listeners"), and ten other bizarre races. A vast, three-tiered highway encircles the planet, and ominous underworld civilizations dating from the prehuman ages thrive beneath the surface. Mysterious "Eyes," remnants from an ancient age of technological marvels, grant powerful abilities to those with the knowledge to use them.

There's plenty more, including a menagerie of exotic beasts, a glossary of Tekumel terminology, even instructions for writing in ancient Tsolyani script. Empire of the Petal Throne is not for beginners, and even experienced referees may have trouble negotiating Professor Barker's dense, scholarly text. The roleplaying rules don't amount to much, but the sourcebook material ranks among the hobby's best.

Buyer's Note: Trade paperback.

Enforcers**½

Complexity: Medium
21st Century Games, 1987

A generic superhero game, Enforcers emphasizes combat to the exclusion of nearly everything else. That's not necessarily bad, considering that comic-book adventures tend to stress punchouts a lot more than, say, hunting for treasure or exploring lost cities. However, players wanting more substance to their superhero campaigns are advised to stick with Champions or Villains and Vigilantes. That said, Enforcers remains a satisfactory game built on standard role-playing systems. It's uncluttered and a lot of fun to read; the enthusiasm of designers Gary Bernard, Charles Mann, and Larry Troth is evident on every page.

Players choose attributes and superpowers for their heroes by allocating points. Characters have both offensive and defensive abilities, which form the basis of the combat system. Combat resolution is fairly complex, involving initiative determination, offensive and defensive modifiers, and the powers of each opponent. Though combat encounters can take a long time to play out, that seems to be the intention.

There aren't many opportunities for actual role-playing in Enforcers, mainly due to the puzzling absence of background information. We're told, for instance, that the game is set in the twenty-first century, but other than brief asides, there's virtually no information about the era. Whether forthcoming supplements remedy this situation remains to be seen; for now, Enforcers is better suited for brief skirmishes than extended adventures.

Buyer's Note: Trade paperback.

Suggested Supplements: Supplements to date have been a little weak. *Knights of Beverly Hills* is an okay adventure, but it suffers from the same inattention to background detail that marred the original game. *The End of A Legend* is a little better, pitting the PC heroes against a colorful criminal mastermind.

En Garde***

....

Complexity: Low/Medium
Games Designers' Workshop, 1975

An out-of-print classic that's worth the search. Set in seventeenth- and eighteenth-century Europe, En Garde is a swashbuckling RPG that owes more to Errol Flynn movies than history texts. What makes it special is the inventive tactical combat system, perhaps the best fencing simulation ever to grace an RPG. Fencing encounters are played out in scenes, each involving specific attack and defense options to produce exciting and realistic results. Characters earn experience points from winning duels, and also gain points from successfully completing social activities, such as debauchery and gambling. A simple, delightfully tongue-in-cheek game.

Buyer's Note: Booklet.

Espionage**

Complexity: Medium
Hero Games, 1983

Espionage is a secret agent RPG based on the Champions superhero game. Unlike the more general approaches taken by Top Secret/S.I. and Mercenaries, Spies, and Private Eyes, Espionage focuses on CIA-type operations and, accordingly, is less frivolous than other spy games and somewhat more difficult. Players decide on a general specialty for their characters, such as covert action or technical services, then purchase their skills from a list of several dozen choices. The resulting characters are tough and versatile, but the poorly organized rules make the process harder than it ought to be.

The game mechanics are also difficult, though they produce realistic and exciting results for those willing to unravel them. The gunplay rules, for instance, cleverly integrate target ranges, multiple shots, weapon types, and misfires to create some genuinely hair-raising encounters. But to assess damage, the referee must juggle stun points and body points to determine if a victim has been stunned, knocked out, killed, or is in some phase of recovery. It can be done, but not without a fair amount of second-guessing.

With its emphasis on realism, Espionage is a little too serious for its own good. There are no tricky gadgets, fantastic weapons, colorful villains, or any of the other exotic elements that make James Bond so appealing. The complicated mechanics are likely to discourage casual players, and even veterans will be scratching their heads over some of the more ambiguous rules. The Danger International game is essentially a revision of Espionage—stick with DI.

Buyer's Note: Boxed set.

Suggested Supplements: The *Border Crossing* adventure gives the game system a nice workout; it's also compatible with Mercenaries, Spies, and Private Eyes. Supplements for Champions and Mercenaries, Spies, and Private Eyes are also compatible with Espionage.

Eternal Soldier*½

Complexity: Medium
Tai-Gear Simulations, 1986

Eternal Soldier is an attempt at a universal system—that is, a game allowing players to take the roles of any type of character for adventures in any era. It's ambitious, but disappointing. For the most part, the rules are derivative (attribute determination is similar to Dungeons and Dragons) and underdeveloped (unusual concepts such as Suffocation Points and Speed Classes are poorly explained). Combat demands a lot of patience from the referee, requiring him to keep track of half-second time segments, as well as skill checks and movement rates. Misguided attempts at humor litter the rulebook; for instance, one of the results under the Artistic Endeavors column of the Success Chart is "Studied art under Pia Zadora." And the illustration choices are downright baffling—what's with the full-page sketch of a cigarette lighter? There may be a good idea or two buried somewhere in Eternal Soldier, but it'll take a determined referee to dig them out.

Buyer's Note: Trade paperback.

Expendables**½

Complexity: Medium
Stellar Games, 1987

Expendables is set in the far future. Players take the roles of interstellar explorers employed by a mysterious corporate entity called the Company. The explorers are charged with the investigation of uncharted planets and sizing up their suitability for economic exploitation. Cynical corporate policy considers employees to be disposable resources, which is why they're called Expendables.

Designers L. Lee Cerny, Walter Mytczynskyj, and Michael Thomas have produced a solid, if quirky, set of game mechanics that are easy to use, even if they don't always make sense. In addition to Strength, Dexterity, Brains, Charisma, Fitness, and Luck, PCs are also rated for Psionic Traits, which the designers matter-of-factly proclaim are possessed by 11 percent of all humanity—oh, really? The Psionic Traits aren't just silly, they're also underdeveloped; a PC with the Trance ability can put himself in suspended animation for four hours in order to slow the effects of poison—wouldn't he still be in bad shape when he woke up? A PC's career determines his skills; an engineer, for instance, is skilled in Electronics, Mechanics, and Radiation Technology. But there are a number of strange choices tucked away in the skill lists; I'm not sure how useful Basket-weaving or Blacksmithing would be in outer space, and this has got to be the only RPG in existence with Proctology as an option.

The game plays well, however, and all of the mechanics are clearly explained and illustrated with plenty of examples. Combat is divided into Battle Turns of five seconds, with players making combat skill rolls and the referee determining the results based on the weapon's damage potential; it's simple, quick, and clean. Nice touches abound, including a brief but adequate space combat system, specialization kits that contain all of the necessary equipment for a given occupation, and a Whole Company Catalog that lists everything from laser microphones and regeneration tanks to sunscreen lotion and portable bathtubs.

Unfortunately, the game neglects to address its premise. Characters are supposed to explore uncharted planets, but the rules for planet creation are ambiguous and, at less than two pages, far too skimpy. The creature-generation system produces boring monsters, and the introductory scenario is dull and difficult to understand. Without sample planets, monsters, and encounters, it's tough to figure out exactly how Expendables is supposed to work.

Buyer's Note: Trade paperback.

Fantasy Hero**

Complexity: Medium
Hero Games, 1985

This is the fantasy spin-off of Hero Games' "Hero System" game series, which also includes Justice Inc., Danger International, and Champions. In fact, Fantasy Hero is basically a Champions variant, substituting spells for superpowers. The game mechanics are interchangeable with other Hero games; character creation involves the distribution of points among a handful of basic attributes, skills derive from attributes and are also purchased with points, and combat resolves by comparing skill levels with dice-rolls.

Fantasy Hero considers magic to be a specialized skill. This means that any type of spell effect is possible, but players must work out the details themselves, as if they were designing superpowers from scratch in Champions. It works, it's versatile, but it's time-consuming and awkward. Worse, because Fantasy Hero isn't tied to any particular campaign world, it's pretty dull.

The streamlined magic system of Advanced Dungeons and Dragons makes Fantasy Hero seem like homework; the sophisticated Ars Magica rules make it look primitive. As a magic supplement for Champions, Fantasy Hero is fine. As a stand-alone game, it's for completists only.

Buyer's Note: Trade paperback.

Suggested Supplement: The *Spell Book* supplement clarifies and corrects the original rules, as well as adding new systems and spells. Essential for unraveling *Fantasy Hero.*

Fantasy Wargaming*

Complexity: Medium
Stein and Day, 1981

Among the worst RPGs ever published, Fantasy Wargaming shows just how badly a game can go astray. First off, the game has nothing to do with "wargaming" per se, but instead is a tired retread of fantasy role-playing, heavy on concepts that seem to be derived from early versions of Dungeons and Dragons, RuneQuest, and other mid-to-late 1970s games. The book is nearly three hundred pages long, and about a third of it is devoted to the legends and lore of medieval Europe; the material is rambling, dry, and mostly superfluous to the game it allegedly supports. Character generation is pointlessly based on astrology; a complex "System of Correspondencies" details which gems, animals, and body parts are associated with various signs of the zodiac, but for no apparent reason, at least as far as I can tell. The magic system is nearly incomprehensible, requiring players to navigate divination tables, ethereal influences, mana accumulation, and a host of other difficult concepts. Other standard RPG elements, such as skill use and scenario suggestions, are all but ignored. Top it off with some distasteful references to Black Masses and you've got a game that I wouldn't touch with a ten-foot broomstick.

Buyer's Note: Hardback book.

Flashing Blades***

Complexity: Medium
Fantasy Games Unlimited Inc., 1984

Set in seventeenth-century France, Flashing Blades is a game of swordsmen and swashbucklers inspired by romantic literature. Designer Mark Pettigrew has an impressive feel for the era, making Flashing Blades the best-ever RPG of its kind.

Characters can be Noblemen, Rogues, Soldiers, or Gentlemen, each with his own benefits and drawbacks. Rogues, for instance, excel at Cut Pursing, while Noblemen are skilled at Horsemanship. In addition, each character has an Advantage, such as a Contact in High Places, and a Secret, such as Compulsive Gambling. The Advantages and Secrets steer adventures in unexpected directions, and also encourage the players to pursue their own agendas, often at the expense of their comrades.

Game mechanics are detailed but not overly complicated. The flexible combat system allows for exciting sword duels, barroom brawls, and flintlock shootouts without the burden of endless computations. Rules for taxing and tithing, guidelines for military campaigns, an overview of French history, and three exceptional adventures complete the package. Low-key and narrowly focused—and perhaps a bit too dependent on the referee to interpret some of the fuzzier rules—the game isn't for everyone. But for those with an interest in the era, Flashing Blades is as good as it gets.

Buyer's Note: Boxed set.

Suggested Supplements: Parisian Adventure includes several high-quality scenarios and some excellent background material about Paris. *High Seas* takes the game to ocean, adding rules for ship combat, piracy, and seafaring expeditions, along with four first-rate adventures; it's impressively researched and, considering the volume of information, an exceptional value.

Freedom Fighters**½

Complexity: High
Fantasy Games Unlimited Inc., 1986

Freedom Fighters is a grim, complicated simulation of guerrilla warfare set in an enemy-occupied United States at some unspecified point in the near future. Players take the roles of rebel fighters charged with ousting the tyrannical oppressors, who might be anyone from foreign armies to Martian invaders.

PC generation is covered in excruciating detail, with over

thirty pages and dozens of charts devoted to every conceivable physical, mental, and attitudinal characteristic. There are fifteen basic attributes, ten personality traits, and a mind-boggling assortment of talents, motivations, and background details. There are separate charts for determining a character's birthplace, eyesight, and ethnicity. Needless to say, a lot of this is unnecessary (a table for determining gender?), and much of it isn't particularly meaningful (what's the point of an ethnicity table?). And in a game that emphasizes realism, the inclusion of psionic powers, such as mental telepathy and thought projection, doesn't make much sense.

The game mechanics are similarly complicated. For instance, there are two formulas for determining how far a PC can jump, one for height (Strength level + Agility level/8) and another for distance (Strength level + Agility level/2). There are more than eight pages of rules for evaluating verbal interactions, including specific Attack and Defense modifiers for Threats, Appeals, and Bribes. Combat encounters require the players to track their characters' Hit Point Total, Unconsciousness Thresholds, Fatigue Limits, and Fatigue Thresholds.

It's a credit to designer J. Andrew Keith that these extremely detailed rules produce surprisingly realistic results, but it takes an enormous amount of time and effort to learn to use them. This is humorless, difficult material that would have benefited from a sharper focus and a skeptical editor with a big red pencil.

Buyer's Note: Boxed set.

Fringeworthy**½

Complexity: Medium
Tri Tac Inc., 1982

Fringeworthy tackles the concepts of alternate realities and interdimensional travel with originality and style. In the near future, the discovery of a complex network of portals and "fringe paths," presumably constructed by an extraterrestrial intelligence, allows instantaneous transmission to a near-infinite number of previously unknown locales. Only a select group of adventurers, such as the PCs, have what it takes to use the portals. These "Fringeworthies" belong to an Inter-Dimensional Exploration Team and agree to follow the portals wherever they might lead and report their discoveries. The portal network is described in convincing detail, thanks to the meticulous background invented by designers Richard Tucholka and Robert Sadler, and works quite nicely as a justification for staging adventures in a startling variety of settings, ranging from medieval fantasy lands to high-tech alien cultures.

The game mechanics are adequate, but don't quite match the invention of the premise. Character creation is an uninspired blend of random attributes and skill selection that's far too time-consuming. Though there's an impressive number of skills available, they're incompletely described, leaving it up to the referee to work out the details. The combat rules produce satisfying results but require a lot of number-juggling. The experience system tends to push abilities to unrealistically high levels, producing characters who are theoretically capable of walking away from a plane crash.

With effort from the referee, all of the systems are playable, though their virtues remain modest. Where Fringeworthy really shines is in its fresh approach to an underexplored topic; no other game covers the ramifications of interdimensional travel as thoroughly as this. It's a hard game to find, but worth the search for those with an interest in the topic.

Buyer's Note: Trade paperback.

Suggested Supplements: The *Rogue 417* adventure sends the transdimensional travelers to a postapocalyptic world where most of the population has been wiped out by a deadly virus; there are a few holes, but overall, it's a good introduction to the game. Material for the FTL: 2448 and Stalking the Night Fantastic games is also compatible with Fringeworthy.

FTL: 2448**

Complexity: Medium
Tri Tac Inc., 1982

Time has not been kind to FTL: 2448. Though its straightforward, uncluttered treatment of science fiction was fresh when the game was first released, FTL has been rendered obsolete

88
....

by the more sophisticated Megatraveller, Star Trek, and Star Wars, which more or less cover the same territory.

With humankind on the rise and cooperation among alien races the norm rather than the exception, the universe of FTL: 2448 is relatively benign. Consequently, the game tends to stress exploration and trade more than interstellar warfare. Players randomly generate basic attributes for their characters, then send them through various training schools to determine their skills. Though there are plenty of skills to choose from—more than two hundred in fact—none of them are defined, nor are their functions explained. Rules for space battles, starship design, and economics are similarly vague.

Though the problems with the rules are frustrating, they're not insurmountable, especially in the hands of an experienced referee. There are thoughtful, inventive sections on stellar law, robotics, and space colonies, and the rules for personal combat strike a nice balance between detail and playability. But though much of FTL: 2448 could be used as sourcebook material for other science-fiction RPGs, the game itself is outdated and hardly worth the effort.

Buyer's Note: Trade paperback.

Future Worlds*½

....

Complexity: Medium/High
Stellar Gaming Workshop, 1987

In its introduction, Future Worlds proposes to blend elements of fantasy and science fiction and to deemphasize science and technology while stressing character development. Sounds good, but what happened? Fantasy takes a distant backseat to a colorless science-fiction setting involving humans and aliens competing for galactic domination—I think (it's pretty vague). The fantasy elements are mostly confined to a brief section discussing a spellcasting group called the Mystics, and about thirty pages of dull spells. Character creation focuses on charts and tables, not personality traits, and the resulting characters are little more than collections of numbers. The combat system is functional but far too convoluted. With few hints as to how this is all supposed to fit together in a cohesive adventure, the Future World referee will have his work cut out for him.

Buyer's Note: Spiral-bound paperback.

Gamma World***

....

Complexity: Medium
TSR Inc., First Edition: 1978, Third Edition: 1986

Apocalyptic role-playing with a sense of humor, Gamma World takes place in a war-ravaged future populated by talking plants, land-dwelling sharks, and friendly robots. Players take the roles of regular humans, mutant humans, mutant animals, or—my favorite—mutant plants, all struggling to survive among the ruins. It's as fun as it sounds.

After rolling for Dexterity, Constitution, and other basic attributes similar to those of Dungeons and Dragons, players choose character types for their PCs, then, if they've chosen a mutant, roll on the Mutation Charts to determine their special powers. Both physical and mental mutations are available, as are specific mutations for plants (Spore Clouds, Dissolving Juices, Thorns, and Accelerated Growth) and animals (Gas Bags, Spines, Bristles, and Antlers). Unlucky die-rolls may result in defective mutations, such as Narcolepsy, Periodic Amnesia, and Allergies. Mutant PCs are one of the game's chief delights; it's possible to wind up as a narcoleptic cactus with antlers and spore clouds.

Rules are kept to a minimum, with virtually all game actions resolved on a single Action Table, color-coded for easy reference. For instance, if the narcoleptic cactus attempts to smack somebody with its antlers, the player rolls a die, factors in a couple of modifiers chosen by the referee, and checks the Action Table; a Red result means that the victim squirmed away, a Yellow result means the victim is stunned, and on a Black result, the victim has been knocked unconscious. An impressive

array of weapons is available for non-antlered characters, ranging from the mundane (dagger, spear, and rifle) to the exotic
(fusion bomb, micromissile, and stun whip) to the downright
bizarre (slither helix, robotic tentacles, and fire hose—fire
hose?).

Though Gamma World may sound like a loony-bin version of
Twilight: 2000, it makes for some exciting adventures as the
PCs explore a high-tech wonderland of mysterious landmarks
and artifacts, encountering some of the most outlandish creatures this side of Dungeons and Dragons. It's a bang-up job by
designers James Ward, David James Ritchie, and Gary Jaquet;
that is, if you don't take your nuclear holocausts too seriously.

Buyer's Notes: Boxed set. The third edition is the one to buy;
look for the cover featuring an armored humanoid riding a giant
mutant wolverine with a gun mounted on its head.

Suggested Supplements: The best adventures are *Alpha Factor*
(an ancient artifact in the Flower Lands) and *Gamma Base*
(showdown in a strange military installation).

Gangbusters***

Complexity: Low/Medium
TSR Inc., 1982

A well-written, attractively designed simulation of G-men,
crime bosses, and bootleggers in the Roaring Twenties, Gangbusters is an overlooked gem, a minor classic by designers Mark
Acres and Rick Krebs. Emphasizing action and adventure over
rules and formulas, Gangbusters may not be the most realistic
treatment of the era, but it's certainly the most fun.

The rules are simple and direct, with players rolling dice to
determine their PCs' basic attributes (Muscle, Agility, Observa-
tion, Presence, Driving, and Luck), then choosing a career path
in law enforcement, private investigation, newspaper reporting,
or crime. Each PC type receives specific instructions for advancement and motivation. The Private Eye, for instance, gains
an increase in his Luck attribute when he reaches Level 5, and

earns the friendship of congressmen and senators at Level 10; he's supposed to maintain good relations with the chief of police and to always get at least part of his fee in advance. Criminals rise in levels by making money through burglary, armed robbery, murder contracts, or bootlegging. Though the game includes a fair amount of background material to give the impression of historical accuracy, the tone of the game is closer to old TV shows (*The F.B.I.* in particular) than history texts—any game with a table to randomly determine a hit man's fees shouldn't be taken too seriously.

The combat rules cover fistfights, ambushes, and gunplay in detail, with an especially nice section on car chases, which can be played out with cardboard counters using the color city map provided with the game. Brief but entertaining sections discussing crime syndicates, bookmaking, NPC encounters, and criminal trials complete the package. Gangbusters works best when players abandon the traditional adventuring party format and divide themselves into teams of good guys and bad guys to compete for control of the city. Gangbusters lacks the depth for an extended campaign, but it's a great way to spend an evening.

Buyer's Notes: Boxed set. Keep an eye out for the second edition trade paperback, scheduled for release in late 1990.

Suggested Supplements: The *Death in Spades* adventure features grim characters, a clever mystery, and plenty of action. Thanks to the unusual presentation, which generates different plots depending on draws from a deck of cards, it can be played more than once.

Gangster**

Complexity: Low/Medium
Fantasy Games Unlimited Inc., 1979

Gangster is a cops-and-robbers game for staging adventures in Prohibition-era Chicago, the drug dens of contemporary New York, or any other setting where criminal activity prevails. Designers Nick Marinacci and Pete Petrone strive for authenticity and are largely successful, even though the game systems don't quite measure up to Gangster's ambitious scope.

Players can take the roles of either police officers or criminals. Regardless of their career path, all PCs determine their basic attributes with die-rolls, then select skills appropriate to their areas of specialization. Bad guys can be Con Men, Forgers, and Pickpockets; good guys can be Drug Experts, Homicide Investigators, and Interrogators. Resolving most actions, including combat activities, requires a single die-roll and a handful of modifiers, with the result compared to the appropriate skill or attribute. Though it's a simple system, it's not particularly satisfying. It lacks the sophistication and versatility of similar reality-based games such as Mercenaries, Spies, and Private Eyes and Top Secret/S.I. Worse, there's little help for the referee; there are no clear instructions for putting together adventures or staging burglaries, bank robberies, and other criminal activities.

The sourcebook material is exceptional. Full-page charts detail the weapons, equipment, and criminal types common to six different historical eras. A lengthy section on the American police system features the history, structure, and responsibilities of municipal and federal law enforcement agencies, while a separate Patrol Guide book discusses police procedures, forensic sciences, and criminal law. Lucid and informative, the sourcebook material could add a touch of authenticity to any RPG with a contemporary setting.

Buyer's Note: Boxed set.

Ghostbusters***

Complexity: Low
West End Games, 1986

Ghostbusters is an oddball of a game, but it's an appealing oddball for a couple of good reasons. First, it can be learned in half an hour, even if you've never seen an RPG before. Second, like the 1984 blockbuster movie of the same name, it's irresistibly silly—how many games come packaged with a Last Will

and Testament and a suitable-for-framing Ghostbusting permit?
As an introduction to role-playing or an entertaining diversion
for more serious gamers, Ghostbusters is hard to beat. It's also
as fun to read as it is to play, thanks to the witty style of designers Sandy Petersen, Lynn Willis, and Greg Stafford (with development assistance from Ken Rolston and Martin Wixted).

As in the film, players assume the roles of intrepid investigators determined to rid the world of spooks, spirits, and
other paranormal nasties. Character creation takes only a few
minutes. PCs are rated for Brains (intelligence), Muscles
(strength), Moves (agility), and Cool (courage), then are assigned specialties that range from astronomy to hairdressing.
Strap on the Proton Pack, gas up the ECTO-1, and it's off to do
battle with barking taxicabs and haunted garbage cans.

The rules are short on charts and tables and long on free-
wheeling improvisation. If a situation isn't covered in the rules,
the referee is encouraged to handle it any way that strikes his
fancy. Most actions are resolved by a roll of the special ghost
die. One face of this die bears the familiar "no ghosts" symbol.
When this symbol turns up, the affected character suffers an
indignity of the referee's choice, such as an exploding Proton
Pack or an unexpected shower of ghost slime. More serious
troubles—say, a herd of rampaging ectoplasmic penguins—may
be avoided by spending Brownie Points. Characters who survive
an adventure in one piece are rewarded with additional Brownie
Points to spend in the next game.

Those with a low tolerance for corny humor will have problems with Ghostbusters. Even for younger players, the game
works best in small doses, as it lacks the depth to sustain a lot
of replay. However, adventures aren't confined to re-creating
scenes from the movie. As the rulebook points out, Ghostbusters encompasses the entire World of Stupid Science—that
is, just about anything you can dream up. UFOs, talking plants,
and even the kitchen sink (especially if it has a haunted drain)
are all potential menaces in Ghostbusters.

Buyer's Notes: Boxed set. The Operations Manual is available
separately, but you need the box to get all the rules. The 1989
publication of Ghostbusters International—the revised edition

of Ghostbusters—means that the original game will become increasingly harder to find.

Suggested Supplements: The *Hot Rods of the Gods* features juvenile delinquents from outer space; great fun, particularly the flying saucer demo derby. *Ghost Toasties* pits the Ghostbusters against a haunted supermarket and is nearly as good as *Hot Rods*.

Ghostbusters International***

Complexity: Low/Medium
West End Games, 1989

The release of the *Ghostbusters II* film marked the perfect opportunity for the re-release of the Ghostbusters game. But instead of reissuing the original, West End Games commissioned a complete overhaul, enlisting the talents of ace designers Aaron Allston and Douglas Kaufman to increase the detail of the original game and make it more appealing to hardcore role-players.

All of the elements that made Ghostbusters so much fun remain intact. Characters are still rated for Brains, Muscle, Moves, and Cool, and are as selflessly devoted to spook-chasing as ever. As in the original game, a roll of the Ghost Die resolves most actions, with the appearance of the ghost face indicating disaster (such as a collapsing building or a fountain of slime spewed by an obnoxious spirit).

New material centers on statistics, charts, and tables to quantify factors that were formerly up to the whim of the referee. For instance, in the original Ghostbusters, weapons caused an indefinite amount of damage. Ghostbusters International includes specific damage ranges for each weapon, as well as maximum ranges and bonus modifiers. GI characters are limited by their Muscles as to how much equipment they can carry, an incidental consideration in Ghostbusters. GI also features precise rules for movement, healing, and other standard RPG mechanics.

Ghostbusters International is more intimidating for novices

than Ghostbusters and much less improvisational. The amount of detail is by no means overwhelming, though fans of the original game are likely to balk at all the new tables and charts. GI is a delightful game, especially in the hands of an experienced referee. But since bigger isn't necessarily better, I'd pass on the new game if I were comfortable with the original.

Buyer's Note: Boxed set.

Suggested Supplements: Ghostbusters II: The Adventure is faithful to the spirit, if not the plot, of the movie sequel, and gives the new rules a thorough workout. For experienced players, the *ApoKERMIS Now* adventure features a bizarre encounter with the mysterious Frog Riders; loads of laughs and surprisingly exciting. The *Tobin's Spirit Guide* sourcebook describes all manner of ghosts, demons, and screwball phenomena that are perfect for spicing up any GI scenario. All of the original Ghostbusters material is also compatible with Ghostbusters International.

Golden Heroes**

Complexity: Medium
Games Workshop, 1984

Players choose generic superhero games so they aren't locked into a specific comic-book universe, enabling them to build their own worlds and customize heroes to their heart's content. However, the rules of Golden Heroes, which superficially resemble those of Champions and Villains and Vigilantes, are so rigid that players might as well pull their characters out of a hat. A PC's basic attributes (Ego, Strength, Dexterity, and Vigor) generate hit points and a random number of superpowers. Though a player has a few options for modifying his hero's abilities, basically he's saddled with whatever powers the dice-rolls dictate, no matter how contradictory or silly. Because the random ability system freely mixes useless powers with the god-like, there's only a remote chance that players will receive PCs of comparable talents.

The combat system is a hodge-podge of weapon classes, target ranges, and power grades bordering on the incomprehensible. Extensive bookkeeping is required to keep track of a hero's private life, including how he spends his free time and what he's been up to in his secret identity—who cares? The rulebooks boast some nice artwork, and the thoughtful referee's tips are applicable to any comic-book RPG, but there's just not enough substance in Golden Heroes to recommend it over the competition.

Buyer's Note: Boxed set.

Suggested Supplements: Though the game itself is disappointing, the Golden Heroes supplements are surprisingly good, particularly *Queen Victoria and the Holy Grail,* an exciting adventure with supernatural overtones.

GURPS****

Complexity: Medium/High
Steve Jackson Games; First Edition: 1986, Third Edition: 1988

GURPS, an acronym for Generic Universal Role-Playing System, is a ambitious design by Steve Jackson that attempts to cover every imaginable genre, setting, and character type in the same game. That it achieves this goal at all is impressive; that it does so with imagination, elegance, and innovation is stunning.

GURPS boasts a remarkably detailed character generation system, and it's based on a mere three attributes: Strength, Dexterity, and Intelligence (a fourth attribute, Health, serves mainly to indicate the amount of damage a character can absorb). Each player receives 100 Character Points to distribute among the attributes, which in turn determines his aptitude in various skills. A player may opt to spend any leftover points on an attractive physique for his PC, or he may choose a hideous appearance and earn extra points to spend elsewhere. Likewise, he can spend points on advantages, such as Acute Vision (cost: 2 points) or Magical Aptitude (at least 15 points) or acquire extra points by taking on disadvantages, such as Overweight (which earns an additional 5 points) or Blindness (a whopping

50 bonus points). GURPS has no character classes; instead, PCs are defined primarily by their skills, also purchased with Character Points. A PC can spend a number of points on skills equal to twice his age; most beginning PCs are eighteen years old, so they can spend 36 points. Attribute ratings limit the levels of skills; for instance, Intelligence limits the levels of mental skills, while Dexterity limits the levels of physical ones. There are more than 150 skills to choose from, ranging from the general (Swimming, Languages, and Cooking) to the extremely specialized (Intelligence Analysis, Spear Throwing, and Nuclear Physics). What makes the system impressive is not only its flexibility but its balance; regardless of how players distribute their initial Character Points, or which advantages, disadvantages, and skills they select, the resulting PCs all seem to have about the same amount of power. Though basic GURPS characters have no specific careers, careful skill selection produces wizards, astronauts, superheroes, or any other character type appropriate to a particular genre.

The slick game mechanics focus on skill rolls, where players roll dice and compare the result to the applicable skill level, and a simple combat system based on a few general maneuvers supplemented by offensive and defensive skill rolls. Advanced combat rules add complications comparable to those of tactical wargames, but the basic system is sufficient to handle most combat encounters. There are clever, polished rules for magic, psionics, and world building, and an outstanding section that teaches referees how to design their own adventures from scratch, taking them step by step through plotting, mapping, and character design. Two clever fantasy scenarios at the end of the book serve as an excellent introduction to the game.

GURPS is a model of organization and presentation, and includes numerous examples to illustrate every facet of the system. Though it's amazing that a game so all-compassing is this smooth, it's not intended for beginners. Experienced players, however, owe it to themselves to investigate this landmark design—it's possible that GURPS may be the only RPG they'll ever need.

Buyer's Notes: The original boxed GURPS sets are now of-

98
....

ficially obsolete. Stick with the third edition, available in both trade paperback and hardcover versions.

Suggested Supplements: GURPS is a three-tiered RPG; that is, players need the basic rulebook, then a sourcebook detailing the genre they're interested in, and finally an adventure supplement appropriate to the genre (the sourcebooks include scenario suggestions, so ambitious referees can skip the adventure supplements if they're on a budget). Best supplements: *GURPS Space* (science fiction), *GURPS Japan* (Oriental fantasy), *GURPS Swashbucklers* (pirates and the high seas), *GURPS Supers* (comic-book heroes), and *GURPS Riverworld* (adapted from the Phillip José Farmer novels). Best adventures: *Unnight* and *Stardemon* (both for *GURPS Space*) and *School of Hard Knocks* (for *GURPS Supers*).

Harn***

Complexity: Medium
Columbia Games Inc., 1983

Not a stand-alone game, Harn is a generic setting adaptable to any fantasy RPG. Of all the generic settings (including City State of the Invincible Overlord, Haven, and Thieves' World) Harn is the least frivolous and most ambitious, supplemented by dozens of sourcebooks that together comprise the enormous *Encyclopedia Harnica*. Harn itself is a vast island lying off the coast of Lythia. It consists of an eclectic assortment of kingdoms, tribes, and communities. Culture, religion, and economics are covered in depth, as is the history of the area; in fact, Harn is closer in style and tone to textbooks than fantasy role-playing supplements. Players expecting a surplus of magic and monsters will be disappointed, but those looking for serious, intelligent adventures can find plenty of them in Harn.

Buyer's Notes: Folder containing two booklets and a large color map. The 1988 Harn World package revises and updates the original material. Both versions are good.

Suggested Supplements: HarnMaster is the rules supplement exclusive to the world of Harn: it's a lavish, detailed RPG resembling a more complicated RuneQuest. It's not essential for enjoying Harn—RuneQuest, Advanced Dungeons and Dragons, Warhammer, or any other fantasy RPG can be adapted without too much trouble—but *HarnMaster* makes a nice alternative for those willing to learn a brand-new set of rules. A number of adventure supplements set in the Harn universe can also be adapted to any fantasy system; the best are *100 Bushels of Rye* and *Staff of Fanon*.

Haven***

Complexity: Medium
Gamelords Ltd., 1984

Like Harn, Haven is not a stand-alone game but a generic setting that can be used with Dungeons and Dragons, RuneQuest, and other fantasy RPGs. Haven is a meticulously detailed city consisting of seven boroughs, each with its own history, notable locations, and scenario suggestions. The personality descriptions are especially impressive; there are literally hundreds of NPCs from all walks of life, fully integrated into a rigid social system, ripe with possibilities for creative referees. Emphasizing realism over whimsy, Haven is grim and gritty; there's less opportunity for magical monsters and flamboyant combat than in City State of the Invincible Overlord or Thieves' World, but there's more potential for pure role-playing. The material is somewhat easier to digest than that of the similarly serious Harn, making Haven the best of the generic settings for hardcore role-players. It's tough to find, but worth the search.
Buyer's Note: Boxed set.

Hawkmoon**½

Complexity: Medium
Chaosium Inc., 1986

As with the Stormbringer game, Hawkmoon is based on the novels of Michael Moorcock, specifically, the History of the RuneStaff and Chronicles of Castle Brass series that detail a future in which nuclear and chemical warfare has reduced the world to a near-feudal state, not unlike that of most conventional fantasy settings. It's an interesting premise, nicely rendered by designer Kerie Campbell-Robson (with assistance from Sandy Petersen).

Game mechanics are similar to those of Call of Cthulhu, Stormbringer, and other Chaosium games, with each player rolling randomly for Strength, Constitution, Size, Intelligence, Power, Dexterity, and Charisma, then deciding his character's nationality. The nationality affects a PC's choice of occupations and skills, and also modifies his attributes and determines his body type. Characters from Espaniya, for instance, are tall and dark, have light or medium bodies, and have exceptional Dexterity and Charisma. Those from Magyaria are fair-skinned, have medium or heavy bodies, and have exceptional Constitution and Dexterity. Skills receive ratings from 1 to 100, and all actions, including combat, are resolved by rolling percentile dice against the applicable skill value.

Though the game is well written and easy to learn—perhaps the simplest of all the Chaosium games—it's not particularly exciting. There's no magic to speak of, and the monsters and other potential adversaries aren't very threatening. Worse, the game doesn't do much with the concept of mixing technology and medieval Europe; there are a few pages of scientific devices, such as flame cannons and mentality machines, but they're nothing special. The section on animal and plant mutations pales before the similar system in Gamma World. Moorcock fans might enjoy this, but the world of Hawkmoon—at least as presented here—probably lacks the depth to sustain the interest of most players.

Buyer's Note: Boxed set.

Suggested Supplementes: Shattered Isle is a pretty good introductory adventure—well written and reasonably exciting. Supplements for the Stormbringer game can also be used with Hawkmoon, since both games are part of Chaosium's Eternal Champion series and share the same basic rules.

Heroes Unlimited**½

Complexity: Medium
Palladium Books; First Edition: 1984, Revised Edition: 1988

Heroes Unlimited is a generic comic-book RPG by Kevin Siembieda that allows players to create just about any kind of superhero they can dream up, including space aliens, mutants, and robots. It's an appealing, versatile system, though it's also unfocused and a little bland.

The game mechanics derive from the Palladium Role-Playing Game, making it compatible with Ninjas and Superspies, Sentinels, and other Palladium products. Character creation is based on the attributes common to all Palladium games, such as Mental Endurance and Physical Strength, and a selection of skills and powers from a remarkably extensive list. Psionic talents, bionic implants, and genetic enhancements are all available to the PC heroes, as is a lengthy arsenal of weapons and equipment. Brief but informative sections on personal backgrounds encourage players to develop identities as detectives, scientists, and secret agents for their PCs.

Mutant and alien heroes seem to have a tremendous power advantage over their Earthbound comrades; though it's inevitable in the comics—compare the mortal Batman to the godlike Superman—it makes for an unbalanced role-playing game. Otherwise, the main problem with Heroes Unlimited is its facelessness. It's not as streamlined as Marvel Super Heroes, as charming as Champions, or as elegant as DC Heroes. It's an excellent source of ideas, however, especially the sections on robotics and equipment, and makes a nice supplement for any of the other superhero games.

Buyer's Notes: Trade paperback. The revised edition is the one to buy. It clarifies the ambiguities of the first edition and features an improved character-generation system.

Suggested Supplements: There are no supplements specifically intended for Heroes Unlimited to recommend. However, it's compatible with all other Palladium games and works especially well with Teenage Mutant Ninja Turtles, Sentinels, Mechanoids, and Ninjas and Superspies.

High Colonies**½

Complexity: Medium
Waterford Publishing House Ltd., 1988

High Colonies is a science-fiction RPG with a strong premise and shaky mechanics. Two centuries in the future, mankind has been chased off Earth by devastating wars and now occupies space stations scattered throughout the solar system. The stations are self-contained environments with unique cultures, ideologies, and legal sytems. Most important, each has its own allies and enemies. For instance, the Evangelic Church of the Chosen, the Kruger Station, and the Ku Klux Klan (perhaps an unlikely choice for a space colony, but an interesting one) are united as the Band of Humanity, which stands in opposition to the Jihad fundamentalists and the Ecumenical Council of Sol, which includes the Roman Catholics and the liberal Church of the Lifeline. Adventures focus on the conflicts between the various colonies; it's an ingenious setting, easily the game's best feature.

The game systems are adequate but uninspired. Basic character attributes stick to the usual Strength, Constitution, Intelligence, Dexterity, and Charisma. Players acquire skills for their characters by expending Skill Points, but the skimpy skill lists don't provide many options. The convoluted combat system would be more at home in a military simulation than a role-playing game, as it requires players to determine initiative, choose firing modes, and factor in a host of modifiers. The inclusion of anachronistic weapons is also puzzling—are we to believe that blowpipes and crossbows will be common in space stations? The most bizarre rules involve damage and healing. Damage affects specific body parts, but healing is determined at random. It's possible, then, that a character who suffered a head wound yesterday will inexplicably heal his arm today.

Rounding out the game are some concise and interesting rules for ship combat, a detailed history of colonial development, well-written sections on aliens and robots, and an exceptionally good scenario set on a mineral-processing colony. High

Colonies has a lot of potential—clearly, designers Eric Hotz and Edwin King are talented guys—but the rules don't quite measure up to the background.

Buyer's Note: Trade paperback.

High Fantasy*½

··

> Complexity: Low
> Reston Publishing Co., 1981

Following the success of Dungeons and Dragons, players were flooded with a deluge of fantasy RPGs, some of them, such as High Fantasy, arriving from unexpected sources. Originally issued by the Twinn-K company in 1978, the game was picked up by a larger publisher, revised and expanded, and reintroduced in both hardback and paperback versions. Apparently the publisher had a lot of confidence in the game, because for a while it seemed to be popping up everywhere. In fact, even though it's been out of print for some time, it doesn't take much searching to turn up a copy of High Fantasy.

But don't go out of your way. Although the game has noble intentions as a simpler alternative to D&D, High Fantasy is dismal—hopelessly derivative, awkwardly written, and virtually unplayable. As with D&D, basic attributes are determined at random, but without any method for offsetting unlucky dice-rolls, players with underpowered characters can't do much other than sit back and watch everyone else enjoy the game. Warriors, Wizards, Alchemists, and Animal Masters are among the available character classes, but it's a mystery why anyone would want to play anything other than a Wizard, since they're overwhelmingly superior. A combat encounter amounts to a single roll of percentile dice, with the results illogical and confusing.

Oddly enough, the book concludes with one of the best solitaire adventures I've ever seen—a clever, challenging scenario that rivals the best of the Tunnels and Trolls solos. Fortunately, it can be adapted to other fantasy systems without too much trouble.

Buyer's Note: Available in both hardcover and softcover editions; the less-expensive softcover is the obvious choice.

IFGS Fantasy Rules***

....

Complexity: Low
Dream Park Corporation, 1989

The IFGS (International Fantasy Gaming Society) organizes, sponsors, and promotes live-action role-playing games across the country. It's an unusual format, where players actually dress up like their characters and act out fantasy adventures in a park, field, or other suitable environment under the supervision of a team of scorekeepers and referees. The *IFGS Fantasy Rules* book shows interested players how to get started.

Because each aspect of the game must be physically represented, live-action role-playing rules are necessarily simple. The IFGS system compares to basic Dungeons and Dragons, including such familiar concepts as alignment, levels, and experience points, with players taking the roles of Fighters, Rangers, Knights, Magic-Users, Clerics, Druids, Thieves, and Monks. There are no character attributes as such; presumably, each PC is as intelligent, strong, and dexterous as the person who plays him. Instead, each character class is defined by his special abilities; Fighters, for instance, can use their "battle fever" skill to inflict increased damage on opponents and can also regenerate lost hit points faster than their comrades. Rangers are exceptionally skilled at untying knots and brewing healing potions, while Knights are immune to all nonmagical diseases and can detect the presence of undead creatures.

The rules provide clear instructions for staging game encounters and resolving actions. Beanbags of various colors represent thrown weapons, while melee encounters are played out with toy weapons (swords are constructed from padded bamboo shafts) with the referee assessing "damage" after each contact. Six different colors of flags indicate different types of spells; red flags denote protective spells, green flags indicate a change in appearance, white flags represent invisibility. To cast a spell, the Magic-User speaks a few magic words (the verbal component), performs some physical gestures (the somatic component), and displays the appropriate flag or other required item (the material component). If playing at night, the Magic-User beams a flashlight on his intended targets. There are similarly clever rules for armor (represented by small cloth squares), flaming oil (a red string tied to a beanbag), and locks (represented by looped and knotted ropes; the more loops, the more complex the lock).

While some may balk at the liberties taken with accepted fantasy conventions—a Knight who detects undead?—IFGS is intentionally unsophisticated so that live-action games can be run as smoothly as possible. Potential players should note that live-action games can be major undertakings, requiring a lot of participants and extensive preparation. But for those interested in giving it a shot, the International Fantasy Gaming Society is the place to begin.

Buyer's Note: Contact the Dream Park Corporation for details. They'll send you some information about the game and tell you how to order the basic rulebook.

Suggested Supplements: The *Fantasy Rules* contain all of the essentials. Scheduled for release in 1990 are the *Game Sanctioning Handbook* (how to prepare an officially sanctioned IFGS game), the *Game Master's Manual* (referee tips), and the *Game Designer's Manual* (how to write and produce games using the IFGS system).

Indiana Jones**½

Complexity: Low/Medium
TSR Inc., 1984

Make no mistake, Indiana Jones is a plain and simple simulation of the movie characters, and has no aspirations to be a generic pulp hero game along the lines of Justice Inc. or Daredevils. Players seeking a 1930s-era RPG with a wide scope and detailed mechanics may be disappointed, but those wishing to relive the adventures of Indiana and Company with a minimum of effort should look no further.

Though the game seems intended for beginners, there are a number of innovative concepts, some of which may horrify purists. The most radical departure from conventional RPGs is the exclusion of a character-creation system; Indiana Jones, Short Round, and other members of the film casts are pregenerated and ready to go. Instead of experience points, Indiana Jones rewards Player Points for successful adventuring; not only do players earn points from the referee, the referee earns them from the players. Instead of advancing in levels, Player Points enable characters to heal more quickly by reducing the severity of wounds.

A single color-coded table resolves the bulk of the game's actions, not unlike the system used in Marvel Super Heroes; if Indy attempts to use his Instinct to avoid a pit trap, a Brown result on the table indicates a Bad Break (he falls in) while a Pink result gives him a Lucky Break (the trap fails to work). A clever Chase Flow Chart generates exciting chase scenes that can be adapted to any setting, or for that matter, any other pulp hero RPG.

Though the game stresses melodramatic combat engagements, the rules discourage the death of the PCs. While that's true to the spirit of the movies—who wants a dead Indy?—hardcore role-players might find it unrealistic. And because the game features an obvious star supported by a cast of lesser characters, it's not particularly suited for a large group of players—who wants to be Short Round when you can be Indy himself? But for small groups of fans willing to share the lead, Indiana Jones can be a lot of fun.

Buyer's Note: Boxed set.

Suggested Supplements: The *Raiders of the Lost Ark* adventure faithfully re-creates elements of the movie, with a few new twists to keep players on their toes. *The Fourth Nail* features a plot to steal a spike used in the crucifixion of Christ—a great premise and an exciting adventure.

Ironhedge**½

Complexity: Medium
Empire Wargames, 1989

Ironhedge, designed by John Brooke, is set on the mythical planet of Ironworld, whose culture resembles that of medieval Europe and whose inhabitants include an array of elves, dwarves, wizards, and other archetypes common to fantasy RPGs.

While the setting may be nothing out of the ordinary, the packaging certainly is. A three-panel referee's screen contains a lavishly detailed map of the planet along with most of the charts necessary for play. An assortment of blank character cards and encounter records are printed in several colors on textured paper—they look so nice that I felt guilty writing on them. Best of all is the "adventure deck," a set of about seventy index-size cards containing maps, diagrams, statistics, and other information relevant to various Ironworld locales. For instance, the Stonehedge card includes three multicolored maps of a bizarre building and its underground labyrinths, descriptions of several interesting encounters, and an eight-line poem to set the stage for the players. The Galley Ships card features diagrams for no less than six different ships, including views of the sides and tops, and complete equipment lists. With beautiful graphics and a staggering amount of detail, the adventure deck is one of the best RPG components I've ever seen.

The game systems are adequate, if a bit underdeveloped, and many concepts—such as experience points, saving throws, and hit points (called Life Points here)—will be familiar to all Dungeons and Dragons players. Characters derive from three basic attributes (Strength, Intelligence, and Dexterity), and can be Fighters, Thieves, Magicians, Alchemists, or Priests. The sketchy magic and combat rules require a lot of referee interpretation; spell descriptions seldom exceed two or three lines, there is less than a full page of naval combat rules, and the techniques for concocting magical potions are extremely vague. And why the sexism? Female characters have Beauty as an at-

tribute instead of Strength and have one less Life Point than
their male counterparts.

Overall, however, designer John Brooke did a nice job.
Though the game systems pale before the presentation, that's
more of a compliment to the packaging than a criticism of the
design. If the rules are set aside, Ironworld functions quite
nicely as a source of supplementary material for D&D and other
fantasy campaigns.

Buyer's Notes: Boxed set. The Ironhedge rules can be purchased separately without the adventure deck, the referee's
screen, and the other Ironworld materials, but since the rules
themselves are nothing special, stick with the boxed set.

Suggested Supplements: Westhedge is an entertaining sourcebook
for adapating the Ironhedge system to an Old West setting,
complete with six-guns, saloons, and stagecoaches.

It Came from the Late Late Late Show**

Complexity: Low
Stellar Games, 1989

Late Show pits the players against drooling zombies, animated
slime blobs, and similarly menacing creeps that will be familiar
to anyone who's ever sat through *Friday the 13th* or *Plan 9 From
Outer Space.* Designer Bradley McDevitt understands his source
material; for instance, the referee is urged to award Fame (comparable to experience points) to PCs who Act Appropriately Stupid, such as following a trail of blood into a dark bedroom. The
type of equipment a PC receives depends on his Fame; the
exceptionally Famous receive Lear jets and .44 magnums,
while lesser mortals will have to make do with bicycles and cattle prods.

Unfortunately, Late Show only hints at the potential of the
premise. The game begs for off-the-wall game mechanics, but
instead we're saddled with mundane character-generation rules
(based on Dexterity, Brains, and other ho-hum attributes), an

unimaginative list of skills (nothing more exotic than Occult Knowledge and Photography), and a convoluted combat system that's desperately out of place in a game this simple. The monsters are pretty bland, and aside from a few brief scenario suggestions, there's not much help for the referee. Worse, the game can't seem to make up its mind whether the PCs are characters in a movie or actors on a set; for example, PCs can die as a result of attacks from monsters, but they also have the option of Walking Off the Set to avoid sticky situations, a rule that drains all the tension out of dangerous encounters. There are a lot of good ideas lurking in Late Show, but the game can't seem to find them.

Buyer's Note: Trade paperback.

James Bond 007***½

. . . .

Complexity: Medium
Victory Games/The Avalon Hill Game Company, 1983

Why James Bond never attracted the audience it deserves remains one of gaming's biggest mysteries. Maybe the concept is old hat, tied too closely with the 1960s. Maybe there were licensing problems somewhere along the line. Or maybe espionage fans prefer the more generic approach taken by Top Secret/S.I. Whatever the reason, the game drifted out of print in the latter half of the 1980s, which is too bad, because James Bond stands as one of the most exciting and inventive RPGs ever published, a masterful effort by designer Gerry Klug (with assistance from Greg Gorden, Neil Randall, and Robert Kern).

Though the rulebook comprises 150-plus pages, referees can begin after studying the first chapter, which introduces the game's two fundamental concepts, the Ease Factor and the Quality Results Table. The Ease Factor measures the difficulty of every action in the game, including fistfights, car chases, gambling, and seduction. The referee assigns an Ease Factor from ½ to 10 for each action attempted by a PC; the lower the

Ease Factor, the more difficult the action. The player multiplies the Ease Factor by the skill or attribute appropriate to the action, then rolls percentile dice and consults the Quality Results Table. The table indicates failure or success; four degrees of success are possible, ranging from the merely Acceptable, through Good, Very Good, and the optimum Excellent. Various tables scattered throughout the rulebook indicate the difference between, say, an Acceptable attempt at safecracking and an Excellent one. Though the system requires a fair amount of page-flipping and interpretation from the referee, it's easy to learn and is remarkably versatile, handling a wrestling match with Oddjob as efficiently as a bridge game with Goldfinger.

Depending on the rank of the character he wishes to create, the referee assigns a variable number of Generation Points to each player; Rookie characters receive 3,000 points, Agents get 6,000, and the "00" PCs receive a whopping 9,000. All physical and personal characteristics derive from these points, including height, weight, and appearance, giving players an exceptional amount of freedom in customizing their characters. With the referee's permission, a player will receive additional Generation Points if he accepts one or more weaknesses for his PC, such as Fear of Snakes or Dependence on Liquor. Interestingly, James Bond characters are assumed to have an unlimited supply of money, allowing them to live the lavish life-styles enjoyed by movie spies.

Skills also derive from Generation Points, and though there are only twenty-four of them, they're broadly defined and therefore usable in a variety of situations; for instance, the Boating skill enables a character to pilot all types of seafaring vessels, as well as gives him a general knowledge of ship mechanics. Each skill lists the modifiers appropriate to specific situations, along with hints to the referee for staging effective encounters. For example, a Seduction attempt involves five separate steps, each requiring a Seduction check at the Ease Factor indicated: The Look (Ease Factor 10), Opening Line (Ease Factor 9), Witty Conversation (Ease Factor 8), Beginning Intimacies (Ease Factor 5), and When and Where (Ease Factor

4). The five steps can take several game-weeks to complete (though it's doubtful that James Bond would take that long).

The combat system is dangerous and melodramatic, using the Quality Results Table to determine damage from an eye-popping array of weapons. All kinds of exotic equipment are available, including cigarette rockets and acid-squirting pens, but PCs must persuade the ever-grumbling Q to let them have it, a nice rule that encourages role-playing.

Hardly a realistic simulation of the spy business, James Bond romanticizes espionage in much the same way as the movie series, complete with unflappable good guys, bizarre villains, gorgeous women, and exotic locales. The game's tone is closer to that of comic books than the gritty realism of the Ian Fleming novels, but no spy game surpasses James Bond in excitement and wittiness, and none is more skillfully designed. As the game and its supplements are out of print and will become increasingly harder to find, I'd advise snapping them up while you still can.

Buyer's Notes: The game is available as a trade paperback or as a boxed set. Aside from the rulebook, the material in the box is mostly superfluous, such as a pad of Character Record sheets and a few dice. The paperback edition is a better buy.

Suggested Supplements: The James Bond adventures are among the most lavishly packaged supplements ever published. The excellent *Dr. No* supplement, for instance, includes a forty-eight-page adventure, a two-panel Gamemaster Screen containing a detailed blueprint of Dr. No's fortress, and a packet of color handouts, including maps, pictures, receipts, and other clues. Along with *Dr. No* are also recommended *You Only Live Twice, Live and Let Die* (the best of all the Bond adventures), *The Man With the Golden Gun,* and *Goldfinger.* Two to avoid: the disappointing *Goldfinger II: The Man with the Midas Touch* and *A View to a Kill.* Though the names of the supplements will be familiar to Bond fans, the adventure plots are different from the movies and novels, sometimes radically so.

The *Q Manual* is an imaginative sourcebook detailing hundreds of guns, gadgets, and vehicles, an invaluable reference that can be adapted to any espionage RPG.

Judge Dredd***

Complexity: Medium
Games Workshop, 1985

Based on the 2000 AD comic-book series, *Judge Dredd* casts players in the roles of futuristic policemen sworn to uphold the law on the mean streets of Mega-City One, "where forty-eight crimes are committed every second." This is a game of extreme violence, but it's violence of the cartoon variety, made palatable by the tongue-in-cheek approach taken by designer Rick Priestley (with assistance from Marc Gascoigne, Albe Fiora, Ian Marsh, and Tony Watkins).

The PC policemen, known as Judges, are rated for Strength, Initiative, Combat Skill, Drive Skill, Technical Skill, Medical Skill, Street Skill, and Psi (for "psychic") Skill. Attribute ratings range from 1 to 100, except for Strength, which ranges from 1 to 3 (Strength 1 means the Judge is small and lean, Strength 2 means he's of average build, and Strength 3 indicates an exceptionally husky body). Each Judge receives a set of standard equipment, including handcuffs, a portable lie detector, and a "Lawgiver" pistol capable of firing armor-piercing shells, incendiary bullets, and other formidable projectiles.

Each game turn comprises six combat rounds, in which each Judge performs a variable number of actions depending on his Initiative score. Each combat round is further divided into ten phases; depending on a particular Judge's Initiative and attempted actions—typical actions include jumping, speaking, listening, aiming, and firing—he's active in some phases and inactive in others. The system requires a fair amount of bookkeeping for the referee to keep track of the rounds, actions, and phases, which can get to be a headache when a large number of characters are involved in a complicated encounter. Still, it's easy to learn and relatively smooth, especially when using a grid map (such as the one supplied with the game) to mark the characters' positions.

More than a hundred pages are devoted to referee's tips, background notes, and descriptions of an exceptionally degenerate array of villains, including the Blitzers (suicidal hit men), the Troggies (subterranean primitives), and the Futsies (psychotic suburbanites). Advanced rules add experience points, special abilities, and techniques for designing city blocks, but the thrust of the game remains unchanged—smoke out the bad guys, pass judgment on them (usually with the Lawgiver), and move on to the next crime scene.

The handsome presentation, featuring a generous amount of artwork from the comics, makes Judge Dredd as much fun to read as it is to play. However, as almost all of the rules are directed to violent encounters, the game lacks depth and it's not likely to sustain long campaigns. But in small doses, Judge Dredd is undeniably exciting, even for players who've never laid eyes on the comics.

Buyer's Notes: Hardback book. Judge Dredd originally appeared as a boxed set, but the hardback includes all of the boxed material in an easier-to-manage format.

Suggested Supplements: Slaughter Margin is an elaborate package containing an exciting introductory adventure and a wealth of attractive play aids. The *Judge Dredd Companion* includes new rules, abilities, and personalities, along with several informative essays on Judge-related topics; an essential sourcebook for those planning extended stays in Mega-City One.

Justice Inc.***

Complexity: Medium
Hero Games, 1984

Justice Inc. is an attractively presented RPG set in the world of pulp heroes, circa 1930. The game covers a variety of genres, among them horror, adventure, mystery, espionage, and science fiction, making it as much of a design kit as a stand-alone game. It's perfect for ambitious referees who enjoy mixing Indiana Jones with H. P. Lovecraft, or Sherlock Holmes with little green men.

The game mechanics, derived from Hero Games' generic

"Hero System," are almost identical to those of Espionage, with adjustments here and there to accommodate the various settings. Players receive a number of Character Points depending on the type of character they wish to play; a Talented Normal receives a modest 50 Character Points, while the exceptionally able Hero receives 75. As in Espionage, players exchange their points for attributes and skills, which include most of the choices from Espionage, along with a selection of Weird Talents (such as Hypnosis, Lightning Calculator, and Simulate Death) and Psychic Powers (like Clairvoyance, Precognition, and Telepathy) to build characters appropriate for mystical and supernatural adventures.

Likewise, the combat rules echo the systems of Espionage, with the addition of a simple routine for car chases and an emphasis on hand-to-hand brawls. Most heroes of the era lacked bulletproof vests or other sophisticated protection, so gunplay tends to be exceedingly dangerous. Players wishing to invent new gadgets or weapons are referred to the rules in Champions, another Hero System game. To create ghosts, players must also scrounge up a copy of Champions. Bad idea—the rules the game needs should be included, instead of an annoying commercial for another product.

A separate Campaign Book includes suggestions for staging adventures in eight different genres (such as Occult, Western, and Action), a comprehensive time line that includes twenty years' worth of World Series results, and several excellent adventures, highlighted by "The Coates Shambler," a nail-biting murder mystery. Though designers Aaron Allston, Steve Peterson, and Michael Stackpole bit off a bit more than they could chew—it's unlikely, for instance, that the horror version of the game will make anybody give up Call of Cthulhu—the clean rules and attention to detail make Justice Inc. far and away the best of the pulp-era RPGs.

Buyer's Note: Boxed set.

Suggested Supplements: A top-notch introductory adventure, *Trail of the Gold Spike* pits a group of investigative heroes against the mysterious Condor at the site of the Gold Spike Mining Company, located deep within the Colorado Rockies; the adventure can also be used with Call of Cthulhu, Mercenaries, Spies, and Private Eyes, and Daredevils. The *Lands of Mystery* sourcebook provides guidelines for putting together a "lost world" campaign involving an undiscovered civilization; it's an inspired treatment, beautifully written, that can also be adapted to Chill, Call of Cthulhu, and Daredevils. Justice Inc. is also compatible with supplements for Champions, Espionage, and Danger International.

Justifiers**

Complexity: Medium
Star Childe Publications, 1988

Justifiers imagines a future world where the invention of the TransMatt has made instantaneous matter transmission a reality, giving greedy corporations access to the stars for new planets to exploit. Players take the roles of Beta Class Humanoid Constructs, who are half-animal/half-humans owned by a monolithic organization called the Corp. Not only must the PCs fulfill their legal obligations to the Corp, they must also earn enough money to buy their freedom. It's an interesting premise, which provides the players with clear goals and gives the referee plenty of room to take the game in any direction he wishes.

The game mechanics stick to standard conventions, with PCs rated for Strength, Dexterity, Intelligence, and other typical attributes, and career choices limited to such standard science-fiction templates as Electrical Engineer and Life Science Specialist. A PC's racial type derives from an animal, which doesn't particularly affect the character's personality, but instead adds ability modifiers; for instance, a PC derived from a cheetah has natural Light Hide armor, receives bonuses to his Agility and Dexterity, and can track prey by scent. Combat involves both melee and missile rounds, modified by weapon choice, armor type, and applicable skills. The system produces acceptable results, but it's frustrating to use, because many of the rules are underdeveloped. It's not clear how dodging works, nor are the rules for surprise and missile attacks completely explained.

In fact, ambiguous rules and spotty writing plague Justifiers throughout. Skills are inadequately described, and many seem unnecessary (how are PCs supposed to use the Civil Law skill? Why is Basic Mathematics, described as the ability to compute 2 + 2, listed at all?). The cross-training rules don't make sense, and the equipment list includes such anachronistic weapons as maces, short swords, and tridents—is this really what we can expect in the twenty-third century? There are some good ideas here, but the game needs a rewrite.

Buyer's Note: Trade paperback.

Suggested Supplements: Two of the sourcebooks, *The Tower* (featuring a planet-spanning zoological laboratory) and *The Corporate Sourcebook* (the lowdown on a space-age corporate giant), contain myriad interesting devices, locales, personalities, and monsters that could be used in any science-fiction game. Nicely organized and well written, they're both worth a look. *Cold as Ice* is a reasonably good introductory adventure, highlighted by an imaginative cast of alien worms.

KABAL*

Complexity: High
Kabal Gaming Systems, 1981

The title is an acronym for Knights and Berserkers and Legerdemain, which is as clever as it gets. KABAL is nicely packaged but hopelessly derivative. Any value it might have as a game is buried beneath a mountain of mathematics: How tall is your character? Roll a six-sided die, multiply the sum by 20, take the square root of the result, and multiply it by 21.5 and you've got his height in centimeters—I think. This is supposed to be fun?

Buyer's Note: Boxed set.

Land of the Rising Sun**½

Complexity: High
Fantasy Games Unlimited Inc., 1980

An eastern cousin of the ultra-detailed Chivalry and Sorcery, Land of the Rising Sun is a thoughtful treatment of medieval Japan, skillfully interweaving imaginative fantasy elements with a scholar's understanding of history. Japanese nomenclature, architecture, and social systems are discussed at length, providing a rich background for Oriental role-playing.

Unfortunately, the background material is much better than the turgid game mechanics it supports. Players can take the roles of a fascinating array of characters, among them intelligent serpent-creatures and shape-changing foxes, but the character-creation system is time-consuming and difficult. The combat rules cover a wide range of attack options with remarkable accuracy, but the rules are so detailed that combat encounters seem to drag on forever. The magic system is the game's best feature, allowing magic-users to become Origami Mages (paper-folders), I Ching Masters, or Herbalists, refreshing alternatives to the familiar Wizards and Priests of Western-based fantasy games.

Though designer Lee Gold explains the game's concepts concisely and clearly, Land of the Rising Sun demands so much from the players that it's more work than fun. However, as a source of ideas, Land of the Rising Sun is worth investigating by any referee interested in an authentic eastern setting. (In 1988, Gold tackled the Orient again in the superb *GURPS Japan*, a sourcebook for Steve Jackson Games' GURPS system.)

Buyer's Note: Boxed set.

Lands of Adventure**½

Complexity: Medium
Fantasy Games Unlimited Inc., 1984

Lands of Adventure is a generic fantasy RPG tied to various "Culture Packs" that detail specific historical settings; for example, the Culture Pack included in the original game details mythic Greece and medieval England. However, the game drifted out of print before the concept could be fully explored, making Lands of Adventure a good idea that never really got off the ground.

The game mechanics, though by no means simple, are a marked improvement over the excessively complex Land of the

Rising Sun, a previous effort by designer Lee Gold. Characters can be humans, giants, elves, dwarves, or even animals. Among their ten basic attributes are the usual Dexterity, Intelligence, and Strength, along with the not-so-typical Prudence (a measure of foolhardiness) and Craft (an aptitude for creating weapons and tools). Some of the attribute rules are downright puzzling; for instance, Intelligence is derived from Craft (shouldn't that be the other way around?) and Gender isn't determined until after all of the other attributes have been calculated. Characters are also rated for Piety, an interesting rule that rewards them for completing pious actions, such as attending religious festivals and offering daily prayers, and penalizes them for blasphemy, such as defiling a deity's holy place or mocking a deity's priest. The combat and magic systems are adequate but routine, though the inclusion of miracles, spell backlash, and combination spells are all nice touches.

The Culture Pack is where Lands of Adventure really shines, containing scholarly, entertaining discussions of Greek and English settings that could easily be adapted into other role-playing systems. The Greek material includes a listing of major festivals, details of sacred plants and animals, and a brief but well-chosen selection of intriguing monsters, such as the Pelasgian Demons and a species of bronze-skinned fire-breathing birds called Stymphalians. The medieval England section is similarly detailed, featuring concise, informative discussions of feudal law and druidism. While it's unlikely that the role-playing rules of Lands of Adventure will replace anybody's favorite fantasy game, the Culture Pack material might be worth a look for referees with an interest in the featured eras.

Buyer's Note: Boxed set.

Living Steel**½

Complexity: High
Leading Edge Games, 1987

Whatever its shortcomings as a game, there's no denying that Living Steel has a nifty premise. The game takes place on the planet Rhand, a high-tech society that serves as a vacation retreat for the Starguild Empire elite. Three factions are battling for control: the Rhand government (an oppressive monarchy that enforces unquestioning obedience from its citizens), the rebel Alpha Team (dedicated to reinstating long-lost ideals of freedom and individuality), and the Spectrals (a vicious alien race bent on wiping out the entire planet with orbiting nuclear bombs and a deadly space virus that transforms humans into bloodthirsty zombies). The players take the roles of Alpha Team members who are hunted by the other two factions; the government wants them executed as dangerous traitors, while the Spectrals see them as uncooperative troublemakers, best suited for zombie food.

It's a terrific setup for some unusually exciting adventures. Not only must the players navigate between the hostile forces of the alien invaders and their own government, they must also scavenge for weapons, supplies, and recruits in a world devastated by nuclear war. The history and politics of Rhand are presented in vivid detail, with anecdotes from Rhand luminaries sprinkled throughout the text to add just the right amount of humor. Befitting a planet of advanced technology, there's plenty of inventive gadgets; Power Armor, for instance, gives players superhuman abilities, while Orca Teleportation Satellites provide instantaneous transportation to any location on the planet.

Living Steel would be a classic if the rules were as good as the background, but for the most part, they're ambiguous and difficult. Character generation takes forever and goes into far more detail than necessary to play a typical adventure. Combat is a nightmare of dice-rolling, table-consulting, and second-guessing; it's similar to the system in the excellent Phoenix Command game, but what's appropriate for the reality-based Phoenix Command is out of place and unbelievable in the world of Living Steel. An Action/Reaction table that supposedly covers the use of noncombat skills is nearly impossible to interpret; the referee would be better off flipping a coin.

Those willing to invest the time could probably whip the game into shape, but it's hardly worth the effort. As Living Steel has too many good ideas to be dismissed out of hand, players should consider using it as a sourcebook for other science-fiction games; either Star Trek or Megatraveller would make a good home for the Spectrals.

Buyer's Notes: The second edition hardback book is the one to buy. Avoid the first edition boxed set, which contains a lot of superfluous material.

Suggested Supplements: Leading Edge says that Living Steel is compatible with the supplements for Phoenix Command, but I'd suggest sticking with the official Living Steel material. It's all good stuff; in fact, the Living Steel supplements are more fun than the game itself. *Operation Seven Swords* is the best of the lot, featuring a detailed look at the Alpha Team organization and their special abilities. Also good is *KViSR Rocks*, a tongue-in-cheek adventure set in a mysterious village of hostile thugs.

Lords of Creation**½

Complexity: Medium
The Avalon Hill Game Company, 1984

How do you reward players for a successful performance in a role-playing game? Designers have struggled with this question since the inception of Dungeons and Dragons. Some games offer players experience points and higher levels of ability, others offer treasure and magic, and in many cases, the satisfaction of a job well done is supposed to be reward enough. Lords of Creation, while not an exceptional RPG, certainly has an exceptonal reward system—an overachieving PC eventually earns the right to create worlds of his own and become the game's referee.

This peculiar rule is the game's most interesting feature. Players begin as Neophytes, determining their Muscle, Speed, Stamina, Mental, and Luck attributes by dice-rolls. The sum of these scores results in the character's Personal Force, the game's most crucial rating. The number of Personal Force points determines a PC's skills and also dictates his current title; as a PC gains experience, his Personal Force level goes up, and he is awarded increasingly higher titles. The ultimate title, of course, is the referee, otherwise known as Lord of Creation. With each new title, a PC acquires a new special ability; the lowly Neophyte has the piddling Dimensional Sight, enabling him to see hidden monsters, while the Lord of Creation has the awesome Construction power, allowing him to create an entire universe (as any referee who has built a game world from scratch can attest, this power isn't necessarily a blessing).

The rest of the game mixes the elegant with the awkward. Adventures can occur in a variety of science-fiction and fantasy settings, and a Book of Foes details monsters and other adversaries for virtually any type of encounter the referee desires; dinosaurs, pirates, goblins, and aliens are just a few of the dozens of available choices. Though designer Tom Moldvay provides helpful tips for staging adventures in the various settings, there's simply too much ground to cover in too little space; if the referee wants to create an adventure with a time-traveling theme, he'll need a lot more information than what's given here. The combat system is fast and simple, but decidedly unrealistic; even low-level PCs can tolerate quite a bit of damage before they pass away. And though the concept of Neophytes, Lords, and other titles is intriguing, it's not clear what they actually represent. Still, for those willing to put up with some murky ideas, Lords of Creation can be an interesting game, unpredictable and decidedly eccentric.

Buyer's Note: Boxed set.

Suggested Supplements: Not much to recommend. *Horn of Roland* and *Yeti Sanction* are routine but well-presented adventures. Either serves as a good introduction to the game.

Mach**½

Complexity: Medium
Alliance Publications, 1983

An out-of-print game that's worth the search for its interesting setting. Mach is a planet shared by several million human colonists and a number of bizarre alien races whose relationships are shaky, to say the least. Alliances are shattered, negotiated, then shattered again, with a mysterious race of tentacled monstrosities lurking in the background who may or may not have the humans' best interests at heart. Despite a few futuristic touches, Mach is decidedly low tech; explorers are much more likely to be attacked with spears or swords than plasma beams or laser guns.

The game mechanics aren't much, comprising a routine character-generation system and a set of overly complicated combat rules. But in the hands of an inventive referee, Mach's intriguing premise could form the basis of a superb adventure for Star Trek, Megatraveller, or other science-fiction RPGs.

Buyer's Note: Boxed set.

Macho Women with Guns***

Complexity: Low
Blacksburg Tactical Research Center, 1989

Here's a game you'll never play with your grandma. Macho Women with Guns features amazonian PCs—rated for Strength, Dexterity, Looks, Health, and, of course, Macho—doing battle with Killer Rabbits, Drunken Frat Boys, and the nefarious Isaac Azathoth in an effort to rack up experience points for the Most Critters Killed (2 points) and the Worst Soliloquy (1 point). Exceptionally macho women may acquire advantages such as Teflon Skin (no damage from icky gunk) and Plastic Surgeon on Retainer (no disfigurement from an attack). Written by Greg Porter (also responsible for the textbook-serious Timelords), Macho Women with Guns is one of the funniest RPGs this side of Paranoia.

Though there are less than ten pages of rules, Macho Women is a slick little game, complete with brief but adequate combat rules covering a variety of assault tactics, including an option for Macho Attacks that allows characters to impress their opponents into submission without actually harming them. A clever section covering random-scenario generation creates instant adventures pitting the Macho Women against the Beastly Boys or Mr. Azathoth in an attempt to rescue an abandoned child or simply destroy everything on the map. The game walks a fine line between satire and adolescent sexism (some characters are Top Heavy, which tends to make them fall over), but overall Macho Women with Guns is so good-natured that its lapses are easy to forgive.

Buyer's Note: Booklet.

Suggested Supplements: Renegade Nuns on Wheels repeats the basic rules from Macho Women and can be used as a stand-alone game, but it works better as a supplement, adding vehicle rules, new skills, and some great new opponents, such as Oddzilla and the BattleWarMechBots. Likewise, *Bat-Winged Bimbos from Hell* includes the basic Macho Women rules but makes a better supplement than a self-contained game; aside from the rules for flight, it doesn't add much to the original, although the Game Name Table—which randomly generates titles for future Macho Women supplements, such as Undead Insurance Salesmen from Planet X—is a lot of fun.

Manhunter**½

Complexity: Medium/High
Kingslayer Publications, 1987

Manhunter is set in a high-tech future where an alliance between the citizens of Earth and a race of enigmatic aliens called the Aglians has resulted in the Aglio-Terran Planetary Defense System, a governing body spanning the entire galaxy. Players take the roles of humans, Aglians, or any of several other well-drawn intelligent species to maintain peace on behalf of the ATPDS or scour the stars in search of adventure.

The character-creation system is quite clever, requiring players to determine levels for eleven basic attributes (Strength, Endurance, Alertness, and so forth), which are then assigned a letter rating based on the character's race. For instance, though a physically frail Aglian and a member of the powerful Ular race might both have Strength scores of 85, the Aglian receives a letter rating of A and the Ular receives a rating of D. To determine each character's actual score, players refer to the Quality Rating Chart and consult the column corresponding to the letter rating; in this case, the Aglian's 85A translates into an actual score of 11, while the Ular's 85D translates into an actual score of 25. Using this system, designer Ramon Moore ensures that each race maintains distinct characteristics, despite the whims of the dice or the desires of the players.

There are excellent sections on robotics, featuring concise and workable rules for robot construction, and some interesting material on the history of the ATPDS, including colorful descriptions of its top ten corporations and backgrounds of its most notorious criminals. Most of the game mechanics, however, are far too complicated, most notably the combat system, whose convoluted formulas slow the action to a crawl (example: a PC's Total Defense score = experience bonus [consult chart 2.1] + total defense stat bonus [add Deftness + speed, then consult chart 2.1] + weapon modifier [consult chart 2.2] + combat skill modifier [consult chart 2.3]). Oddly, there's a magic system tacked on to the end of the rulebook; though playable, it's jarringly out of place in this setting.

Manhunter has a number of good ideas, but it's hard to tell how they're supposed to fit together. A sample adventure would have helped, as would a sharper focus. Still, for a first-time designer, Manhunter is an impressive effort.

Buyer's Note: Trade paperback.

Man, Myth, and Magic*½

Complexity: Medium
Yaquinto, 1983

Man, Myth, and Magic has been out of print for some time, but since the game and its supplements pop up in stores and at conventions from time to time, potential buyers should be forewarned to keep their distance. Presumably the game can be set in a past era, but there's nothing even remotely plausible about the concept, since Nazis can pop up in ancient Rome as easily as a mastodon might trample the soldiers at Gettysburg. Character generation is equally absurd, because nearly everything is determined at random; one PC might be an elf, the next a Roman gladiator, and another a tribal witch doctor. Nobody ever claimed that fantasy had to make sense, but there ought to be a semblance of internal logic, a feature that Man, Myth, and Magic utterly lacks.

Any potential for goofy fun is lost in a mishmash of awkward, ill-conceived game mechanics. The magic system is unimaginative, the combat rules are confusing, and the introductory scenarios are dull and nearly impossible to run if the players stray too far from the rigid story line. There are some nice graphics, particularly the maps of Stonehenge and the Great Pyramids, but they hardly justify the purchase of a game this muddled.

Buyer's Note: Boxed set.

Suggested Supplements: Ascent to Hell, a bizarre adventure that takes place in some of the less frightening chambers of the netherworld, is as good as it gets.

Marvel Super Heroes***½

Complexity: Low
TSR Inc., 1984

Marvel Super Heroes is intended as a smooth introduction to role-playing for fans of the comics, and as such, it's an unqualified success. It's a snap to learn, loaded with action, and neatly captures the anything-goes lunacy that's been a hallmark of Marvel Comics since the early 1960s.

Designers Jeff Grubb and Steve Winter made the game as user-friendly as possible, beginning with the virtual elimination of tables, formulas, and other number-heavy mechanics. Instead of numerical ratings for Fighting, Agility, Strength, Endurance, Reason, Intuition, and Psyche, characters are assigned single-word "Ranks." There are ten Ranks in all, ranging from the paltry Feeble (representing Aunt May's Strength or Man-Thing's Intuition) to Remarkable (Spider-Man's Endurance or Wolverine's Fighting) to the godlike Unearthly (the Hulk's Strength or the Watcher's Reason). Popularity, Resources (a measure of wealth), Magical Limits, and just about every other skill, trait, and modifier likewise receive Ranks instead of numbers. For instance, an unemployed hero like Spider-Man may have Feeble Resources, while millionaire Tony (Iron Man) Stark is blessed with Incredible Resources.

A single Universal Table handles all of the game's actions, completely forgoing numbers in favor of Ranks. If the Hulk wishes to use his Unearthly Strength to uproot a skyscraper, the controlling player throws percentile dice and checks the Unearthly column on the Universal Table. Similarly, if Spider-Man wants to see if he can afford an operation for Aunt May with his Feeble Resources, his player throws dice and checks the Feeble column. There are four ranges of results, each indicated by a different color. If the roll indicates a White result, the attempt fails. Green, Yellow, and Red results indicate varying degrees of success, as interpreted by the referee. More impressive than the system's simplicity are the satisfying results it produces; though too formless for the precision required by "serious" RPGs, the results are perfectly in tune with the casual logic of the comics.

The Battle Effects Table supplements the Universal Table during combat encounters. Opponents engage in dueling dice-throws, based on the Ranks of the appropriate powers and abilities. The Battle Effects Table details the results of a successful attack, ranging from Slams and Stuns on Slugfest column, and Misses and Bull's-Eyes on the Shooting and Throwing column. The loser subtracts the indicated damage from his current number of Health Points. It's possible for a hero to die, but as in the comics, it's not likely. Each character has a number of Karma Points that he can spend to bail himself out of life-threatening situations; heroes earn additional Karma Points by successfully fighting crime and being good citizens.

Admittedly, Marvel Super Heroes has a narrow focus. The game presumes familiarity with the Marvel Universe, and players who've never heard of Captain America or the Fantastic Four (are there any?) won't find much to like, though it's possible to invent new characters and even duplicate heroes from other comics companies. And some may find it hard to keep the Ranks straight; I can never remember if Remarkable is better than Incredible, or vice versa.

I believe it's more difficult to design a simple game than a complicated one, so Marvel Super Heroes strikes me as a triumph. Those offended by the idea of characters explaining the rules ("Web-head hadda go save somebody, so he asked me to take over for a while," says the Thing in the Battle Book) should probably stick to the more sober-minded Champions or Superworld. But for beginners who can't wait to start web-slinging, or experienced players looking for a whimsical diversion, Marvel Super Heroes is an excellent choice.

Buyer's Note: Boxed set.

Suggested Supplements: There's a mountain of supplements available for Marvel Super Heroes. Here are some of the best:

Expansions: The Marvel Super Heroes Advanced Set adds all of the complications bypassed in the original game, including numerical ranges for Ranks, modifiers for combat, and a more detailed movement system. Expanded rules for superpowers makes it easier to create characters from scratch, and new statistics are provided for all of the major Marvel heroes. Though the Advanced Set retains the style and tone of the original, it's aimed at sophisticated players. The *Ultimate Powers Book*, a supplement to the Advanced Set, features descriptions of hundreds of superpowers for customizing original characters and revitalizing old villains.

Sourcebooks: The *Gamer's Handbook of the Marvel Universe* is a beautiful multivolume set detailing the backgrounds, personalities, and abilities of every major Marvel character; the definitive reference work for the serious MSH player. The *Deluxe City Campaign Set* provides all the maps, encounters, and staging tips

128
....

necessary for putting together an extended campaign set in New York City; one of the best treatments of a contemporary setting ever published. Players interested in spellcasting heroes should investigate the *Realms of Magic* supplement, which expands the rules for magic from the original set and also includes game statistics for Marvel's most popular wizards.

Adventures: Among the best introductory adventures are *Cat's Paw* (featuring the original members of Alpha Flight), *Breeder Bombs* (X-Men), and *Murderworld* (Fantastic Four); all are well-written and easy to run, even for beginning referees. Also interesting is *Gates of What If*, an alternate universe adventure where Dr. Doom is a good guy. Ambitious players should try the four-volume Future in Flames series (*Nightmares of Future Past*, *X-Potential*, *Reap the Whirlwind*, and *Flames of Doom*), which feature a future Earth where super-powered mutants are hunted down and imprisoned in camps. The Elders of the Universe series (*Cosmos Cubed*, *Ragnarok and Roll*, and *Left Hand of Eternity*) is an excellent outer space campaign starring the Watcher, Galactus, and other high-powered characters.

Masters of the Universe*½

Complexity: Low
FASA Corp., 1985

In the mid-to-late 1980s, the "Masters of the Universe" cartoon show commanded a devoted following of grade-schoolers. The action figures of He-Man and his fellow Masters flew out of the toy store shelves at an unprecedented rate, and their continuing popularity seemed assured—at least until the Teenage Mutant Ninja Turtles came along. Still, what a great idea for an introductory role-playing game, right?

Well, sort of. Colorful stand-up figures are provided for all of the notable characters, and the attractive game board of Snake Mountain makes for a nice playing field. The game is simple, brief, and does a pretty good job of introducing basic role-playing concepts, such as Strength and Agility attributes, skill levels, and magic points, to novices.

However, Masters of the Universe has some big problems. The rules are presented in a comic book, an idea more clever than practical—just try sorting through the word balloons to find the rule you need (thankfully, there's a rules summary at the end of the comic). Regardless of what the box says, this is primarily a board game, not a role-playing game; players search Snake Mountain for the crown jewels, then must escape with them off the board. More seriously, Masters of the Universe completely misjudges its audience. From my experience, the Masters' biggest fans are well under eight years old; this game is just too hard for them. Older players—say, ages eight through twelve—will probably find it beneath their dignity. Bullwinkle and Rocky or even Marvel Super Heroes is a much better choice for beginning role-players.

Buyer's Note: Boxed set.

Mechanoids***

Complexity: Medium
Palladium Books, 1985

Concise rules, a slick presentation, and a fascinating setting add up to a gem of a game. Mechanoids never got the attention it deserved and remains an overlooked classic of science-fiction role-playing. It's a stylish and inventive simulation of alien invasion from the prolific Kevin Siembieda.

As in Heroes Unlimited, Robotech, and other Palladium products, the basic rules derive from the Palladium Role-Playing Game, though here they're stripped down and streamlined, making this the easiest to learn of all the Palladium titles. Basic attributes include Physical Strength, Intelligence Quotient, and Speed, with a PC's hit points dependent on his Physical Endurance. Players choose career templates called Occupational Character Classes for their PCs, which come complete with appropriate skills; Communications Engineer, Field Scientist, and Commando are among the possibilities. PCs with psionic abilities have paranormal talents such as Levitation, Invisibility, and others that read suspiciously like magic spells; in fact, victims resist psionic attacks with successful saving throws in much the same way as Dungeons and Dragons characters resist magical attacks. This psionic/magic system contrasts too sharply with the high-tech setting of Mechanoids and should've been left on the drawing board. The combat system, on the other hand, is a winner; the attacker rolls a die, and if the result is greater than the opponent's Armor Rating and all dodging attempts fail, the attack succeeds. Roll for damage, and that's it—quick, simple, and elegant.

But where Mechanoids really shines is in its vivid setting. The game begins after a human colony on a distant planet is attacked by the Mechanoids, a savage alien race resembling giant mechanical insects. With the Mechanoids wielding a mind-boggling array of cybernetic devices, the humans, including the PCs, are hopelessly outclassed. Though the odds are stacked against them, the PCs have no choice but to fight for survival or submit to the invaders. The situation is desperate, and the result is a level of tension seldom achieved in a role-playing game.

Though the game mechanics lack the intricacies of Megatraveller or even Siembieda's own Sentinels, they're more than adequate to support the premise. While Mechanoids is easy to master, those not up to learning a new game system should be able to adapt the background to other space-age RPGs without too much trouble. However they use it, science-fiction fans shouldn't miss Mechanoids.

Buyer's Notes: Trade paperback. *Mechanoids* updates the material presented in the 1981 game-book trilogy, *Mechanoid Invasion*, *The Journey*, and *Homeworld*. The trilogy is vastly inferior to the 1985 paperback described here.

Suggested Supplements: There are no supplements to recommend specifically for Mechanoids. However, Mechanoids is compatible with other Palladium games, Robotech and Teenage Mutant Ninja Turtles being particularly good choices.

MechWarrior***

···

Complexity: Medium
FASA Corporation, 1986

MechWarrior is not a stand-alone game; rather, it's the role-playing supplement to BattleTech, the granddaddy and undisputed champion of robotic tactical board games. BattleTech itself is terrific, a versatile combat system that avoids the awkward mechanics of similar games, yet is detailed enough to please the most obsessive giant robot fan. Though the BattleTech setting is nicely textured, featuring a universe ravaged by the Succession Wars and MechWarriors competing in violent contests for power and honor, the game focuses almost exclusively on combat. Role-playing seems like an afterthought, as PCs exist mainly to pilot the giant machines.

That's not to say that MechWarrior is superfluous. It features intelligent, streamlined rules for creating characters based on a mere four attributes: Body, Dexterity, Learning Ability, and Charisma. Players buy skills from a modest selection of choices, most of them combat-oriented, such as Tactics, Brawling, and Gunnery. Successful adventures result in the acquisition of experience points, which increase a PC's class level from Green to Regular to Veteran to Elite. There's also a brief but adequate system for determining the PCs' Battle Mechs (big machines), along with their military units, which can range from Lances (four Mech units) to Companies (twelve Mechs). Interestingly, because a large number of characters might be needed to fill out a unit, players often control more than one PC.

MechWarrior PCs aren't especially interesting as personalities, but within the narrow focus of Battletech, they function quite well. Because the MechWarrior combat system is essentially an extension of the parent game, ownership of Battletech is mandatory.

Buyer's Notes: Trade paperback. BattleTech—a prerequisite for MechWarrior—is a boxed set.

Suggested Supplements: The BattleTech expansion sets take the original game in new directions; they're attractively packaged and clearly explained, but as the layers of complexity add up fast, they're recommended only to experienced players. The best: *AeroTech* (battles in the sky) and *City Tech* (battles in an urban setting).

The sourcebooks explore the history and personalities of various cultures of the BattleTech universe; they're well-written and fun to read, even for casual players. Recommended: *Sorenson's Sabers*, *House Kurita*, and *House Marik*.

The Mega Role-Playing System *½

Complexity: Medium
Mega Games Ltd., 1989

Maybe the last decade's worth of role-playing games didn't all reach Scandinavia, or maybe something got lost in the translation. In any case, this Norwegian design might have generated some interest if it had been published in the 1970s, but now it's little more than a curious anachronism.

Mega is yet another generic fantasy RPG with few original twists of its own, save for a modestly interesting character-generation system based on attribute ranges (which establish limits for the abilities of each race) and development levels (which generate formulas for determining individual ability levels). The rest of it reads like warmed-over Dungeons and Dragons, complete with routine combat rules and magic systems that are more likely to elicit yawns than interest. Skip it.

Buyer's Note: Hardback book.

Megatraveller ****

Complexity: Medium/High
Games Designers' Workshop, 1987

For years, Traveller was the undisputed champion of science-fiction role-playing. A game of unprecedented magnitude, there was no aspect of spacefaring adventure that Traveller didn't handle, and handle exquisitely. True, the original game lacked a few details, such as robotics, alien races, and high-tech hardware, and the historical background wasn't fully developed, but a string of supplements eventually pulled everything together, creating a classic in the process.

Then along came Megatraveller, a complete redesign of the original Traveller by Marc Miller (with assistance from Frank Chadwick, Joe Fugate Sr., and Gary Thomas) that stands as one of the most remarkable gaming achievements of the last decade. Not only does Megatraveller retain the scope and appeal of Traveller, it expands on the strengths of the original with a bonanza of inspired new material.

Nowhere is the improvement more evident than in Megatraveller's redefinition of the Traveller universe. The original Traveller was set in a far future dominated by the Imperium, a model of stable and efficient government that encompassed some ten thousand star systems. Megatraveller finds the Imperium in chaos, thanks to the assassination of the Emperor by a scheming pretender to the throne named Dulinor. The Imperium is crumbling, as rival factions squabble for power and rebel groups threaten anarchy. It's an exciting background, artfully detailed, and offers unlimited potential for adventures.

The boxed set consists of three thick volumes, all of them models of clean organization and vivid writing. The *Player's Manual* explains the rules for character creation, skill acquisition, and combat techniques. Character creation is based on a PC's personal background and occupation, with Military Officer, Diplomat, Merchant, and Asteroid Miner among the career choices. As with most of the Megatraveller rules, character generation is complicated, but produces satisfying and realistic results. The *Referee's Manual* expands on the combat rules introduced in the *Player's Manual*, adding rules for starship and surface vehicles, along with a comprehensive section on vehicle construction. The book also addresses one of the original game's major deficiencies with the inclusion of helpful tips for staging Megatraveller adventures. The final volume, the *Imperial Encyclopedia*, is an invaluable reference book featuring absorbing essays on the technology and cultures of the Mega-traveller universe.

All of Traveller's best features, including the excellent rules for starship design and world creation, are present in Mega-traveller, but with numerous clarifications and a host of new options. There's an increased emphasis on interstellar trade in Megatraveller, as the eternally indebted Traveller PCs will be happy to hear. Rules for psionics, library data, and task resolution have been streamlined and improved. A superb design in a gorgeous package, Megatraveller is the pinnacle of science-fiction role-playing.

Buyer's Notes: Boxed set. The *Player's Manual*, *Referee's Manual*, and *Imperial Encyclopedia* are available separately, but all three are needed to appreciate the game to its fullest.

Suggested Supplements: The *Referee's Companion* features rules for large-scale combat, mapping techniques, and suggestions for running extended campaigns; a must-have for serious referees. The *Rebellion Sourcebook* provides detailed information about the various factions vying for power in the Imperium, along with an excellent introductory scenario; another essential purchase. Skilled referees should be able to adapt virtually all of the original Traveller supplements to the Megatraveller universe; especially recommended are the modules in the Aliens series.

Mekton II**½

Complexity: Medium
R. Talsorian Games, 1987

A game of giant robots, Mekton II has more in common with tactical military simulations than RPGs. Inspired by Japanese cartoons, the Mekton constructs are enormous humanoid machines outfitted with all sorts of high-tech weapons and gizmos. Designing the robots is fun and simple, easily the most enjoyable part of the game. The combat rules are as detailed as those of tactical wargames; they're fairly easy to use, if somewhat sketchy in places (it's unclear, for instance, exactly how skills affect combat results).

The character-creation rules are the game's weakest feature, apparently included for the sole purpose of generating pilots for the robots. Though the PC pilots can have backgrounds, families, and other personal characteristics, they're essentially irrelevant to the focus of the game. It's possible to design a campaign setting from the information presented in the *Algol Sourcebook*, but I'm not sure it's worth the trouble, because it's merely a way to kill time until the next robotic showdown. As a role-playing game, Mekton II isn't much, but as a tactical simulation of robot warfare, it's reasonably fun.

Buyer's Notes: Trade paperback. Avoid the inferior first edition, entitled simply Mekton, published in 1984 as a boxed set.

Merc**

Complexity: Medium
Fantasy Games Unlimited Inc., 1981

Merc filled a niche when it was first released, but the subsequent publication of a number of more sophisticated games covering the same ground have rendered it obsolete. The subject is contemporary warfare, with players taking the roles of mercenaries engaged in covert (or not so covert) military actions around the world. The game's best feature is its character-creation system, which generates a wide variety of physical and mental characteristics, along with specialties ranging from Interpreter/Interrogator to Martial Arts Expert. Though lacking detail, the combat system smoothly resolves everything from grenade tossing to hand-to-hand skirmishes.

Trouble is, everything Merc does, some other game does better. The action is much more intense in Recon, the combat system pales before that of Phoenix Command, Mercenaries, Spies, and Private Eyes is more elegant, and Top Secret/S.I. is more versatile. Merc is not a bad game, but its day has come and gone.

Buyer's Note: Boxed set.

Suggested Supplements: Merc Supplement 1 clarifies many of the rules of the original game, while adding new ones for vehicles and airborne operations; essential if planning an extended campaign. *Campaign Book 1: Rhodesia* features scenarios for Rhodesian guerilla warfare; sketchy in places, but adequate overall.

Mercenaries, Spies, and Private Eyes***½

Complexity: Low/Medium
Blade Games, 1983

A spin-off of Tunnels and Trolls, Mercenaries, Spies, and Private Eyes is a beautiful game and a remarkable design. In a rulebook that barely exceeds one hundred pages, author Michael Stackpole covers three related but distinct genres—modern warfare, espionage, and hardboiled detective—with rules that are simple enough for novices yet sophisticated enough to satisfy the most experienced players.

All MS&P characters derive from a set of standard attributes, including Strength, Intelligence, and Constitution, of which Intelligence is the most crucial. A PC receives a number of Skill Points equal to his Intelligence score, which can be used to buy skills from a list of nearly one hundred options. A Sherlock Holmes type, for instance, might opt for such skills as Forensics and Disguise, while a would-be Indiana Jones might choose Horsemanship and Bullwhip. The Special Interests skill is a catch-all category that allows for characters to specialize in any obscure talent of the player's choice, such as Occult Practices, Ancient Architecture, or even Fantasy Role-Playing Games.

The game mechanics refine and streamline many of the systems introduced in Tunnels and Trolls. Determining the success of an action, whether it's an attempt to jump a chasm, decode a secret message, or fire a rifle, requires the player to roll two six-sided dice and add the appropriate attribute (if he's trying to decode a secret message, he'd use Intelligence). If the dice-roll exceeds the necessary "to hit" number, the action is successful. "To hit" numbers are modified by skill levels and the referee's general assessment of difficulty; for instance, a ten-foot chasm would have a higher "to hit" roll than a five-foot chasm. Virtually any type of action can be resolved quickly and satisfyingly with this versatile system.

Combat also involves "to hit" rolls. Opponents engaged in melee combat each roll a die and add their combat modifiers; the opponent with the highest roll wins the round, and the loser suffers an amount of damage equal to the difference in their die-rolls. Missile combat (defined as any attack involving projectiles, including bullets, arrows, and spears) is a bit more complex, requiring that the attacker modify his roll by the weapon type, range, target size, and movement of the attacker and target. Still, even the most involved combat engagements rarely take more than a few minutes to resolve, and the results are exciting and realistic.

There are detailed sections for staging adventures in a variety of genres, with an especially helpful chapter on designing mysteries, explaining the art of planting clues, how to determine motives, and how to create a cast of plausible suspects. Because the game stresses simplicity, detail is necessarily understated, perhaps too much so for players who insist on precision; for instance, there isn't much meaningful distinction between the various weapon types, and establishing "to hit" levels is always an educated guess. Still, it's a lot of fun, and easily one of the most ingenious private eye/secret agent RPGs ever published.

Buyer's Note: Trade paperback.

Suggested Supplements: Stormhaven describes a mysterious estate on an island near Vermont, loaded with creepy NPCs and plenty of adventure springboards; a perfect setting for a Doc Savage/Indiana Jones flavored campaign, it also can be used with the Espionage rules. *The Adventure of the Jade Jaguar* is a solo adventure, similar to the solitaire Tunnels and Trolls supplements, and features an exciting rescue in the jungles of Latin America.

Metamorphosis Alpha**½

Complexity: Low
TSR Inc., 1974

Essentially, this is Dungeons and Dragons in space. Players find themselves aboard an immense interstellar spacecraft containing all sorts of dangerous animal and plant mutations. Exploring the labyrinths of the spacecraft is not unlike roaming a cavern net-work or other dungeonlike enclosure, and, in fact, Meta-morphosis Alpha is closer in spirit to a D&D variant than a new game system.

Though the rules are a bit dated—understandable, as they're more than a decade and a half old—Metamorphosis Alpha still has potential for an evening or two of fun. Its true value, how-ever, is as a collector's item. The game is not only one of the first science-fiction RPGs, but it is also one of TSR's earliest efforts following the success of D&D. A would-be collector could do worse than hoarding a few copies of Metamorphosis Alpha.

Buyer's Note: Booklet.

Middle Earth Role Playing**½

Complexity: Medium/High
Iron Crown Enterprises, 1984

Virtually every fantasy RPG owes a debt of gratitude to *Lord of the Rings:* what could be more natural than a game based en-tirely on J. R. R. Tolkein's classic books? Middle Earth Role Playing attempts just that, and if it's not entirely successful, blame it on the difficulty of duplicating the charm of the novels in a set of role-playing rules.

The game mechanics basically streamline those in Iron Crown's Rolemaster game. Where Rolemaster is awkward and chart-heavy, MERP is smooth and . . . well, it's still chart-heavy, but not excessively so. Players roll up Strength, Agility, Constitution, and the rest of the usual attributes, then choose racial types from a selection that includes dwarves, elves, half-elves, and hobbits. PCs choose from a variety of skills, such as Riding, Public Speaking, and Disarming Traps, and each has a specific profession, such as Scout, Ranger, or Mage. Nearly every profession has access to spells, which are cast by expend-ing Power Points. When a PC has spent his Power Points, he's finished casting spells for the day, but he recovers them again after eight hours of rest. The game drags a bit during combat encounters, since combat resolution involves quite a few modifiers and a fair amount of table checking, but it's nothing an experienced referee can't handle.

MERP is more likely to find favor with casual Tolkein fans than Middle Earth fanatics, because even though it's a pretty good fantasy game, it doesn't measure up to the novels. Combat plays a much larger role in the game than it does in the books, and where magic was a phenomenal event in *Lord of the Rings*, it's commonplace here. More troubling, the Middle Earth of the game isn't all that different from any other fantasy setting based on medieval Europe. Designer S. Coleman Charlton did a commendable job overall, but I suspect that it's impossible to capture the essence of Tolkein in an RPG.

Buyer's Notes: Trade paperback. There's also a boxed version that includes all of the rules from the paperback, along with an introductory adventure and other supplementary materials. Players on a budget can get by with the paperback.

Suggested Supplements: Nearly all of the MERP supplements are first-rate products, well presented and crisply written. As each focuses on a specific aspect of the Middle Earth mythos, they're closer in spirit to the source material than the game itself and are recommended to Tolkein fans as well as gamers. The best: *Mirkwood, Moria, Lorien,* and *Isengard*.

Midnight at the Well of Souls*½

Complexity: Medium
TAG Industries, 1985

Fans of novelist Jack Chalker may be tempted to investigate this game, which is based on the author's superb Well World novels, but they're advised to avoid it. The premise has a lot of potential (the Well World is a gigantic computerlike mechanism divided into sections, each of which houses a unique race of intelligent beings), but the game doesn't do much with it. Though there's an ambitious system for generating worlds, similar to the one in the FTL: 2448 game, the results are little more than bland lists of numbers.

The game mechanics are unimaginative and superficial. Character creation involves the usual random determination of attributes and the expenditure of skill points on run-of-the-mill skills. Combat is number-heavy and seems to be excessively dangerous—a couple of bad dice-rolls, and good-bye, PC. Worst of all, the game fails to capture any of the charm of the Chalker books, a flaw that's hard to overlook, considering the title.

Buyer's Note: Boxed set.

Morpheus**

Complexity: Medium
Rapport Games, 1990

Morpheus explores the connection between role-playing and dreaming by casting players as imaginary characters participating in adventures set in a "mind park" operated by the Mindgamer's Organization for Recreational Programs Harnessed by Electroencephalic Utility Systems (Morpheus, for short). The rationale for Morpheus—something about a neural link that taps into the nervous system—is secondary to its purpose; namely, to allow for any type of adventure the referee can dream up without the constraints of reality-based rules.

There are only three character types in Morpheus: the Alterationist, who can transform and mutate himself at will; the Invocationist, who can alter reality and heal other characters; and the Gadgeteer, a high-tech warrior who can create any kind of mechanical device. Characters are rated for Imagination, Confidence, Ego, and Reputation, and receive a fixed number of Dream Points to buy special talents. Each PC also receives a Feat Roll rating derived from his Confidence and Imagination scores. Presumably, the Feat Roll can resolve any type of attempted task, but it's up to the referee to work out the details, a problem that plagues Morpheus throughout. Are there any limits to the types of weapons a Gadgeteer can create? What exactly is the function of Confidence? Do all of the dream creatures respond to a PC's Reputation in the same way? It's anybody's guess.

Morpheus is intentionally unrealistic and encourages players "to run amok." Designer Devi Durham has a lot of fun with the concept, but without guidelines more specific than the vague suggestions offered here, it doesn't take long for a game to degenerate into chaos. Morpheus bursts with inventive ideas, but it'll take a determined referee to shape them into a coherent, playable game.

Buyer's Note: Trade paperback.

The Morrow Project**½

Complexity: Medium/High
Timeline Inc., 1980

The Morrow Project is the most graphic and chilling RPG depiction of near-future nuclear carnage ever published. The PCs are part of the Morrow Project, a top-secret organization that recruits civilians and cryogenically freezes them so they'll survive the coming nuclear holocaust. After awakening in a devastated world, the PCs face the long task of rebuilding civilization. Unlike the superficially similar Gamma World, which includes a menagerie of bizarre monsters that would be right at home in a fantasy game, Morrow Project is anything but frivolous.

The game includes an impressive amount of background material, beginning with a detailed examination of how a nuclear attack might affect the United States. Charts and statistics show the most likely targets of hostile missiles, the performance capabilities of various warheads, and the consequences of nuclear-related blasts. Weaponry and vehicle information is similarly detailed, with comprehensive statistics for M-16s, Stoner carbines, laser guns, airscouts, and hovercraft. Weather, terrain, lifeforms, and medicine receive extensive coverage; in short, there's everything needed to create a convincing postapocalyptic setting.

Considering the detail evident elsewhere in this game, the character creation rules are surprisingly fuzzy. Die-rolls determine the usual primary attributes (Strength, Constitution, etc.), with the majority of secondary attributes dealing with physical characteristics, such as Body Structure Points and Blood Points. Strangely, PCs aren't rated for Intelligence, nor do they acquire skill specialties as do PCs in similar games. Worse, aside from assignments to scientific, reconnaissance, or other specialty teams, PCs have no particular attitudes, emotions, or backgrounds. With the personality of a slide rule, a Morrow Project PC isn't much fun to play.

The game comes alive in the combat rules, the most detailed treatment of violent encounters this side of Aftermath. Attack success depends on the weapon employed, the type of target, and a host of modifiers including range, penetration ratings, armor class and visibility. Victims don't merely suffer damage, they are burned, poisoned, radiated, bled, and shocked with excruciating precision. Though the rules border on the excessive, they produce realistic results for those with the patience to navigate them.

As a game, Morrow Project has too many ambiguous rules for casual players, though hardcore science-fiction fans might enjoy it. But as a sourcebook of nuclear holocaust, it's without peer, unreservedly recommended to anyone with an interest in the subject.

Buyer's Note: Trade paperback.

Suggested Supplements: There are a number of excellent adventures, but all tend to be as detailed and starkly written as the game itself and are not recommended to beginners. The best: *Damocles* (strange occurrences in the wastelands of Michigan) and *Operation Lucifer* (a search for an unexploded nuclear bomb).

Multiverse**½

Complexity: Medium
T.C. International, 1989

Give Multiverse credit for ambition. It attempts no less than to generate role-playing settings in "an infinite number of dimensional planes that overlap our own." That's a mighty tall order, and what's surprising is how well designer Troy Christensen pulls it off. The systems are clever, the presentation is clean and professional, but the game isn't quite comprehensive enough to meet its lofty goal.

Character creation involves the assignment of 30 Racial Points and a variable number of Personal Points and Experience Points to a PC's attributes, characteristics, and skills. Characters also receive "bio-options" that give them special abilities based on the gravity type of their homeworlds. There are dozens of possible bio-options, ranging from exotic body appendages, such as gills and multiple arms, to powerful psionic powers, such as telepathy and temperature control. The dozen available character classes include Viking, Philosopher, and Wizard—an awfully skimpy list, considering the scope of the game.

The most interesting feature of Multiverse is its "floating decimal point" rule for resolving actions. Each ability rating is expressed as a single whole number followed by a decimal point and two more numbers. Depending on the difficulty of the task in question, the decimal "floats" either to the right or to the left. For instance, if a character has an 8.17 rating in his Pistol skill and attempts a near-impossible task, such as shooting down an advancing tank, the decimal floats one place to the left, resulting in a 0.817 percent chance of success (rounded up to 1 percent). If he attempts a task of average difficulty, like shooting a bad guy from a moderate distance, the decimal floats one place to the right, resulting in an 81.7 percent chance of success (rounded up to 82 percent). Applicable modifiers affect these results in various ways, but basically, that's all there is to it. It's a clever system, easy and versatile.

Though quite detailed, the rest of the Multiverse rules are

clearly explained and user-friendly. Trouble is, it's hard to tell what we're supposed to do with them. There aren't any adventure outlines, nor are there any meaningful suggestions for designing campaign worlds; we're shown how to arrive at technology levels and gravity types, but how do you invent cultures, personalities, and histories for these places? Multiverse has a lot of potential, but the premise is too broad to be handled adequately in a mere sixty-seven pages.

Buyer's Note: Trade paperback.

Muskateers*

Complexity: Low
Task Force Games, 1985

Set in seventeenth-century France, Muskateers is a ho-hum board game and a dismal failure as an RPG. Players take the roles of colorless pregenerated characters, then push die-cut counters around on a map of a palace, attempting to free prisoners or search for jewels as directed by one of nine sketchy scenarios. There's no background material, nor are there rules for character creation or any evidence of a thoughtful attempt to explore the role-playing possibilities of an interesting era. What's left is a mildly entertaining tactical combat system and a lot of missed opportunities. For the real thing, check out Flashing Blades.

Buyer's Note: Boxed set.

Mutazoids***

Complexity: Medium/High
Whit Productions Inc., 1989

Imagine a cops-and-robbers RPG set in the future, where the cops are Dirty Harry–type anarchists and the robbers are bug-eyed nightmares from the *Late Show*, and you've got the general idea of Mutazoids. More precisely, during a disruptive period of the twenty-first century, a virus plague released by the Organization of Cultural Freedom munched its way into the DNA of victims across the world, resulting in bizarre mutations called Mutazoids. The Mutazoids, who sport tentacles, multiple eyes, and other repulsive deformities, are now second-class citizens, eternally at odds with the regular humans. Somewhere in the middle are the Acceptables, mutations who are only slightly deformed, but are nonetheless denied equal rights. A police force called the Enforcers carry out the laws of the land by whatever means necessary.

Most players take the roles of the peacekeeping Enforcers, although the rules also allow them to become Mutazoids and Acceptables. Regardless of the character type chosen, all PCs randomly generate seven primary attributes (including Constitution, Dexterity, Intelligence), then determine seven calculated attributes (Movement Rate, Hit Points, and so forth) from the primaries. Mutazoids and Acceptables randomly determine their deformities on the Physical Description Chart to see if they end up with sucker mouths, storage humps, or any of dozens of other delights.

The combat mechanics are extremely detailed, but the level of complexity is about right for a game that stresses violent encounters as much as this. Whether opponents bite, grapple, punch, slash, tackle, or trip one another, each option has its own line of combat statistics in the Hand to Hand Maneuvers Chart. Brass knuckles, throwing stars, and baseball bats are among dozens of weapons available to the PCs, and if all else fails, they can blow each other to bits with a choice of five types of explosives.

Mutazoids has a lot of nice touches, such as a Universal Task Roll Table that resolves virtually all of the game's actions and a fascinating section on the twenty-first-century legal system, complete with detailed descriptions of mutant and human misdemeanors and some clever rules for handling trials. There are a couple of minor glitches; for instance, allowing players to become either Enforcers or Mutazoids creates a lot of procedural headaches for the referee, and there aren't nearly enough suggestions for designing adventures. But overall, designer Ken

Whitman has done an impressive job of creating an attractively chaotic RPG environment.

Buyer's Note: Trade paperback.

Ninjas and Superspies**½

Complexity: Medium
Palladium Books, 1988

Erick Wujcik, the designer of the outstanding Teenage Mutant Ninja Turtles game, mixed Bruce Lee movies with *The Six Million Dollar Man* and came up with Ninjas and Superspies, a modern-day RPG concerning a secret network of martial arts masters and superpowered spies struggling for world domination.

The game systems derive from the Palladium Role-Playing Game, with players rolling dice to determine their PCs' basic characteristics, selecting Occupational Character Classes, then choosing skills and powers based on the PCs' personal histories. Players can become Wired Agents (spies outfitted with cybernetic implants to give them superpowers), Gadgeteers (specialists in bizarre weapons and equipment), or Operatives (standard secret agents). An interesting section on cover identities provides spies with covert backgrounds, enabling an Operative to maintain a secret life as a Diplomat or Courier, or a Wired Agent to pose as a Journalist or Computer Consultant.

Though there are plenty of espionage elements, martial arts dominate the game. The nearly forty different martial arts forms range from the familiar (Jujutu and Tae Kwan Do) to the exotic (Bok Pai and Zanji Shinjinken), and include their entrance requirements, skill costs, disciplines, costumes, stances, cultural skills, and philosophies. As a PC gains experience in his chosen form, he gains new skills; for instance, a specialist in Isshin-Ryu Karate gains bonuses on his Melee Attack and Parry/Dodge skills when he reaches 3rd Level, and earns an additional Martial Arts Power when he reaches 4th Level. Additionally, PCs learn to draw on a spiritual energy called Chi to improve their concentration and focus their abilities. Combat itself is complicated but exciting, marred only by a few awkward concepts carried over from the Palladium Role-Playing Game, such as using both Structural Damage Points and Hit Points to keep track of damage.

Though the rules for cybernetics are entertaining—for instance, there's a section entitled "Basic Eye Replacement" that describes options for Video-Nerve Interface Eyeballs, Container System Eyeballs, and for cyborgs on a budget, Glass Eyes—they don't integrate convincingly with the martial arts rules, as if material for two different games had been crammed into the same book. There are few guidelines for the referee, and the brief scenario outlines only hint at the game's possibilities. However, the martial arts rules receive the most comprehensive and coherent treatment ever presented in an RPG, making Ninjas and Superspies a must-buy for players interested in the topic.

Buyer's Note: Trade paperback.

Suggested Supplements: There are no supplements to recommend specifically for Ninjas and Superspies, but it's compatible with material for other Palladium games, Heroes Unlimited and Teenage Mutant Ninja Turtles in particular.

Oriental Adventures***½

Complexity: Medium/High
TSR Inc., 1985

Oriental Adventures is an Advanced Dungeons and Dragons variant set in the Eastern world of Kara-Tur. The basic rules, including combat, magic, and character generation, are similar to those of AD&D, and concepts such as Armor Class, hit points, levels, and alignment remain unchanged. However, the resemblance ends there. Oriental Adventures features its own character classes, races, spells, and most important, a unique design approach that skillfully integrates game mechanics with background material. It's a vivid setting and a fascinating set of rules, courtesy of veteran designer David Cook.

As in AD&D, the character-generation procedure begins by randomly determining Strength, Dexterity, Constitution, and other basic attributes. But unlike AD&D, where players select PC races from such standard fantasy types as elves and dwarves, OA races are truly exotic. For instance, players can opt to be hengeyokai, a race of intelligent, shape-changing animals; korobokuru, dwarflike recluses with bowed legs and a knack for farming; or spirit folk, the descendants of humans and nature spirits whose life forces are linked with rivers and trees. Character classes include Barbarian, Bushi (a mercenary or bandit), Kensai (a master of the sword or other weapon), Monk, Sohei (a warrior monk), Samurai, Shukenja (a holy man, comparable to the priest class of AD&D), Wu Jen (a powerful magic-user), Yakuza (a jack-of-all-trades with ties to the underworld), and Ninja, whose background is kept secret even from the other PCs. Each class has its own advantages and disadvantages; the Kensai, for instance, is immune to fear but is forbidden to wear armor, while the Monk excels at unarmed combat but may not own land or horses.

In addition to their combat skills, all PCs receive a variable number of practical skills, such as Silk Making, Calligraphy, Origami, and Tea Ceremony, each filling a fixed number of Proficiency Slots as determined by the PC's class. Detailed rules provide PCs with families, birth ranks, and personal histories, which in turn help determine their beginning Honor, expressed as Honor Points. Honor Points are awarded or withdrawn throughout the game depending on the PC's actions. For instance, Ninja lose honor if their true identity is revealed, Samurai earn Honor for leading a victorious force in battle, and spirit folk lose honor for allowing their life force tree or river to be damaged. The resulting characters are richly textured, clearly motivated, and a lot of fun to play.

The combat rules stick to AD&D conventions, with the addition of an excellent martial arts system that allows players to design their own attack styles, and special "ki" powers that enable PCs to temporarily enhance their fighting prowess by focusing their inner energies. Samurai can increase their strength to superhuman levels by focusing their ki, while Kensai use ki to cause maximum damage with their specialized weapon. Ninja focus their ki to walk across water and pass through walls.

Oriental Adventures is not for beginners. Though it's possible to play with the rulebook alone, a familiarity with AD&D is presumed, and a general understanding of Oriental culture and traditions is helpful. Additionally, Oriental Adventures has yet to catch up with the second edition Advanced Dungeons and Dragons rules, so the referee will have to make a few adjustments when switching between systems. For experienced players, Oriental Adventures is sheer delight. A sophisticated, challenging game, it's the best Eastern-flavored RPG ever published.

Buyer's Notes: Hardback book. Though it's likely that a second edition Oriental Adventures conforming with the second edition Advanced Dungeons and Dragons rules will be available someday, it's not here yet. Most players and referees will find the second edition *AD&D Player's Handbook* and *Dungeon Master's Guide* essential for enjoying the current edition of Oriental Adventures.

Suggested Supplements: Kara-Tur: the Eastern Realms is a boxed set of sourcebooks featuring the histories, personalities, and cultures of the various lands of Kara-Tur; indispensable for serious players. The best adventures: *Ochimo the Spirit Warrior* (an investigation of a haunted island), *Mad Monkey vs. the Dragon Claw* (confrontations with the mysterious Cult of the Black Leopard), and *Blood of the Yakuza* (a sourcebook with several scenario outlines set in Wa, an island country of Kara-Tur based on feudal Japan). The *Monstrous Compendium Volume Six* provides combat statistics and ecological notes for the spirit creatures and other monsters exclusive to Kara-Tur.

Other Suns**

···

Complexity: Medium/High
Fantasy Games Unlimited Inc., 1984

Other Suns is a game of space travel and interstellar exploration rendered in excruciating detail. Character creation involves the calculation of about two dozen characteristics, many requiring lengthy formulas and a lot of math. The combat system gives opponents numerous defensive and offensive options, but keeping track of special hits, fumbles, endurance, accumulated damage, and other factors gets tedious mighty fast.

If Traveller didn't exist, Other Suns would look a lot better than it does, but comparisons are inevitable, and there's nothing that the latter does better than the former. Like Traveller, Other Suns includes extensive rules for ship construction and planet design, but they lack the elegance of Traveller and are difficult to use. The best section of Other Suns deals with a variety of alien races, detailing their appearance, weaponry, and attitudes. This could make a good source of ideas for other science-fiction games.

Buyer's Note: Boxed set.

Palladium Role-Playing Game**½

···

Complexity: Medium
Palladium Books, 1983

It's inevitable that any fantasy RPG will be compared to Advanced Dungeons and Dragons, and in order to attract more than a small cult of admirers, a new game must find a way to distinguish itself. Designer Kevin Siembieda includes all the right elements in the Palladium Role-Playing Game, and everything works, but there's nothing exceptional—no new systems, no new approaches, no new insights. The character classes (Thief, Ranger, Priest, and so on) aren't dramatically different from AD&D, nor are basic concepts such as alignment, experience points, and saving throws. The combat system strives for originality but mistakes complexity for realism. Damage, for instance, applies to both a character's physical body and to his armor, meaning that players must keep track of hit points as well as something called Structural Damage Capacity.

Though the game mechanics aren't much, there are a number of interesting background elements easily adaptable to other fantasy RPGs. The magic section includes appealing rules for purchasing spells (they're available from clergymen and alchemists), scroll conversion (which changes a scroll into a usable form, a process where the wizard risks blindness, transformation into a goat, and other penalties), and magic guilds. Sections on religion, fairy lore, and druids are informative and fun to read.

I can't imagine many players preferring this to AD&D, RuneQuest, or any of the other established fantasy games. All things considered, the Palladium Role-Playing Game is more memorable for the games it spawned, such as Heroes Unlimited and the excellent Teenage Mutant Ninja Turtles, than as an alternative to AD&D.

Buyer's Note: Trade paperback.

Suggested Supplements: Like the Palladium Role-Playing Game itself, most of the supplements tend to be well done but unmemorable. The best is probably *Book Two: Old Ones*, which includes a variety of adventures, suitable not only for PRPG, but other fantasy RPGs as well. Palladium has also published an outstanding series of thoroughly researched, profusely illustrated sourcebooks usable in any game, PRPG included. The titles: *Compendium of Weapons, Armour, and Castles, Palladium Book of Weapons and Assassins,* and *Palladium Book of Weapons and Castles of the Orient;* all first-class.

Paranoia****

· ·

Complexity: Medium
West End Games Inc., First Edition: 1984; Second Edition:
1987

Imagine a game where players desperately compete to betray each other, where the referee is the players' worst enemy, where logic is shunned and senselessness is the norm, where character death is not only frequent but guaranteed, and everything is played for laughs. Welcome to Paranoia, a brilliant, revolutionary RPG written by Dan Gelber, Greg Costikyan, Eric Goldberg, and Ken Rolston that defies categorization and stands as one of the most thoroughly enjoyable games of the last ten years.

Inspired by *Brave New World* and *1984*, Paranoia is set in a future world where personal freedom is a thing of the past and citizens are slaves of a dictatorial government. A superintelligent entity known only as the "Computer" (played by the referee) oversees all aspects of life in Alpha Complex, the vast underground city where the game takes place. The Computer enforces a strict caste system, assigning citizens to color groups according to their security clearances. At the high end of the spectrum are the Ultraviolets, the Computer's most trusted allies. At the low end are the Infrareds, dull-witted drones who comprise the bulk of the population. The players are lowly Reds, superior only to the miserable Infrareds, whose job is to serve the Computer as all-purpose flunkies, or "Troubleshooters." The Computer directs its Troubleshooters to investigate and correct crises throughout Alpha Complex, each crisis forming the basis of a new adventure.

The twist here is that the Computer's faulty circuits have left it deranged, violent, and extremely paranoid. The most insignificant legal infractions, the slightest deviations from standard procedures, and all accusations of treason, substantiated or not, are punished by immediate execution. Laws undergo arbitrary changes, standard procedures vary from day to day, and accusations of treason abound, as exposing traitors is one of the few surefire ways of rising through the ranks and earning the Computer's trust. The referee is encouraged to make life as miserable as possible for the Troubleshooters by fostering an atmosphere where betrayal is rewarded and bold action is brutally punished.

It sounds oppressive, but it's all quite hilarious, thanks to the tongue-in-cheek approach permeating every aspect of the game. For instance, Secret Societies, such as Death Leopard and the First Church of Christ Computer Programmer, flourish in Alpha Complex, even though membership guarantees instant execution. Naturally, all PCs are assigned to Secret Societies at the beginning of the game. Not only must they keep these memberships secret from the Computer, but also from each other, because the Computer rewards any PC who betrays his friends. Likewise, mutants are considered to be impure and therefore must be eliminated. And naturally, all PCs are assigned a mutant ability, such as X-Ray Vision or Telekinesis, at the beginning of the game, and again, these powers must be kept secret from both the Computer and the other players. Weapons invariably self-destruct as soon as they're used, resulting in the user's execution, because destroying Alpha Complex property is a treasonous offense. To boost morale in Alpha Complex, the Computer regularly flashes messages throughout, along the lines of "Happiness is Mandatory" and "Just Say No to Secret Societies"—noncompliance is punishable by you-know-what. And though death is inevitable, it's hardly the end of the world, as each PC is actually a member of a large clone family; when one clone meets his maker, the player is allowed to activate a brand-new one to continue his Troubleshooting career.

Elaborate rules are provided for character creation, combat resolution, and other game mechanics, but they're essentially irrelevant, because the referee is encouraged to make up everything as he goes along. Obviously, this puts a lot of pressure on the referee, and the success of a Paranoia adventure depends directly on his improvisational skills as well as his sense of humor. Likewise, players used to the rigid structures and cooperative emphasis of traditional RPGs may have trouble with a game this chaotic. But Paranoia isn't intended for beginners. This is sophisticated, intelligent role-playing at its most subversive, a satiric masterpiece that should delight any experienced player with a taste for the bizarre.

Buyer's Notes: The first edition is obsolete, featuring overly complicated rules and a number of ambiguities; stick with the second edition. There are two second edition formats, a trade paperback version and a boxed set containing the rules, the *Complete Troubleshooter* sourcebook, and a twenty-sided die. The sourcebook is fun but not crucial, and experienced players presumably have a die already; the trade paperback contains everything you need to play.

Suggested Supplements: All of the Paranoia supplements are hilariously written and a delight to read, even if you never intend to use them in an actual game. Best sourcebooks: *Acute Paranoia* (new rules, Secret Societies, and personalities) and *Crash Course*

Manual (what happens to Alpha Complex when the Computer dies). Best adventures: *Yellow Clearance Black Box Blues* (a strange black box triggers mysterious deaths), *The Iceman Returneth* (a frozen High Programmer thaws out), *Don't Take Your Laser to Town* (Troubleshooters in the Old West), and *Send in the Clones* (the secret behind the treasonous tunes playing in the corridors of Alpha Complex).

Pendragon****

Complexity: Medium
Chaosium Inc., 1985

Set in feudal Britain in the days of King Arthur, Pendragon is a masterful design by Greg Stafford that perfectly captures the grandeur and romance of the era. With brilliant game mechanics, a gorgeous presentation, and remarkable insight, Pendragon is as close to a work of art as a role-playing game can get.

Combining elements of traditional folklore, classic fiction, and historical fact, the world of Pendragon is richly imagined and vividly detailed. An imaginary time line sets the perimeters for the campaign, a seventy-five-year period beginning in the year 495, when wars with hostile tribes raged across Britain prior to the ascension of Arthur, through the year 570, when the banishment of Lancelot foreshadowed the Dark Ages. Sections on chivalrous behavior, religious customs, the responsibilities of knighthood, and dozens of other fascinating topics bring the era to life.

Wisely, the game discourages players from taking the roles of Lancelot, Guenevere, and other familiar stars of Arthurian legend. Instead, players invent original knights and squires who are just beginning their careers. By adhering to religious ideals, defending the helpless, completing heroic tasks, and fulfilling other noble goals, the PCs accumulate Glory Points; if they earn enough of them, they're eventually recognized as Knights of the Round Table.

Though characters are rated for basic attributes (including

Strength, Dexterity, and Appearance), skills (such as First Aid, Heraldry, and Folklore), and background data (Homeland, Religion, Age, Ancestry) much the same as in other games, Pendragon adds two new categories—Personality Traits and Passions—that dramatically shift the focus from traditional RPGs. There are a dozen Personality Traits, each consisting of two opposite tendencies; for instance, one set consists of Chastity and Lustful, another set includes Generous and Selfish. Both tendencies of every trait exist in every character. Tendencies are assigned numerical values whose total always equals 20. A character who has a rating of 15 in Chastity must have a rating of 5 in Lustful; should his Chastity rise to 16, Lustful drops to 4. Players use the Traits as informal guidelines to shape their PCs' personalities. They are also used by the referee to resolve conflicting emotions, personality disputes, or moral tests; should a knight encounter a seductive maiden, the referee may ask the player to make a successful die-roll against his PC's Chastity score to see if he resists her charms. Additionally, a PC's religious background can affect his traits; Christians, for instance, promote Chastity as a virtue, while Pagans consider Lust to be virtuous. Players are not required to adhere to their Traits at all times, but penalties and bonuses are awarded if Traits are cleverly used and are interpreted in creative ways.

Passion ratings indicate a PC's most intense personal values, such as an unwavering Loyalty to a liege or king, a deep Love for a mate or deity, or a consuming Hatred for a villain or race. Should a PC remain true to his Passions, he earns Glory Points. Should he find himself in a situation where his Passions conflict—for instance, if he meets a Hated enemy while on a mission to prove his Loyalty to his liege—the referee may call for Passion rolls to help resolve the dilemma. The player weighs the results of the Passion rolls, responds to the situation, and is awarded or penalized depending on the wisdom of his decision.

Because the Traits and Passions function more as general guidelines than strict rules, Pendragon places an extraordinary emphasis on actual role-playing as opposed to resolving violent confrontations. Though combat is possible (detailed in a terrific set of rules that cover jousts, duels, and tournaments), players spend most of an adventure dealing with interpersonal conflicts. Pendragon is a game about values and emotions, not swords and monsters. Though not especially complicated, Pendragon is best suited for mature players and sophisticated referees capable of appreciating the subtleties.

Buyer's Notes: Boxed set. A trade paperback edition is planned for a 1990 release.

Suggested Supplements: Without exception, the Pendragon supplements are first-rate products. The *Pendragon Campaign* sourcebook provides invaluable suggestions for staging a long campaign, complete with scenario breakdowns covering the entire Arthurian era. *Tournament of Dreams* and *The Grey Knight* are both exceptional adventures, as much fun for the referee as for the players.

Phoenix Command***

Complexity: Medium/High
Leading Edge Games, 1986

Less of an RPG than a meticulous combat system, Phoenix Command is made to order for role-players who relish every smack and slash of a combat encounter. Though it can be used as a stand-alone game, Phoenix Command is more useful as a supplement and reference book for Recon, Top Secret/S.I., Price of Freedom, Twilight 2000, or any other RPG with a military setting.

The focus of the game is contemporary small arms, with dozens of weapons ranging from rocket launchers to shotguns rendered in lavish detail. Weapon statistics apply to the Phoenix Command game, but they can be converted to other games with a minimum of effort. The system is brutally thorough; not only does it take into account such standard combat modifiers as movement and firepower, but it also considers aim factors, tactical maneuvers, and a host of other factors. In spite of its complexity, the combat system plays quite well and produces astonishingly realistic results.

As a role-playing game, Phoenix Command is merely adequate; its rules for character generation and skill levels stick to tried and true conventions, and the scenario suggestions are fairly routine. But as a combat system, Phoenix Command is top of the line, rivaling the best tactical wargames in detail and sophistication.

Buyer's Note: Trade paperback.

Suggested Supplements: For the truly obsessed, the *Advanced Phoenix Command Supplement* adds yet another layer of complexity; good ideas and a nice presentation. *Phoenix Command Hand to Hand* does for melee encounters what the original game does for small arms combat; it's an excellent expansion.

Pirates and Plunder*½

Complexity: Low/Medium
Yaquinto, 1982

Pirates and Plunder is more memorable for its presentation than for its value as a game. P&P allows both the players and referee to begin play as soon as they open the box. The rulebooks are formatted as a series of programmed adventures, with each adventure introducing a new set of rules. The referee begins by reading the prologue to the players, explaining that they're pirates who've been captured by the Spanish. At this point, the rules lead the players and the referee through character generation (a workable but uninspired system based on randomly determined attributes), after which the narration continues. The PC pirates are subsequently imprisoned and must fight for their food, thus introducing the basic combat rules (again, straightforward but nothing special). And so it goes, with one miniadventure after another introducing advanced combat, experience points, and other concepts.

It's an admittedly painless way to learn the game, at least as far as the players are concerned. For the referee, it's not quite as easy; many rules are inadequately explained, and the entire game suffers from sloppy editing (the first episode refers to the stamina attribute, but there's no definition for stamina anywhere in the game). Incredibly, none of the game takes place at sea—a stunning oversight for a game presumably about piracy.

The game is out of print. But in spite of its flaws, the learn-as-you-go concept is an approach worth pursuing; for that reason, Pirates and Plunder is worth investigating for would-be designers.

Buyer's Note: Boxed set.

Powers and Perils*½

Complexity: High
The Avalon Hill Game Company, 1984

Powers and Perils was a major disappointment at the time of its release, especially because the Avalon Hill Game Company is renowned for its quality products, including Squad Leader, Diplomacy, and other classic wargames. Undeniably ambitious, with five rulebooks comprising 200-plus pages, P&P is a hodgepodge of unfocused ideas and absurdly complex systems that's nearly impossible to play.

Nowhere is this obsession with detail more evident than the character-creation system, which requires over forty pages of rules and dozens of charts to explain. Virtually every aspect of a PC, regardless of how trivial, requires the player to navigate complex formulas and an alphabet soup of head-scratching abbreviations. For instance, the formula for a character's Portage Ability (how much weight he can carry) is $(S \times 2) + (StB \times 20)$, while his Magic Defense Value equals his Mana Level + $(MEL)/2$, rounded up, unless he's untrained, in which case it's something else; you'll have to page through the rules to find out what "StB" and "MEL" stand for. All of this might be acceptable if the end result produced interesting characters, but they're only colorless lists of numbers, no more realistic than the most basic Dungeons and Dragons PCs and far less interesting than, say, Element Masters characters.

The combat system is surprisingly straightforward, but nothing out of the ordinary. The magic system is based on an interesting arrangement of classes called Magic Paths, each with its own laws and spells, but using magic involves even more formulas and tables, and it's hardly worth the effort.

Completing the game are a detailed list of about a hundred creatures and a book of treasures and encounters. The creature list is unexceptional and spotty—where, for instance, are the aquatic monsters? The encounter and treasure lists, on the other hand, are comprehensive and imaginative, easily the game's best feature. An introductory adventure, "County Mordara" is also included, but as it requires a thorough understanding of the game systems, only the most determined players will be able to slog through it.

Buyer's Note: Boxed set.

Suggested Supplements: The *Book of Tables* collects all of the charts from the original game into a single booklet, organizes all of the crucial formulas on Adventure Record Sheets, and includes encounter tables and other important referee information on three Gamemaster Screens. This is not a great product—there's no index for the tables, making it only a mild improvement over the rulebooks—but it's as good as it gets for Powers and Perils.

Price of Freedom***½

Complexity: Medium
West End Games, 1986

West End Games made their mark in role-playing with the humorous Ghostbusters and Paranoia games. Price of Freedom looked like a change in direction; this was no game of goofy spirits or bumbling clones, but a grim simulation of the near future in a Communist-occupied USA. But a flip through the rulebook, littered with jingoistic slogans like "Free Minds and Free Markets" and "Better Red Than Dead," suggested something else: Not only was Price of Freedom an action-packed military RPG, its satiric edge cut harder than Paranoia, and it was every bit as funny as Ghostbusters. A landmark RPG, courtesy of ace designer Greg Costikyan (of Toon and Star Wars fame).

Price of Freedom begins a few years after the USSR has conquered the United States and turned it into a prison camp for patriots. Players assume the roles of average American citizens trying to loosen the grip of the Soviets. Because the reds have total nuclear supremacy, conventional military operations are out of the question, forcing the PCs to form makeshift guerrilla bands. A typical adventure might find the PCs attempting to sabotage a Communist submarine base off the coast of New Jersey or plotting to free an imprisoned scientist from an internment camp in Kansas. With sophisticated weaponry for the most part unavailable, the PCs must make do with shotguns, pitchforks, and pickup trucks.

To create a character, the player distributes 50 points among attributes such as Strength and Intelligence and 150 points among skills such as Computer Science and Locksmithing. A skill or attribute is successfully used when a twenty-sided dieroll is less than or equal to the skill or attribute number. If a PC performs particularly well, his skills and attributes may be improved at the end of an adventure at the discretion of the referee. Rounding out a character are his Physical Tag (his most striking physical feature, which might be a bald head, a garish tattoo, or a cute dimple), his Personality Tag (a brief attitude description, such as Proud, Religious, or Depressed), his Passion (money, alcohol, sex, or anything else of obsessive importance to him), and his Interest (essentially, a less-obsessive Passion).

The combat system is quite detailed, and comparable to a conventional board game, complete with hex maps and counters. The basic rules—which involve line of sight, unit activation, and other elements familiar to veteran wargamers—may be too complicated for novices. However, a simpler version can be used, or the combat rules can be ignored altogether, reflecting Costikyan's anything-goes philosophy that encourages improvisation. (In fact, Costikyan's commentary, laced throughout the rulebooks, is never less than fascinating, particularly in his insightful discussions of how to stage adventures and set up campaigns).

The packaging is gorgeous, the premise is outrageous, and the execution is brilliant, flawed only by a narrow approach that limits its long-term playability. Inexplicably, Price of Freedom never caught on—maybe the satire was a little too subtle, or maybe the humor was a little too black—but it's nevertheless a classic, one that deserves a closer look from those who may have missed it the first time around.

Buyer's Note: Boxed set.

Suggested Supplements: The only official adventure released to date is *Your Own Private Idaho*, but it's a good one, an exciting contest between a small American resistance group and an immense Soviet military division in the forests of Idaho.

Prince Valiant***½

Complexity: Low
Chaosium Inc., 1989

Based on the brilliant Hal Foster comic strip, Prince Valiant is a near-perfect introductory RPG. Players take the roles of Knights of the Round Table in the age of Camelot, jousting for the king's honor, rescuing damsels in distress, and engaging in a variety of other knightly activities. A single page of rules introduces newcomers to the game, while a lengthy section of advanced rules adds enough detail to satisfy the most sophisticated role-players. An impressive design from Greg (RuneQuest, Pendragon) Stafford.

For many players, an RPG without dice is like a movie without popcorn, but Prince Valiant forgoes dice entirely, substituting an ingenious system using ordinary coins from the players' pockets. There are only two basic attributes—Brawn and Presence—each of which is rated for a particular number of coins. Sir Fox, for example, might have a Brawn rating of five coins, while his companion, Sir Swan, might have a Brawn of two coins. When the knights encounter a situation involving the use

162
....

of Brawn—say, opening a stuck door—players flip the indicated number of coins. Any result of "heads" means the knight has successfully opened the door; with five coins, Sir Fox has a clear advantage over his companion. In many cases, the number of heads indicates the degree of success; if Sir Fox gets "heads" on all five of his coins, he may actually rip the door off its hinges. Coin flips also resolve combat encounters and the use of skills; if Sir Fox pits his Hunting skill (one coin) against that of Sir Swan (three coins), the number of "heads" determines who catches the evening meal.

The game is packed with other clever touches. A knight's achievements are measured by Fame points (roughly equivalent to the experience points of other RPGs). The character with the highest Fame total serves as the party leader. Fame points can also be exchanged for higher coin ratings in various skills. Knights have no hit points; instead, they take damage by losing coins from their Brawn ratings (which may be recovered by resting or applying a Healing skill). The referee can add spice to an adventure by introducing NPCs who wield one or more Special Effects, such as a powerhouse opponent who can Terrify his opposition, or a seductive maiden who can Incite Lust.

Excellent sections on staging adventures, the history of the original comic strip, and magic and monsters complete the game. My only reservation is that the focus of the game seems too narrow for extended play; this could've been alleviated somewhat with the inclusion of a long adventure instead of the brief scenarios included at the end of the book. However, players who feel constrained by Prince Valiant can find solace in Stafford's Pendragon game, a more sophisticated treatment of the same concepts.

Buyer's Note: Trade paperback.

Privateers and Gentlemen***

Complexity: Medium
Fantasy Games Unlimited Inc., 1983

There are few finer examples of historical RPGs than Privateers and Gentlemen, an elegant blend of tactical miniature games and role-playing designed by Jon Williams. Set in the Age of

Fighting Sail in the late eighteenth century, the game balances simplicity with detail to produce a vivid and compelling re-creation of naval warfare.

The miniatures rules, included in their own book, do more than merely supplement the role-playing elements of Privateers and Gentlemen, comprising instead an entirely separate game. The battles are small-scale—basically ship against ship—with vessels rated for crew capabilities, firepower, and hull strength. As the emphasis is on maneuver and gunplay, while downplaying descriptions of actual ships, hardcore wargamers may find these rules too simple for serious military simulations. However, they're quite exciting and easy to learn, complementing the dramatic elements of the role-playing game quite nicely.

The role-playing rules feature a complex character-generation system that not only includes ratings for such standard attributes as Strength and Intelligence, but also for Intuition (which gives access to the referee's information) and Social Level (a measure of both personal and familial status). Most characters begin their careers as newly commissioned lieutenants. Specific shipboard assignments are determined at random, which is not particularly satisfying, as the wrong die-roll can confine a PC to the role of a lowly commander with little or no decision-making power (although this can be remedied by allowing the players to choose their own assignments, with the referee reserving the right to veto inappropriate selections). Man-to-man combat, sea encounters, and NPCs are all neatly handled by thoughtful and clearly explained rules.

Poor organization and awkward editing makes the referee's job harder than it should be, and some of the rules—particularly in the miniatures section—lack precision, requiring an inordinate number of judgment calls. More troubling is the lack of scenarios; it's up to the referee to put together an adventure with virtually no guidance from the rules, which isn't easy considering that both ship-to-ship engagements and role-playing encounters are required to create a successful scenario.

Still, Privateers and Gentlemen stands as an exceptional product by a designer who clearly knows his stuff. Though not for everyone, even players used to spaceships and magic wands might be surprised to find out how much fun military history can be.

Buyer's Notes: Boxed set. The miniatures rules are available separately in the Heart of Oak set.

Suggested Supplements: Two supplements with a Mediterranean setting provide the game's badly needed adventures. *King Over the Water* features a nail-biting battle that takes place during a raging sea storm. *Decision at Djerba* is a collection of miniadventures stemming from an attempted blockade of enemy warships and can be used as a sequel to *King Over the Water.*

Psi World**½

Complexity: Medium
Fantasy Games Unlimited Inc., 1985

Psi World is set in a future society where certain individuals—including the PCs—are blessed with spectacular psionic powers. Depending on the adventure and the inclinations of the referee, the psionic PCs are either feared outcasts who are hunted by the police or revered heroes who use their abilities for the benefit of mankind. It's an interesting premise for an RPG (though a fairly common one in both science fiction and comic books), generally well done and reasonably engaging.

The rules are brief but thorough, with a couple of interesting twists in the character-generation department. In addition to his mental abilities, a Psi PC is differentiated from a Norm (a regular person) by his level of education; Psi characters aren't allowed to progress as far in the school system as Norms, giving the Norms access to higher skills. The effect is admirable—the higher skills of the Norms offset the superior powers of the Psi, placing them on more or less equal grounds—but the rationale is shaky; if the Psis have such advanced minds, couldn't they educate themselves?

There are two categories of skills, Level and Non-Level. Level Skills, such as unarmed combat and firing guns, can be acquired at varying levels of proficiency, while Non-Level skills, such as swimming and rock climbing, are all or nothing—a character either swims or drowns, with nothing in between. Again, the effect is nice (it encourages specialization and limits individual ability) but the logic is troubling; as can be observed at any public pool, people do indeed swim at different levels of skill.

Psionic powers are divided into major and minor classifications, and PCs can choose either a single major power (such as Empathy, Teleportation, and Precognition) or two minor powers (such as Pyrokinesis and Mind Meld). Though the major powers also allow the use of a number of subdisciplines (for instance, Empathic Healing and Detect Emotion are among the subdisciplines of Empathy), the minor powers are more formidable and hence more fun to use. Of course, strip away the psionic packaging, and what you've got is a magic system—a limited one at that. Psi World is an interesting alternative to standard fantasy RPGs, but its focus is ultimately too narrow for extended play.

Buyer's Note: Boxed set.

Suggested Supplement: The Hammer Shall Strike supplement adds another major power (Animalist) along with several new minor powers; not essential, but it considerably expands the scope of the original game.

Recon***½

Complexity: Medium
Palladium Books, 1986

Recon—or more precisely, Revised Recon, as it's based on a set of miniatures rules of the same title—is a gem. It's a thorough and ingenious presentation of contemporary guerrilla warfare, designed by the team of Erick Wujcik, Kevin Siembieda, Matthew Balent, and Maryann Siembieda, who clearly know their subject. Emphasizing the war in Vietnam (with options for other grim settings), Recon does an impressive job of capturing the tension of jungle warfare fought under the most extreme conditions imaginable.

Characters are derived from only three basic attributes: Strength, Agility, and Alertness. Each PC then chooses two Military Occupational Specialties from a list including Demolitions, Grenadier, and Heavy Weapons, which in turn determine his secondary skills, encompassing everything from Locate Food and Detect Dangerous Animals to Forward Observer and Demolitions Disposal. The hardware available to the Recon team is detailed in nearly forty pages of weapon descriptions. It's all impressively researched, succinctly explained, and illustrated with detailed artwork.

The rules show remarkable insight into the tactics and operations used in Vietnam-era engagements. The game systems are outstanding, especially those for combat, which include rules for garrote, bayonet, and knife fighting, as well as for hand-to-hand encounters. Completing the package are tips for staging adventures, a generous sampling of Vietnam scenarios, rules for adapting the game to mercenary characters, and even the original Recon miniatures rules. If there's a problem, it's that the game's narrow focus limits its appeal to mature players with an interest in the military. That aside, Recon is a prince of a game, easily the definitive treatment of its subject.

Buyer's Note: Trade paperback.

Suggested Supplements: The *Advanced Recon* expansion adds rules for new character types, random encounters, and adventuring in Laos; it's an excellent book, comparable in quality to the original game. While not an official supplement, *The Palladium Book of Contemporary Weapons* provides statistics and diagrams for dozens of modern arms, perfect for use in Recon scenarios.

Reich Star***

Complexity: Medium
Creative Encounters, 1990

Nazis in space—what a concept! Reich Star imagines a future where the Third Reich not only triumphed in World War II but has spread its tyranny through the galaxy. Tension persists between the Reich and the Empire of Nippon, Earth's other dominant power, resulting in assassination attempts, bombing of government installations, and other acts of brutal terrorism. With freedom a thing of the past, life for the common man is a nightmare of abuse and neglect. Only the most dedicated freedom fighters—such as the PCs—stand a chance of restoring justice and banishing the Nazi regime.

The game mechanics aren't especially innovative, but they're clearly explained and quite thorough. Characters are built on Strength, Constitution, Dexterity, and other familiar attributes, and can become Mercenaries, Smugglers, Explorers, or other types appropriate to a science-fiction setting. Each PC receives a variable number of Luck Points that can be spent to temporarily boost his attributes in times of extreme danger; for instance, a PC with a Strength rating of 12 can boost it to 15 for a few rounds by spending three of his Luck Points. Skills are purchased from a pool of points equal to a PC's Intelligence rating; if he runs out of points, he can acquire a few more by accepting a Disadvantage or two, such as Blindness or Clumsiness (it's similar to the system in the Champions game). Combat involves a lot of numbers and tables, but it's reasonably smooth. It's also disgustingly precise; there are specific damage guidelines for brain damage, internal bleeding, and just about every other type of physical trauma.

Lengthy sections detail the history, personalities, and technology of the Reich Star universe, and there are a lot of references to the Reich empire; we're told, for instance, about the Class III starport that the Reich operates on the moon, as well as the shock troops of the Wehrmacht infantry. However, these Nazis have only tenuous connections with their real-life counterparts; they might as well be Martians. Still, designers Ken Richardson and Simon Bell have a lot of fun with the premise, producing a solid science-fiction RPG in the process. Reich Star is about as realistic as a Roger Corman movie, but in the hands of an experienced referee, it can be just as exciting.

Buyer's Note: Trade paperback.

Ringworld**½

Complexity: Medium/High
Chaosium Inc., 1984

Ringworld—based on the novel of the same name by Larry Niven—takes place on one of science fiction's most memorable locales, a ring-shaped planet 1 million miles wide and 6 million miles in diameter that contains nearly 30 trillion inhabitants and a startling variety of races. It's a terrific setting, but only a so-so game.

Though the game systems are adequate, they're nothing out of the ordinary. In addition to such standard attributes as Strength, Intelligence, and Constitution, PCs also are rated for Defects (either physical or psychological), Home Worlds (their different gravities affect the PCs' characteristics), and Chronological Age (thanks to the advent of the Fountain of Youth–like boosterspice, a PC's Chronological Age can differ significantly from his Physiological Age). A PC's age, education, and intelligence determine his Occupation Points, which are used to purchase skills. The PCs have access to an impressive array of high-tech gadgets, including interstellar spacecraft, ultraintelligent computers, and a wide range of sophisticated weaponry. Because the Ringworld natives tend to be on the primitive side, they aren't particularly threatening, and violent encounters are usually cakewalks for the well-armed and highly skilled PCs.

The combat system is based on one-second impulses, with each action requiring a specific number of impulses to complete. It's an exciting, easy-to-use system for the players, but it's a lot of work for the referee, who must keep track of a host of modifiers along with a running total of how many impulses have passed since combat began. Some flow charts or impulse tables would help, but as it stands, it's pretty much up to the referee to devise a workable routine for handling combat encounters. In fact, there's not much help of any kind for the Ringworld referee; not only does he have his hands full managing a planet roughly the size of 3 million Earths, the game presumes he has a basic understanding of physics, embryology, and other sciences. And unless he is familiar with the original novel, it's unlikely that the referee will have a clue as to how to stage an adventure.

The strength of Ringworld is its background material. The planet's history, races, flora and fauna, technology, and culture are covered in fascinating detail, addressing many of the questions left unanswered in the novel (however, Niven fans are forewarned that the game overlooks the events in the original novel's sequel, *Ringworld Engineers*). There's a lot of material for ambitious referees, making Ringworld quite useful as a source of ideas for Megatraveller and other high-tech science-fiction RPGs.

Buyer's Notes: Boxed set. Ringworld is getting very hard to find, and looks to be a potential collector's item.

Suggested Supplements: For those using Ringworld as a source of ideas rather than a stand-alone game, the *Ringworld Companion* is indispensable, containing several new alien races, a number of new gadgets, and some much-needed maps.

Robotech**½

Complexity: Medium/High
Palladium Books, 1986

In the introduction to Robotech, the scene is set on a future Earth "after the decimation by the Zentraedi and the destruction of the SDF-1 and 2." If that doesn't ring a bell, Robotech is probably not the giant robot game for you. But for fans of the Japanese television series *Macross* on which the game is based, Robotech is giant robot heaven, a remarkably detailed simulation of the Zentraedi and company that's as certain to satisfy the obsessed as it is to baffle the uninitiated.

Characters are rated for eight basic attributes, including Intelligence Quotient, Mental Endurance, and Physical Beauty, and can select an occupational specialty from several ready-to-play templates, among them Destroid Pilot, Veritech Fighter, and

Communications Engineer. The resulting PCs are colorful and able, if somewhat overwrought; I'm not convinced that seven different alignment types are necessary (is there a meaningful difference between Principled and Scrupulous PCs?), and I doubt if a character's Physical Beauty will be relevant very often in Robotech adventures.

But that's nitpicking, because the focus of Robotech isn't on the PCs but on the giant mechanical nightmares they control. And in its treatment of the Destroids, Veritechs, and assorted Mecha, Robotech is faultless. Every nut, bolt, and circuit is lovingly detailed, with special attention paid to attack and defense mechanisms. The Super Veritech entry, for instance, features statistics for speed (with and without boosters, including notes for both Guardian and Battloid modes), height and width (in feet and meters), main and secondary engines (the Super Veritech has an FF-2001 Fusion Turbine in each leg), and weapons systems (two short-range medium warhead missiles and a pair of missile launching pods that can be jettisoned if necessary). The combat rules may seem excessive—for instance, there are combat statistics for nearly thirty different types of missiles—but they allow players to relish every smack, crunch, and spurt of a Mecha assault, which is what Robotech is all about.

For those who aren't familiar with the material, reading Robotech is like going to a party where you don't know any of the guests. Many terms, including "Zentraedi" and "Mecha," are used before they're defined, and the history of the conflict isn't presented until the end of the book. And there are barely any suggestions for putting together adventures. Presumably fans of the series will know what to do with all of this, but others probably won't have a clue.

Buyer's Note: Trade paperback.

Suggested Supplements: The sourcebook supplements focus on specific aspects of the Robotech universe, all of them introducing new characters, rules, and weapons. Because each adds an additional layer of detail, they're best taken in sequence, beginning with *Book Two: Defense Force Manual* (including comprehensive information about the postapocalyptic setting) and

Book Three: The Zentraedi (maps, diagrams, and statistics concerning this race of warrior aliens). Players who are still on board after *Book Three* will find further enlightenment in *Book Four: Southern Cross* (more weapons and robots, and the outline for a new war), and *Book Five: Invid Invasion* (a new race of evil aliens). The game mechanics are derived from the Palladium Role-Playing Game, so Robotech is theoretically compatible with such games as Heroes Unlimited and Teenage Mutant Ninja Turtles, but I think it'd take an awfully determined referee to put them together.

Robot Warriors***

Complexity: Medium
Hero Games/Iron Crown Enterprises, 1986

As giant robot games go, Robot Warriors is about as good as it gets. Designers Steve Perrin and George MacDonald took a modular approach to the rules, introducing enough basic concepts in the first chapter to get eager players on the battlefield with a minimum of preparation. Successive chapters add more layers of detail, exhausting every aspect of robotic combat by the end of the book.

The basic game is pretty simple. Each player is assigned a giant robot, whose control systems are rated for Dexterity, Speed, and Total Mass. When a robot attempts to pummel his neighbor, the player makes an attack roll, the referee determines if the attack was successful, and damage is assessed to the enemy. Game objectives vary but generally boil down to a bunch of giant robots pounding each other into scrap metal. There's not much in the way of subtleties, but it's clean, quick, and reasonably entertaining.

The second section of the book provides suggestions for building the perfect robot. Depending on the scenario, each player begins with a variable number of Construction Points with which to purchase Systems (the microelectronic gadgetry that controls the robot) and Mass (the robot's bulk, which determines its armor, weaponry, and movement rate). Along the way, a robot may acquire one or more Disadvantages, which not only give it a personality of sorts, but also make it more challenging to operate. Typical Disadvantages include Limited Turning Radius, No Hands, and Unluck, a condition of accident-prone robots that causes their foot assemblies to lock up or buildings to fall on them. Advanced combat rules set the stage for all kinds of interesting encounters, including robots that toss cars at each other, robots that whiz through outer space, and robots that transform into different shapes.

Chapter 4 introduces role-playing elements in the form of human pilots. Players design their pilots from a typical array of attributes (Strength, Intelligence, Constitution, and so forth), then choose skills such as Electronics, Weapon Familiarity, and Demolitions that will enhance their chances of survival on the battlefield. Though the role-playing opportunities would seem to be limited, Perrin and MacDonald provide a number of imaginative scenarios, including a guerrilla war against a force of alien invaders and a battle with a bizarre creature called the Devourer of Worlds. Like all games of this genre, Robot Warriors doesn't have much to offer hardcore role-players, but for those who enjoy a good demolition derby, it's hard to beat.

Buyer's Notes: Trade paperback. Creative referees can adapt Robot Warriors to the Champions and Danger International games.

Suggested Supplements: Robot Gladiators outlines an interesting campaign based on robotic arena combat; short on role-playing, but long on action.

Role Aids***

Complexity: Medium
Mayfair Games Inc., 1983

Though many companies have published generic supplements, none have matched the consistent quality of Mayfair's Role Aids series. Each volume is about a hundred pages long and features an in-depth look at a particular race or character type, including cultural and historical backgrounds, personality profiles, and a number of well-developed scenarios. The material can be adapted to a variety of fantasy games but is especially suitable for Dungeons and Dragons and Advanced Dungeons and Dragons.

All of the books are excellent, but among the best are *Dragons* (by Cory Glaberson, featuring an excellent essay on dragon physiology), *Elves* (by Cheron Fitzgerald Carr and Delbert Carr, Jr.; great material on elven villages), and *Undead* (by Laurel Nicholson and John Keefe; terrific new monsters and several nail-biting adventures). As is the case with all generic supplements, the Role Aids books are necessarily incomplete; referees will need to edit and develop the material to make it compatible with their game of choice.

Buyer's Note: Trade paperback.

Rolemaster**½

Complexity: High
Iron Crown Enterprises, First Edition: 1982; Revised Edition: 1988

If Rolemaster isn't the most detailed fantasy RPG ever published, it's not for lack of trying. Designers Kurt Fischer, Peter Fenlon Jr., S. Coleman Charlton, Bruce Neidlinger, Terry Amthor, and Leonard Cook originally released the game as five separate books intended for use as supplements for existing fantasy games. Four of the books were then packaged in the same box as a self-contained game, with the fifth (*Campaign Law*) available separately to complement the boxed set. Later revisions combined the five books into three, and the boxed set of three books now stands as the complete and official Rolemaster set.

The seams still show. Rolemaster reads more like a collection of supplements than an integrated system, although the latest revision goes a long way toward improving the organization and fuzziness of the original books. The sheer volume of material remains impressive, if not downright intimidating. But it works better now as a game that it used to, although it's still an extraordinarily complicated one and by no means for beginners.

Arms Law, the first of the Rolemaster books, has now been combined with its sequel, *Claw Law*, into a single volume. The subject is combat, and it's covered in staggering detail, with tables including hundreds of entries to handle every conceivable weapon type and combat encounter. The *Arms Law* material covers a multitude of swords, arrows, maces, and other battlefield arms, while *Claw Law* does the same for the bites, scratches, stomps, and stings of the animal world. If a die-roll determines that a given attack is successful, the player is referred to the appropriate chart, where he cross-references the weapon with the armor type of the victim. In addition to suffering the indicated amount of damage, the victim may also be inflicted with a critical hit; another roll on a different table tells exactly what has happened (for instance, the victim may be sliced up, punctured, or otherwise mutilated). Though the combat rules are reasonably smooth, sorting through all of the charts is a real pain, especially when a lot of characters are involved.

Spell Law addresses the use of magic and is the most successful of the Rolemaster books. The system assigns magic users into three different categories, or "realms," each of which has access to spells from a wide array of choices—hundreds of them, in fact. The system features many interesting concepts, among them a unique method of magical healing where the wizard empathically transfers the wounds of a comrade to himself. The procedure for spellcasting is similar to that of combat, with die-rolls determining success or failure of an attempted spell, and various tables detailing the fate of the victim.

The final book, *Character Law and Campaign Law*, combines the original *Character Law* and *Campaign Law* books into a single volume. The emphasis here is on character creation, and while the systems break no new ground, they're nicely handled. Die-rolls determine basic attributes, but players can assign the rolls to any attributes they like to maximize the potential of their chosen character class. Considering the detail of the rest of

Rolemaster, the skill section is surprisingly skimpy. The campaign material attempts to unify the disparate elements of Rolemaster with varying degrees of success; the general suggestions for designing a campaign world are interesting, but there's inadequate guidance for designing adventures that effectively exploit the game systems.

Though each book has something to recommend it, the whole of Rolemaster is less than the sum of the parts. The game is too complex for all but the most experienced players, with its merits overwhelmed in detail. Worse, Rolemaster lacks the flavor of classic fantasy RPGs such as Advanced Dungeons and Dragons and RuneQuest, coming off instead as a dull collection of numbers and tables. Taken individually, however, the Rolemaster books—*Spell Law* in particular—contain a wealth of ideas that imaginative referees will find quite useful.

Buyer's Notes: Boxed set. The three volumes of Rolemaster—*Arms Law and Claw Law, Spell Law,* and *Character Law and Campaign Law*—are available individually.

Suggested Supplement: The Rolemaster Companion is an information-packed sourcebook that expands on virtually every aspect of the original Rolemaster game, including an especially helpful section on magic.

RuneQuest****

Complexity: Medium/High
Chaosium Inc., First Edition: 1978; Second Edition: 1979; The Avalon Hill Game Company, Third Edition: 1984

In the late 1970s, while other publishers scrambled to copy the success of Dungeons and Dragons by cranking out slavish imitations, Chaosium responded with RuneQuest, the first truly original alternative. Its innovations were both numerous and startling; character classes and experience levels were nowhere to be found, all PCs had access to magic, and with the world of Glorantha as its background, RuneQuest boasted the hobby's first fully developed fantasy setting. Fans recognized RuneQuest as an instant classic, and its appeal remains undiminished. The game has evolved and expanded in the ten years since its initial publication, and the Avalon Hill edition— a masterful collaboration by Steve Perrin, Greg Stafford, Steve Henderson, Lynn Willis, Charlie Krank, Ken Rolston, and Sandy Petersen—now stands as the definitive version.

Though there are ratings for Strength, Constitution, and other basic attributes, RuneQuest PCs are primarily defined by their skills. Skill categories include Agility (encompassing such talents as Climbing, Dodging, and Swimming), Knowledge (Animal Lore, First Aid, Martial Arts), and Perception (Listening, Searching, Tracking), each of which receives a rating from 0 to 100. When using a skill, players throw percentile dice and check the result against the applicable skill rating to determine success or failure. For instance, if a PC's skill rating for Listening is 20, a roll of 20 or less enables him to overhear a conversation in the next room. Successfully used skills may be increased in subsequent adventures by as much as six percentage points. Though the referee must remain alert to abuses from greedy players—any successful use of a skill theoretically results in an increased level—it's an elegant, innovative system that proved to be so versatile, it eventually was adapted to other Chaosium games, including Call of Cthulhu, Stormbringer, and Elfquest.

All RuneQuest PCs have Power ratings that translate into an equivalent number of Magic Points. Each spell requires the expenditure of Magic Points; a character can cast spells as long as he has Magic Points, completely regenerating them after a day's rest. The game includes three distinct schools of magic, Spirit Magic, Divine Magic, and Sorcery, all of which are available to every PC, within a few cultural restrictions. Even with its limited number of spells, magic predominates in RuneQuest to a degree unheard of in most other RPGs, making it a particularly satisfying game to players for whom magic and fantasy are synonymous.

RuneQuest tends to be combat-heavy, and the rules are appropriately detailed. Attackers make offensive die-rolls, defenders counter with Parry or Dodge skill rolls, and the referee selects the appropriate modifiers. A successful attack results in damage to specific body parts. It's a realistic system, but it can also be quite slow, interminably so for those less interested in tactical combat than in role-playing encounters.

Combat aside, the rest of RuneQuest is an unqualified success. With its thoughtful, vivid discussion of religion (based on deities who command the power of the Great Runes associated with the creation of Glorantha), culture (including sections on ship transport, elder races, and mysterious cults), and economics (tables are provided for mercenary rates, freight costs, and retail sorcery), no fantasy game comes close to matching RuneQuest's integration of game mechanics and background detail. The magic rules and skill systems have become industry standards, often copied but never outdone. In short, RuneQuest is a classic—a masterpiece of fantasy role-playing.

Buyer's Notes: The boxed Deluxe RuneQuest includes all of the material available in the Player's Box and Gamemaster's Box; as you need everything to play the game, buy the deluxe set. Some of the earlier Chaosium editions are still around, but they're not as good as the Avalon Hill edition. Owners of the earlier versions should note that first edition and second edition RuneQuest characters aren't fully compatible with third edition standards without a few adjustments. The third edition also pushes Glorantha a bit farther into the background than the earlier editions, making it easier for referees to adapt material from other fantasy games.

Suggested Supplements: Most of the Avalon Hill supplements are lavish boxed sets containing both adventures and sourcebook material. The best of them: *Griffin Island* (an outline for a wilderness campaign set on a bizarre island; one of the best fantasy supplements ever published), *Gods of Glorantha* (a superb presentation featuring dozens of RuneQuest religions), and *Land of Ninja* (RuneQuest in feudal Japan). Disappointing: *Monster Coliseum* (routine treatment of gladiatorial combat) and *Vikings* (a subject that doesn't work well with the RuneQuest concepts). Also recommended are *Snakepipe Hollow* and *Apple Lane*, exceptional adventures released in the tried-and-true single-book format. Of the original Chaosium material, the *Questworld* boxed set features a number of excellent introductory scenarios, though the referee will have to make the necessary adjustments if he's using the third edition rules.

Sandman**½

....

Complexity: Low
Pacesetter Ltd., 1985

Sandman is a truly original, unquestionably bizarre, and extremely frustrating RPG. It's billed as an "Instant Adventure"; play can begin almost immediately, as there are less than three pages of rules for the referee, and the players need no briefing of any kind to get started. In fact, the first encounter finds the PCs awakening on a train with no idea of who they are, where they are, or how they got there. As the adventure progresses, they acquire clues to their identities and abilities, gradually piecing together their true mission and the reason for their amnesia. Their ultimate goal: to discover the identity of the godlike "Sandman" who's behind it all.

Each new scenario finds the PCs undergoing radical and abrupt transformations; a PC who appears as a twentieth-century medical doctor in the first scenario may find himself as a spellcasting dwarf in the next, while a PC who's a broom-riding witch may suddenly change into a Roaring Twenties gangster. Locales also undergo wild and unexpected changes; a modern airport abruptly changes into a medieval forest, a Mediterranean pirate vessel changes to a rocket ship on its way to another planet. The players have no control over these changes, nor are the reasons behind them immediately clear. Even the referee remains in the dark for much of the game; however, he's likely to notice that many of the sequences are suspiciously similar to famous motion pictures, among them *Casablanca*, *Bonnie and Clyde*, *Peter Pan*, and *Saturday Night Fever*.

Smooth writing, clear organization, and a number of clever play-aids make the referee's job remarkably easy. A Prop Book contains cut-apart maps, clues, and other handouts to be distributed to the players at key points in the adventure. There are several comic strips called Pictograms that summarize the various scenarios, enabling the referee to track the PCs' progress with ease. Poetry Cards provide the players with cryptic information regarding their whereabouts and the Sandman's true identity; although only marginally helpful (sample line: "And looking backward as the sand collapses / Into excessive darkness, sight replotted / Out of its hall of mirrors . . .") they add to the game's air of lunatic mystery. No RPG has ever managed to sustain a hallucinatory atmosphere as successfully as Sandman, a tribute to the ingenious work of designers Mark Acres and Andria Hayday.

But there's a problem, and it's a big one. Sandman was originally conceived as a series of linked games, but the company went belly-up after the first set was published, leaving its mysteries unresolved. The true meaning of the Poetry Cards, the fate of the PCs, and the secret of the Sandman will never be revealed, unless the referee invents the answers himself. Sandman is the role-playing equivalent of a movie with the last twenty minutes forever left on the cutting room floor.

Buyer's Note: Boxed set.

Sentinels***

....

Complexity: Medium/High
Palladium Books, 1987

Sentinels may look like a revision of Palladium's Robotech, but it's a stand-alone RPG, though to the casual reader it's virtually identical in tone, subject, and approach to the earlier game. Like Robotech, Sentinels focuses on giant robot battles portrayed in Japanese cartoons. This time around, the game centers on the "untold stories" of the Robotech universe, which is probably quite significant to fans of the series; to the less obsessed, it means giant robot battles on other planets, accurately described in the introduction as "World War II in space."

Like Robotech, the rules for Sentinels derive from the Palladium Role-Playing Game; in fact, the rules for Robotech and

Sentinels are essentially the same. Characters are rated for eight basic attributes, then select their occupational specialties from a number of pregenerated templates, among them Veritech Pilot, Cyclone Rider, and Bio-Maintenance Engineer. As in Robotech, the real stars of the game are the machines, and Sentinels includes some charmers, such as the Ikazuchi Command Carrier (a half-mile-long spacecraft), the Vindicator VF-IV (a cross between an Alpha and a VF Veritech, for those keeping track), and the Destroid REF Cyclops (an all-terrain reconnaissance vehicle that looks like a bloated fish). The combat rules are excruciatingly detailed, but perfectly appropriate for a game where combat is everything.

With its expanded skill lists, extensive background material, and brief but adequate introductory scenarios, Sentinels emphasizes role-playing more than Robotech and is therefore a more interesting game. It's not for newcomers—players who've never heard of Macross, Mecha, or other elements of the Robotech universe won't have a clue as to what this is all about—but fans of the Japanese cartoons will find plenty to enjoy.

Buyer's Note: Trade paperback.

Suggested Supplements: The best supplement is the original Robotech game. All official Robotech supplements are also compatible with Sentinels.

Shadowrun***

Complexity: Medium/High
FASA Corp., 1989

Shadowrun is cyberpunk with a twist. The cyberpunk elements include a grim future where monstrous corporations virtually run the planet and computer programmers are capable of plugging their brains into high-tech machinery. The twist: Magic exists side by side with the computers, taking the form of elves, dragons, wizards, and other fantasy archetypes. There's a convoluted rationale to explain it all, involving recessive DNA or some such nonsense, but it's just an excuse to mix fantasy in a pot of hardcore science fiction and see what crawls out.

Presuming you can swallow the premise, the results aren't bad at all. Characters range from mercenary soldiers of fortune to magic-wielding wizards to computer-hacking "deckers," each with his own skills, equipment, and personal contacts. Mind implants can increase the talents of nonwizardly types (magic and technology aren't necessarily compatible), and a Matrix program is available to generate mind-bending computer landscapes for deckers to explore. The magic system is terrific fun, comprising two distinct categories of spells; Hermetic Mages draw their power from books and rituals, while Shamans derive theirs from natural sources. Ritual summonings, astral travel, and other magical activities receive detailed, imaginative treatments.

Unfortunately, fuzzy and overly complicated rules plague Shadowrun throughout. All game mechanics stem from a common procedure of Success Tests, where players roll dice against their ratings in applicable skills and attributes. But interpreting the results involves as much guesswork as mathematics, and it can take a seemingly endless number of dice-tosses to figure them out. Combat is draggy and dull, involving far too many dice-throws and an excess of confusing modifiers.

Still, the merits of the setting surpass the awkwardness of the rules, and designers Bob Charrette, Paul Hume, and Tom Dowd are to be applauded for their smooth integration of such diverse elements; any game where a fire-breathing dragon can turn up as a corporate chairman is worth checking out.

Buyer's Note: Hardback book.

Suggested Supplements: FASA has supported the game with a library of first-rate material. *Mercurial, Dream Chipper*, and *DNA/DOA* are all exciting and bizarre scenarios, enthusiastically recommended. The *Sprawl Sites One* sourcebook features an assortment of unusual locales that can be used as adventure springboards or as background for original Shadowrun characters.

Shadow World***

Complexity: Medium
Iron Crown Enterprises, 1989

Not a stand-alone game, Shadow World is a generic setting that can be used as a supplement for any fantasy RPG. Rather than focusing on a single city or country, Shadow World presents an overview of an entire planet called Kulthea, a sprawling network of islands and small continents separated by vast stretches of sea. As most of Kulthea is uncharted, the rulebooks concentrate on such general topics as geography, climate, and history, making Shadow World easily adaptable to any campaign.

Comparable to Warhammer in its grim atmosphere, the minions of evil in Shadow World draw strength from a mysterious energy called Unlife, while the forces of good are represented by energy fields encircling the world known as the Flow of Essence. The Flow can be used to channel magic, or its streams can be ridden to different worlds, a convenient method of transporting characters from other games to Kulthea.

In addition to the World Guide, the set also includes an Inhabitants Guide describing the flora and fauna of Kulthea, along with a beautiful glossy map to hang on the wall. Conversion notes are provided to ease the transition from Advanced Dungeons and Dragons or RuneQuest to Shadow World, though players of Rolemaster and Fantasy Hero can get started right away, because Shadow World is particularly compatible with those systems. As with any generic setting, the referee will have to do a fair amount of preparation to incorporate the material into an ongoing campaign, and the lack of scenarios means he'll also have to put together an adventure from scratch (unless he also springs for a Shadow World supplement).

Buyer's Note: Boxed set.

Suggested Supplements: The supplements focus on specific areas of Kulthea and contain both background material and adventure ideas. Best bets: *Demons of the Burning Night* (an uncharted island riddled with undead) and *Kingdom of the Desert Jewel* (underground strongholds and monstrous invaders).

Skull and Crossbones*½

Complexity: Medium
Fantasy Games Unlimited Inc., 1983

A sketchy treatment of role-playing in the pirate-infested Caribbean, Skull and Crossbones tries to cram too much in too little space. While the thirty-two-page rulebook covers character creation, combat, and other role-playing basics, the systems are derivative and nothing is explored in detail. Characters can be gunners, navigators, and other seafaring types who scramble for experience points in order to become a Pirate King. There's a brief but adequate section for ship-to-ship combat, but sea encounters, tips for staging adventures, and other crucial elements are all but ignored. Designers Gerald Seypura and Anthony Le Boutillier have an obvious affection for their subject, but they just weren't given enough room to do it justice.

Buyer's Note: Boxed set.

Suggested Supplements: Pieces of Eight fleshes out the original game with rules for NPCs, voodoo, and ships, and also includes some modestly interesting scenarios. Though sketchily written, it goes a long way toward making Skull and Crossbones a playable game.

Skyrealms of Jorune***

Complexity: Medium
Skyrealms Publishing Inc., 1987

There's both bad news and good news to report about Skyrealms of Jorune. The bad news is that it doesn't amount to much as a game. Though all the rules are in place, they're adequate at best (a skill-based character-generation system that produces reasonably interesting PCs) and ambiguous at worst (a clumsy combat system that leaves a lot of the fine-tuning up to the referee). It's playable, but not without effort, and I suspect the fuzzy rules will discourage most beginners.

The good news is that Skyrealms features a remarkable fantasy setting, second only to Empire of the Petal Throne in originality, detail, and texture. The game takes place on Jorune, a mysterious planet enveloped by a magical energy called Isho, and populated by a bizarre race known as the Shantas. Shantan culture has been suppressed by devastating encounters with human visitors, yet the Shantas continue to thrive, thanks to their bizarre technology based on the manipulation of the Isho. For instance, they can appear anywhere on the planet by utilizing special warp gates, and they can enhance their sensory perception by constructing strange statues called Cle-Eshta to tap the Isho. Players take the roles of Tauther, a class of people who aspire to become fully recognized citizens, known as Drenn. A Tauther PC acquires Social Points en route to Drennship as a result of successful missions and quests, which usually stress role-playing skills more than combat techniques.

The culture, history, and personalities of Jorune are rendered in exquisite detail, with vivid writing and beautiful illustrations by the design team of Andrew Leker, Mark Wallace, Amy Leker, and Miles Teves. Though the game mechanics won't raise too many eyebrows, the setting is startlingly different from those typical of fantasy RPGs, making it well worth the purchase for anyone who's bored with endless variations of medieval Europe.

Buyer's Note: Boxed set.

Suggested Supplement: Check out *Campaign Jorune: Ardoth,* a fascinating look at one of Jorune's strangest cities, complete with maps, background material, and adventure ideas.

Space: 1889***½

Complexity: Low/Medium
Game Designers' Workshop, 1988

Taking its cue from the writings of H. G. Wells, Edgar Rice Burroughs, and Jules Verne, Space: 1889 imagines that Thomas Edison discovered the basics of space travel in 1870 and, within a few short years, rocket ships were as common as zeppelins and English colonists were building summer homes on Venus. It's a charming premise and one of the most imaginative RPGs of the last decade.

PCs are rated for Strength, Intellect, Endurance, Agility, Charisma, and the all-important Social Status to create Diplomats, Explorers, Merchants, Nobility, Master Criminals, and other characters indigenous to Victorian England. Attribute ratings suggest appropriate skills, which in turn generate Cascade Skills, a series of related abilities (Marksmanship, for instance, might include a Cascade Skill of Bows, while a Crime skill might include a Cascade Skill of Forgery). It's a terrific system, producing playable, well-rounded PCs in just a few minutes.

The rest of the game is similarly elegant. To resolve an attempted task, the referee determines its difficulty rating, then the player rolls a number of six-sided dice equal to the rating of the applicable skill or attribute; if the dice total exceeds the difficulty rating, the attempt succeeds. For instance, if a PC is attempting to lift a heavy rock, the referee may set a difficulty level of 12; if the PC's Strength is 3, he throws three six-sided dice, and the total must equal or exceed 12 in order for him to lift the rock. Weapons are also rated in terms of dice; if a PC uses a club with a 2 rating, the player throws two dice to see if his attack succeeds.

What makes Space: 1889 a joy is its delightful setting, rendered in loving, whimsical detail by designer Frank Chadwick. Mysterious lizardmen lurk in the shadows of Venus; the English explorers fend them off with lightning cannons and electric rifles. Savage barbarians on Mars stand ready to defend the planet's greatest resource, the liftwood trees, whose antigravitational properties power magnificent cloudships. Victorian noblemen pack their gramophones and Gatling guns, then board ether fliers for a trip to the moon. Familiarity with the source material isn't necessary but it's helpful; a referee who's read Wells's *From Earth to the Moon* or Burroughs's John Carter novels will understand exactly how to stage an adventure.

Buyer's Note: Hardback book.

Suggested Supplements: Tales from the Ether, a superb anthology of short adventures, is a great introduction to the game; try the "Burning Desert" scenario first, an exciting visit to the tin mines of Mercury. Advanced players should investigate the *Beastmen of Mars* adventure, featuring an expedition to uncover the red planet's darkest secrets.

Space Master**½

....

Complexity: High
Iron Crown Enterprises, First Edition: 1985; Second Edition: 1988

With page after page of tables, charts, and numbers, Space Master is the most demanding outer space RPG ever published. It's playable and well written, but the design team of Kevin

Barrett, Terry Amthor, S. Coleman Charlton, and Tod Foley leave nothing up to chance—if it can be expressed in numbers, that's how you'll find it in Space Master.

The character creation and combat systems alone take up most of the 128-page Player Book. Creating a PC involves temporary and potential statistics, stat bonuses, skills and skill ranks, racial modifiers, and a host of charts and tables. The Language Skill Chart fills an entire page, as do the Racial Statistics Chart and the Secondary Skill Development Cost Chart. The Experience Guidelines Table is a two-pager, and I had to read it half a dozen times to figure it out. It took me all afternoon to create a single PC, and even though it was kind of fun—a game in itself, in fact—it may not be everyone's idea of a good time.

In terms of complexity, the combat rules put all other systems to shame and defy summarization. Suffice it to say that there are rules for every conceivable type of personal and vehicular combat encounter, with innumerable formulas and tables for providing precise, detailed results. To pick an example at random, the two-page Static Action Chart lists six categories of Basic Modifications (including nine levels of Difficulty, ranging from Routine to Absurd, and six levels of Lighting, ranging from No Shadows to Pitch Black; all modifiers include statistics for Speed and Strength, Hiding, Disarm Traps, Pick Locks, Maneuvers—which are applied to rolls on the Personal Maneuver Chart—and Perception) and five categories of Special Modifications—that's page one. Does it work? It seems to, though playing out a simple duel between two characters took me about two hours to complete. As for large-scale combats, I can't say—I gave up. I suspect they work just fine, providing the players and referee hang in there long enough to see them through to the bitter end.

Space Master features excellent, detailed systems for planet creation, robots, psionics, and the most comprehensive equipment catalog for science-fiction gaming I've ever seen. There are some general guidelines for setting up near-future, science-fantasy, and time-travel campaigns, but these are surprisingly brief. The Terran Star Empire—Space Master's "official" setting—is discussed at length, but only in the broadest terms; we're exploring planets, establishing colonies, and warding off hostile aliens, sort of like we do in Megatraveller, except that the universe of Space Master is not nearly as interesting.

Complicated rules aren't necessarily bad. A lot of players like the challenge of dense systems; some wargamers, for instance, are willing to spend years unlocking the secrets of Advanced Squad Leader or Campaign for North Africa; why should roleplayers be any different? Be warned, however, that there's no such thing as a casual player of Space Master—this is science fiction for accountants.

Buyer's Notes: Boxed set. The revised second edition is the one to buy; it has a picture on the cover of two teenage boys engaged in a shootout with a laser-wielding robot. Though the second edition is compatible with all of the first edition supplements, it isn't compatible with *Tech Law* and *Future Law*, two basic first edition rulebooks.

Suggested Supplements: Beyond the Core and *Action on Akaisha Outstation* both feature several interesting adventure ideas along with background material describing specific areas of the Space Master universe; either is a good place to start a campaign.

Space Opera**½

Complexity: High
Fantasy Games Unlimited Inc., 1980

Traveller revolutionized science-fiction role-playing with its thorough rules and unlimited potential for expansion, but its emphasis on adventure offended hardcore fans who liked their science fiction strict and serious. For them, Space Opera provides a challenging alternative. It's an unforgiving game system that does for science fiction what Chivalry and Sorcery does for fantasy; namely, it tests player tolerance for tables, charts, and formulas.

Players take the roles of explorers and star soldiers in a grimly militaristic universe where instability is the norm. Characters are based on their planet of origin as well as their generated attributes. Though the system produces well-rounded PCs, it's painfully convoluted, a problem that plagues Space Opera throughout. The rules for starship design require a background in physics to appreciate, and the combat rules rival the detail of tactical wargames. Every part of the game's mechanics is based on complicated routines—a simple scenario can take a weekend to complete.

The rules are workable, but they're also dated and dry, especially in light of such streamlined, action-intensive games as Star Trek and Star Wars. For players with time on their hands who consider Star Trek too childish and Star Wars too simple-minded, Space Opera might be worth a look.

Buyer's Note: Boxed set.

Suggested Supplements: Alien Base serves as a satisfying introductory adventure to Space Opera, featuring the search for a missing survey ship and an encounter with alien slavers. *Operation Peregrine* contains some interesting background material concerning a bizarre sector of outer space and a complicated but enjoyable adventure involving a kidnapped religious leader. *Casino Galactica* is the best of the Space Opera supplements, a sourcebook describing the facilities and personalities of one of the galaxy's most notorious playgrounds.

Stalking the Night Fantastic*½

Complexity: Medium
Tri Tac Inc., 1983

Investigating the supernatural is a great idea for an RPG, as evidenced in Call of Cthulhu and Beyond the Supernatural, but you wouldn't know it from Stalking the Night Fantastic, which is neither scary nor particularly exciting. The PCs are members of Bureau 13, a top-secret agency responsible for stamping out ghosts, demons, and other occult minions. Character generation

involves rating over a dozen attributes, many of them unnecessary and several downright redundant (in the context of the
game, there's no clear distinction between Dexterity and
Agility). For some reason, there are two discrete combat systems; a simple one for NPCs and monsters and an enormously
detailed one for the PCs. The results are wildly inconsistent; a
wounded NPC, for instance, may continue to function without
any ill effects, but a wounded PC may suffer shattered bones
and spurting arteries (combat tends to be graphic). There's an
above-average encounter section that includes confrontations
with witch doctors, space aliens, and Shapeless Disgusting
Things, but it's not interesting enough to offset the game's considerable deficiencies.

Buyer's Note: Trade paperback.

Star Ace**

Complexity: Low/Medium
Pacesetter Ltd., 1984

Star Ace is a toddler's-eye view of science fiction, where common sense is about as relevant as it is in *Alice in Wonderland*.
While swashbuckling adventurers and drooling green monsters
abound, the laws of physics are nowhere in sight. Star Ace is
just the game for players who find Star Trek and Star Wars too
scientific.

Actually, Star Ace is similar to the *Star Wars* movies, at least
in spirit. The players assume the roles of freedom-fighting
space guerrillas (sort of like Han Solo) up against an evil empire
of galactic bad guys (sort of like Darth Vader). Characters increase in aptitude and notoriety as they progress through the
ranks from Rookie to Ace, becoming more skill-efficient as they
gain experience. It's an easy system to learn, but not particularly conducive to role-playing, because PCs advance more
quickly as a result of violent encounters than from interacting
with other characters.

As with other Pacesetter games (Chill and Timemaster), all

actions are resolved on a single table. Theoretically, players roll dice, the referee checks the table, and that's all there is to it. But in practice, each roll is subject to numerous modifiers that must be dug out of the text, requiring endless page-flipping and second-guessing from the referee. What was intended as a time-saver turns out to be a nuisance.

Star Ace clearly isn't intended to be an accurate simulation, but there's a fine line between simplicity and silliness. If you thought the thunderous explosions in the *Star Wars* movie were annoying (no sounds allowed in a vacuum, say the laws of physics), wait till you get a load of Star Ace's spaceships—apparently they accelerate instantly, maneuver at random, and consume no fuel. PCs can earn money by selling goods, but there are few hints as to how cargo is acquired in the first place, and prices are determined at random. The NPCs are caricatures, and the aliens aren't derived so much from a Saturday matinee movie as they are from the cartoon that precedes it.

Buyer's Note: Boxed set.

Suggested Supplements: Both *Goodbye Kankee* and *First Strike on Paradise* are good introductory adventures that feature nonsensical plots, goofy locales, and scores of ridiculous creatures; in short, everything that Star Ace finds so appealing. The *Aliens* sourcebook provides historical and cultural data for more than a dozen bizarre races, such as the Crystal Folk, the Hawkmen, the Ferm, and the Blinkers, most of whom could be incorporated into other science-fiction RPGs without too much trouble.

Star Frontiers***

Complexity: Low/Medium
TSR Inc., 1982

Star Frontiers is to science-fiction role-playing as basic Dungeons and Dragons is to fantasy: a streamlined, easy-to-learn game stressing general concepts while minimizing complicated mechanics. Star Frontiers earns a qualified recommendation; it's an excellent game for beginners, but experienced players may be disappointed that it lacks the scope of more elaborate science-fiction games such as Megatraveller.

Character generation is similar to D&D, with players determining Strength, Dexterity, Intelligence, and other basic attributes by rolling dice and consulting tables, then choosing their PCs' races. Humans, of course, are among the character races, along with a delightful assortment of aliens, including the shape-shifting Dralasites, the insectoid Vrusks, and the simian Yazirians, whose underarm webbing enables them to soar through the air like flying squirrels. Players select skills from three main areas (Military, Technological, and Biosocial), with each choice including several subskills; for instance, the Medical skill, which is part of the Biosocial group, includes both Diagnosis and Surgery. Though players have only limited freedom in customizing their characters, the system produces interesting PCs that are more than adequate for the modest demands of the game.

The combat rules compare favorably with simple tactical wargames, using grid maps to track movement, and weapon types, target positions, ranges, and skill levels to resolve attacks. Rules for hand-to-hand and vehicle combat add variety. Weapon choices mix the expected (laser guns) with the unusual (electric swords).

Purists will probably be appalled at the rest of Space Frontiers. Planet generation and alien cultures are addressed only in passing, as are the specific mechanics of space travel. There's a list of suggestions rather than specific procedures for creating monsters. And the monsters provided are adorably goofy, not unlike the monsters featured in basic D&D.

Does any of this matter? Only to fussbudgets. Science-fiction fans who take their cues from comic books instead of textbooks will be right at home with Star Frontiers.

Buyer's Note: Boxed set.

Suggested Supplements: The Knight Hawks boxed set is a major expansion covering ship design, economics, and a campaign outline for the Second Sathar War; superb material, and a notch more complicated than the original game. *Zebulon's Guide to Frontier Space* is an entertaining sourcebook describing new aliens, skills, and equipment. Best adventures: *Mutiny on the Eleanor Moraes* and its sequel, *Face of the Enemy* (featuring a crashed spaceship and the exploration of a mysterious planet).

Star Hero***

Complexity: Medium
Hero Games/Iron Crown Enterprises, 1989

An intelligent, comprehensive science-fiction RPG, Star Hero includes just about everything necessary for an exciting outer space campaign except a detailed setting. With lucid rules by designers Paula Woods and Sam Bowne, Star Hero is not only a solid, self-contained game, it's also useful as a sourcebook for other science-fiction RPGs.

Star Hero is based on the "Hero System," and the basic rules will be familiar to anyone who's played Champions, Danger International, or any of the other Hero Games products. Players roll up Strength, Dexterity, Constitution, and other basic attributes, then spend Hero points to increase their PCs' skills and characteristics. Skills common to other Hero games are available, such as Ambidexterity and Disguise, along with some new choices pertinent to space exploration, such as Planetology and Robotics. Indecisive players can take the easy way out and opt for a "package deal" template such as Starship Pilot or Scientist that comes ready-made with all the appropriate skills.

Rules for skill use carry over from the Hero System, where a single die-roll is matched with an applicable skill level to check for the success of any action. Combat also derives from the Hero System, with the defender's Defensive Combat Value (a function of Dexterity) subtracted from the attacker's Offensive Combat Value, modified by weapon types and various maneuvers, then checked against a die-roll; the system is a little awkward, but it's versatile and produces realistic results. The sections new to Star Hero are also the best in the game, including simple rules for starship construction and combat, an excellent chapter on future technology, and ingenious guidelines for creating new alien races.

Although the book ends with a general outline for a campaign based on an intergalactic alliance of humans and aliens, it's too sketchy to be of much use. In fact, the lack of a focused campaign setting, such as those offered in Megatraveller and Star Wars, is the game's biggest drawback; the referee will either have to build a universe from scratch (a mighty tall order), or graft the Star Hero rules onto a preexisting setting. Still, those looking for a simple, comprehensive overview of science-fiction role-playing should enjoy Star Hero, as will fans of other Hero Games who can use this to expand their campaigns into outer space.

Buyer's Note: Trade paperback.

Suggested Supplements: As yet, there are no supplements available for Star Hero. However, supplements for other Hero games are compatible with Star Hero, particularly those of Champions, Danger International, and Robot Warriors.

Star Trek***½

....

Complexity: Medium
FASA Corp., 1983

Star Trek the RPG faithfully simulates the characters, universe, and attitude of "Star Trek" the television series. With its simple mechanics and clear presentation, along with the obvious affection of designers Guy McLimore, Jr., Greg Poehlein, and David Tepool for the source material, Star Trek is a fan's dream come true.

Though the game furnishes complete statistics for Captain Kirk, Mr. Spock, and other familiar characters from the series, players can create new characters from scratch if they wish, utilizing a simple system of randomly determined attributes (Strength, Endurance, Intelligence, Luck, Dexterity, Charisma, and Psionic Potential), racial modifiers (Vulcans, for instance, earn bonuses to their Strength, Endurance, and Intelligence, while Humans are penalized for Psionic Potential), and skill ratings (including Administration, Negotiation, Shuttlecraft Pilot, and Warp Drive Technology). A die-roll, with appropriate modifiers, determines the successful use of a skill. It's not clear how all of the skills function in the game—I'm not sure, for instance, what we're supposed to do with Administration—while others, such as Negotiation, would be better handled by role-playing instead of a die-roll. Still, the PCs are well rounded and interesting, perfectly suited for the demanding life of an *Enterprise* crewman. The characters of the TV show, who presumably will be used more often than original PCs, are accurately rendered, complete with special skills reflecting Captain Kirk's expertise in the life of Abraham Lincoln and Lieutenant Sulu's knowledge of ancient firearms.

The combat rules derive from tactical wargames, with PCs moving on a square grid and expanding Action Points (based on their Dexterity) to execute combat actions. Range, weapon type, and concealment modify the attacker's chance to hit his target, with successfully attacked victims subtracting damage from their Endurance ratings. Though not particularly realistic, combat is quick and exciting, as in the TV series. The system for starship combat skillfully blends tactical maneuvers with role-playing by making each player responsible for a specific duty, such as engineering, navigation, or communications. With the captain acting as coordinator, the engineer allocates power to the engines, the navigator mans the deflectors, and so forth, with the decisions of all players crucial to a successful showdown. It's exciting and fun for everyone, and Star Trek's most innovative feature.

The game includes some brief but interesting background notes concerning the Star Trek universe, along with some good rules for generating new worlds for the crews to explore. As in the series, the game is episodic and lends itself better to single adventures than extended campaigns; those seeking a broader canvas and more sophisticated mechanics are better off with Megatraveller. But role-players comfortable with the simplicity of the series need look no further—the game is a flawless reproduction.

Buyer's Notes: Boxed set. Both deluxe and basic versions are available. The deluxe set includes the Starship Tactical Combat Simulator, essential for staging starship battles, and that's the version to buy. Stick with the second edition, clearly labeled as such on the front of the box, which cleans up the ambiguities of the first edition.

Suggested Supplements: FASA has supported the game with a mountain of sourcebooks and adventures, most of them pretty good. Best sourcebooks: *The Klingons* (detailed information about Star Trek's notorious aliens), *The Romulans* (as good as *The Klingons*), *The Next Generation First Year Sourcebook* (concerning the second TV series—an excellent update), *Trader Captains and Merchant Princes* (great rules for creating traders and conmen), and *Star Fleet Intelligence Manual* (espionage in the future). Best adventures: *A Matter of Priorities* (an exciting adventure featuring the players as Klingons; requires the *Klingon* sourcebook), *Orion Ruse* (integrates characters from the *Trader Captains* supplement, which is necessary to run the adventure), *The Vanished* (an engaging mystery), *The Dixie Gambit* (action-packed encounters). Disappointing adventures: *Demand of Honor* (sketchy) and *Denial of Destiny* (routine).

Star Wars***½

Complexity: Medium
West End Games, 1987

What many feared would be a quickie rip-off of the megahit films turned out to be one of the biggest role-playing surprises of the decade. Star Wars is a delight, a beautifully written, thoroughly entertaining RPG that not only captures the spectacle and humor of the movies, but is also an inspired design, courtesy of role-playing veteran Greg (Toon, Price of Freedom) Costikyan.

There are twenty-four character templates to choose from, each representing a personality common to the Star Wars universe, such as Bounty Hunter, Ewok, Smuggler, and Wookie. Each comes complete with background notes, personality profiles, and even a sample quote (Bounty Hunter: "Don't try it, buddy. I'm only going to tell you once."). Characters are further defined by six basic attributes (Dexterity, Knowledge, Mechanical, Perception, Strength, and Technical) and a number of skills appropriate to their types; for instance, the Bounty Hunter excels in skills related to his Dexterity, such as Dodge and Blaster, while the Ewok's exceptional Perception makes him better at Searching and Hiding.

Skill ratings are expressed in terms of dice; a 3D rating in Dodge means that three dice are used to resolve the use of that particular skill. To check the success of an action, the player throws the number of dice indicated for the applicable skill, and the referee compares the result to the action's Difficulty Number. Simple tasks, such as firing at point-blank range, have a Difficulty Number of 5, while very difficult tasks, such as firing from a distance at a moving target, have a Difficulty Number of 30. While most games have strict limits on the number of actions that can be taken in a single round, Star Wars characters are limited only by their skill dice; for a 5D skill, the first attempt uses five dice, the second attempt uses four, and so on until the player runs out of dice. In tight situations, players can call on the Force by spending a Force Point to double the number of dice normally available to a particular skill; a 5D skill, for instance, temporarily becomes a 10D skill. As in the movies, calling on the Force can be risky; the referee awards a Dark Side point to players who use the Force for evil, and a player who succumbs to the Dark Side loses control of his character to the referee.

The rules encourage quick play and intense action, and the clear presentation ensures that novice players are as at home as veterans. Comprehensive tips on staging adventures make the referee's job a snap. And it's as much fun to read as it is to play, thanks to Costikyan's breezy style and the inclusion of hilarious color ads scattered throughout the rulebook, such as those announcing a new line of R2 droids from Industrial Automation ("Machines for the Future") and interstellar vacations from Galaxy Tours ("Your four-week fantasy voyage begins on the remote, romantic desert world of Tatoonie . . ."). With its rigid ties to the Star Wars mythos, some may find the game's focus too narrow. But I can't imagine a fan of Luke Skywalker being disappointed with a simulation as inventive and colorful as this.

Buyer's Note: Hardback book.

Suggested Supplements: The *Star Wars Sourcebook* contains detailed background material and game statistics for a multitude of aliens, spaceships, vehicles, and personalities; a fan's dream, and a must-have for serious players. The Galaxy Guide sourcebooks describe specific Star Wars eras and locales in loving detail; the most interesting are *Yavin and Bespin* (a fascinating cloud city) and *The Empire Strikes Back* (characters and hardware from the movie). The best adventures: *Battle for the Golden Sun* (encounters in a water world), *Starfall* (exploration of a wrecked Imperial starship), and *Scavenger Hunt* (strange aliens and a mysterious garbage heap).

Stormbringer***½

Complexity: Medium
Chaosium Inc., 1981

Based on the novels of Michael Moorcock, Stormbringer is set in the Young Kingdoms, without a doubt one of fantasy's dreariest and most doom-laden worlds. The bloodthirsty cultists, brutish slave owners, and slovenly drug takers of the Young Kingdoms are a far cry from the friendly wizards and adorable elves populating most other fantasy settings, and designers Ken St. Andre and Steve Perrin have done a chillingly effective job of bringing it all to life. The game uses the conflict between Law and Chaos as a rich subtext; this conflict was also the source of endless torment for Prince Elric, the protagonist of the novels.

Game mechanics derive from the systems used in Rune-Quest, Call of Cthulhu, and other Chaosium-developed products. Players randomly roll for Strength, Constitution, Size, Intelligence, Power, Dexterity, and Charisma, then determine their characters' nationalities. Instead of humans, dwarves, and elves, Stormbringer characters are natives of particular kingdoms, all of whom have strikingly different appearances, abilities, and characteristics. The people of Myrrhyn, for instance, are winged humanoids with sleek bodies and sharp wits, while the inhabitants of Nadsokor are little more than depraved beggars, disease-ridden and repulsive. Obviously, a few unlucky die-tosses can create profound disparities among the PCs, but because a pretty face and a charming personality aren't necessarily pluses in the world of Stormbringer, the repulsive characters are often more fun to play.

Magic receives an outstanding treatment, forgoing the usual spells and ability levels in favor of an innovative system using five power ranks. Each successive rank enables a magic user to call on increasingly potent entities. Sorcerers of the First Rank can summon and control lesser elementals capable of minor feats of magic, Second Rank sorcerers can call on lesser demons, while sorcerers of the Fifth Rank can contact the godlike Lords of Law and Chaos. Magic is always risky, even in the lower ranks where a grumpy demon may decide to turn on the caster, making for some interesting situations.

There are equally interesting rules for plant lore (used to develop herbal preparations to increase or decrease attributes), creating magical weapons (such as the "stormbringer" sword of Elric, whose magic derives from the demon inhabiting it), and religion (detailing the cults of Law, Chaos, and the Four Elements). This is not a game for beginners; the rules presume familiarity with role-playing (especially games with similar systems, such as RuneQuest), and the distinctions between good and evil are not as rigidly defined as they are in most fantasy RPGs. But sophisticated players, particularly those familiar with the Moorcock novels, should find Stormbringer to be an exceptionally rich and entertaining experience.

Buyer's Notes: Stormbringer is available as a boxed set, a hardback book, and a softcover book. The hardback and softcover books contain all of the boxed material as well as the *Stormbringer Companion* sourcebook. The softcover version, which includes some minor revisions from the hardback, is the best buy.

Suggested Supplements: Owners of the boxed version of Stormbringer will find a wealth of useful material in the *Stormbringer Companion* sourcebook, which details creatures, characters, and treasures relevant to the Young Kingdoms, along with several brief but interesting introductory scenarios. Advanced players should check out the *Stealer of Souls* and *Black Sword* adventures, which together form the basis for a lively, absorbing campaign. The Stormbringer and Hawkmoon games are both part of Chaosium's Eternal Champion series, meaning that the games share a common system and all of the supplements are compatible.

Super Squadron***

....

Complexity: Low/Medium
Adventure Simulations, 1983

Super Squadron is a superhero RPG that comes from Australia, courtesy of designer Joseph Italiano. It's easy to play yet comprehensive, with an especially good section on character creation. A player begins his heroic career by randomly determining the origin of his alter ego. Based on his origin—he might be a Mutation, an Alien, or Self-Developed—the PC receives a variable number of superpowers. The resulting hero is remarkably complete; where other superhero RPGs might outfit a spellcasting character with energy blasts, ESP skills, and similarly pedestrian powers, the spellcasters of Super Squadron receive honest-to-goodness spells, each with its own detailed description. There's a refreshing emphasis on the hero's private life, including suggestions for romance and marriage; Super Squadron characters can even have children.

The game systems, while nothing special, compare favorably to those of Villains and Vigilantes, though the Super Squadron rules are more ambiguous and have a few holes (for instance, it's awfully easy for an escaping character to elude capture). Though Super Squadron is unlikely to replace Villains and Vigilantes or Champions as anyone's favorite generic superhero game, it's an entertaining alternative for those who enjoy roleplaying as much as bashing bad guys.

Buyer's Note: Boxed set.

Supervillains*

···

Complexity: Medium
Task Force Games, 1982

Supervillains is allegedly a board game/RPG combination, but there's a lot more board-gaming than role-playing, and it's dismal board-gaming at that. Players move little cardboard super-people, like Speedo and the Invisible Semi-Man, on a featureless map supposedly representing New York City. When they encounter enemies, they try to beat them senseless or blast them to pieces with their superpowers. Players take turns moving and fighting, with each turn taking one hour of game time; these aren't particularly speedy superheroes, Speedo notwithstanding. The rules are so full of holes that the players are virtually forced to invent their own game. As for the role-playing elements, they exist mainly to introduce random encounters to the board game, extending the length of the battles and little else. If a player wants rules for personalizing Invisible Semi-Man, he'll have to borrow them from some other RPG.

Buyer's Note: Boxed set.

Superworld***

···

Complexity: Medium
Chaosium Inc., 1983

Superworld is an expanded and revised version of the supplement of the same name included in Chaosium's Worlds of Wonder game. Taking a serious approach to a frivolous subject, the prolific Steve Perrin did a bang-up job, creating one of the most fully realized and shamefully overlooked superhero RPGs ever published.

A character's Strength, Constitution, Size, Intelligence, Power, Dexterity, and Appearance are determined randomly. The sum of these basic attributes is used to compute the character's Hero Points, which are used to buy skills and superpowers. There is a vast array of powers to choose from—a whole bookful, in fact—enabling players to duplicate any existing hero from the comics, as well as to create an infinite number of variants. Characters short on Hero Points can earn more of them by taking on one or more Power Disadvantages, such as a Side Effect (the use of a particular superpower might accidentally harm innocent bystanders) or a Burnout Chance (a power may fizzle out after it's used). Handicaps further complicate a hero's life, ranging from the life-threatening (a special vulnerability to a particular substance) to the merely irritating (anti-hero editorials from a self-righteous newspaper editor).

The game mechanics are smooth and exciting, particularly the combat system, which encourages melodramatic slugfests comparable to those in a comic book. Two excellent introductory adventures, a booklet of reference tables, and a handful of blank character sheets complete a remarkably generous package. Though the game has a few glitches (it's difficult to create exceptionally powerful heroes, and PCs must spend Hero Points to acquire regular weapons—couldn't they just buy them at a gun shop?), none are particularly troubling. A first-class game.

Buyer's Note: Boxed set.

Suggested Supplements: Bad Medicine for Dr. Drugs is a goofy, engaging adventure in which the PC heroes investigate a drug problem at the local high school. The *Superworld Companion* adds rule variants, new powers, and some hints for converting the Superworld system to the Villains and Vigilantes and Champions games.

Swordbearer**½

Complexity: High
Fantasy Games Unlimited Inc., 1985

Swords and sorcery for grad students. Swordbearer is an ambitious attempt by B. Dennis Sustare to rework some of the more conventional concepts of fantasy RPGs and create a sophisticated alternative for those bored with Advanced Dungeons and Dragons and RuneQuest. It doesn't all work, but the results are interesting.

Following an adequate but routine character-creation section, Swordbearer introduces the concept of Activity Spheres, which are detailed groupings of related talents, such as Fighting, Magic, and General Knowledge. By specializing in a Sphere, a PC learns skills more quickly. Skill selection has few limits, enabling players to customize their characters to their hearts' content. With experience and increased status, characters acquire new skills and improve the old ones. It's a clever system that promotes the development of a PC's personality as well as his talents.

The character-creation system also does away with the concept of money, substituting instead a numerical rating for Social Status to indicate a character's purchasing power. A lowly Status 1, for instance, indicates slaves and indentured servants, while barons, counts, and other nobility receive Status 17 or higher. All goods and services have Status ratings, as do treasures. If a Status 7 PC wants a Status 7 item, he is assumed to have enough funds to purchase it. If a Status 5 PC finds a Status 9 treasure, his Social Status is raised accordingly. Though the system does away with a certain amount of bookkeeping, it also requires a lot of interpretation from the referee. Players who salivate over the contents of every treasure chest and keep track of every gold piece in their pockets aren't likely to be satisfied with a monetary system this abstract.

The game offers the referee two choices of time scales for combat encounters; "instant" combat breaks down the action into segments of four seconds, while "period" combat involves twenty-second segments. Players announce their actions for each instant or period, with the referee determining the results based on weaponry, speed, and a host of other modifiers. It's complicated but surprisingly flexible, allowing the referee to adjust the intensity of combat encounters according to the current situation and the needs of the players.

In the end, however, Swordbearer's complexity overwhelms its clever ideas. The simplest combat engagements can take ages to complete, and even modest mathematical errors (such as neglecting to factor in surprise) can produce wildly inaccurate results. The magic system requires characters to locate and identify an appropriate "node" of energy, align the node to a spell, then resolve the attempt by consulting an alignment equation ([5 × current power of aligned mode] − [25 × strength of node to be aligned] + 75). The material is clearly presented, and referee hints abound, but the amount of effort required to master the game mechanics make Swordbearer virtually unplayable.

Buyer's Note: Boxed set.

Swordtag*½

Complexity: Low
Adventurers' Guild, 1988

Swordtag is a brief set of rules for live-action fantasy role-playing, where players don makeshift armor and chase each other with phony swords in a city park or somebody's backyard. The game mechanics are heavily influenced by Dungeons and Dragons, involving Thieves, Mages, and Warriors rated for Life Points (read: hit points), skill levels, and alignment. They're very simple and nothing special. More interesting are the suggestions for simulating fantasy encounters in real-life settings. For instance, designer Brett Dougherty explains how to manufacture swords from dowel rods and foam pipe insulation and how to make a Wand of Light from a paper towel tube and a flashlight. Mages cast spells by tossing Ping-Pong balls or dried beans at their victims. A recipe for a magical potion might include water, food coloring, and a drop of vanilla flavoring.

However, Swordtag is more of an outline than an actual game; in spite of some engaging ideas, there's barely enough information to stage a brief encounter, let alone an entire adventure. The magic rules are unclear, and the combat system is virtually nonexistent. Many of the simulation suggestions are impractical (how exactly do you construct a "hidden switch" required by the Staff of Light?) or just plain silly (to create a dragon, round up three to six friends, throw a blanket over them, find a dragon head mask, and give them a bucket of water to simulate a dragon breath attack). For a more sophisticated treatment of live-action games, try IFGS Fantasy Rules.

Buyer's Note: Booklet.

Talislanta***½

Complexity: Low/Medium
Bard Games, 1989

A fantasy game without elves or dwarves? In Talislanta (consisting of two books: the *Handbook and Campaign Guide* and the *Chronicles of Talislanta*), designer Stephan Michael Sechi neatly sidesteps all of the stereotypical elements of medieval-based RPGs to create a unique fantasy setting that defies categorization, populated by spirit trackers, botanomancers, exomorphs, and mandragores. It's as if H. P. Lovecraft had written *Alice in Wonderland* with Hans Christian Andersen and William S. Burroughs as technical advisors.

The game world is detailed in the *Chronicles of Talislanta* book, organized as a series of essays covering the continent's key cities, personalities, and historical incidents. Entertainingly written from the perspective of the great wizard Tamerlin, the book introduces the skyfaring Dream Merchants of Phantas, the water-dwelling Imrian slave traders, and the dual-brained Sindaran humanoids, among dozens of other fascinating races and characters. Unusual locales include the Labyrinths of Sharna, the Ur Forest of Krag, and the Jungles of Chana, all bursting with potential for compelling adventures. Because the Talislanta game mechanics are confined to a separate book, all of the *Chronicles* material can be easily adapted to other RPG settings.

The Talislanta *Handbook* rules are a model of clarity and elegance, with a single Action Table resolving all of the game activities. When a character makes an attack, casts a spell, or uses a skill or attribute, he rolls a twenty-sided die, adds any modifiers determined by the referee, then consults the appropriate column on the Action Table. An attempt to cast a spell, for instance, may result in a Maximum Effect (the spell inflicts the maximum possible damage or achieves an otherwise perfect result), Spell Failure (no effect), or Magical Mishap (the spell rebounds on the caster or has some other undesired result). It's simple, quick, and versatile, and typical of the game's admirable avoidance of charts and formulas.

Character creation involves the selection of a template from nearly a hundred exotic possibilities, among them the Yassan Technomancer, the Zandir Charlatan, and the Sunra Aquamancer. Each template comes ready-made with physical characteristics, abilities, skills, equipment, and personality notes. The nomadic Yassan Technomancer, for instance, has exceptional manual dexterity, is skilled in engineering, and wears a hooded yellow tunic, while the Sunra Aquamancer is a magic-using amphibian skilled in navigation who wears a silk headband and rainbow-colored boots. Players customize these templates by increasing and decreasing two attributes and adding a new skill of their choice. Distinctive, enthralling characters can be created in a matter of minutes—it's an inspired system, one of the best of any fantasy RPG.

The remainder of the rulebook includes a clever magic system, a detailed language guide, and a bizarre selection of weapons and equipment unique to the world of Talislanta. There's a formidable amount of information here, perhaps too much for the novice referee. In fact, with so much unfamiliar ground to cover, the lack of structure is the game's biggest flaw (more examples of play would've been helpful). But for the adventurous, Talislanta is role-playing nirvana.

Buyer's Notes: The *Handbook and Campaign Guide* and the *Chronicles of Talislanta* are trade paperbacks and must be purchased separately. Players on a budget can get by with just the *Handbook,* but both volumes are needed to fully enjoy the game. The second edition *Handbook* is the one to get, identifiable by the multicolored warrior on the cover.

Suggested Supplements: Sorcerer's Guide expands on the magic system introduced in the *Handbook,* adding rules for magical research and alchemical technique; because the *Handbook* covers the subject more than adequately, the *Sorcerer's Guide* is recommended only for completists. The *Naturalist Guide*, a scholarly treatise on the flora and fauna of Talislanta, is an essential reference for referees planning long campaigns; the offbeat monsters can also be used to enliven other fantasy games. The various *Cyclopedia Talislanta* volumes combine historical notes with engaging scenarios, each tied to a specific region of Talislanta; all are recommended.

Teenage Mutant Ninja Turtles***½

Complexity: Medium
Palladium Books, 1985

Teenage Mutant Ninja Turtles, the comic book, may sound like kid's stuff, but it's not. Created by Kevin Eastman and Peter Laird, *TMNT* has attracted fans ranging from preschoolers, who like the cartoonish characters, to adults, who appreciate the satiric edge. Teenage Mutant Ninja Turtles, the role-playing game, is equally sophisticated and just as fun, thanks to a terrific design by Erick (Ninjas and Superspies) Wujcik.

Players aren't restricted to mutant turtles; a variety of modified animals are available as PCs. Character design begins by selecting an animal type (anything from a dog to a cat, or an aardvark to an elephant), then mutating it by applying Biological Energy Points. The Bio Points can cause the animal to shrink, enlarge, gain human features, or acquire any number of superpowers. Skills, education level, and alignment complete the character. For those eager to get started, pregenerated statistics for many of the comic's major characters are provided, among them April O'Neil, Splinter, and, of course, Michaelangelo and the other teen turtles.

Completing the game are excellent rules for psionics and combat, including a brief but thorough discussion of martial arts and plenty of hints for first-time referees on how to stage adventures. The five scenarios range from the introductory "Terror on Rural Route 5," which pits the players against a mutant bull and a gang of television-educated pigs, to an exciting advanced adventure called "The Terror Bears," starring a gang of bloodthirsty bear cubs. Amply illustrated with scenes from the comics, Teenage Mutant Ninja Turtles is a perfect blend of whimsy and adventure. Recommended to all role-players with an appreciation for the bizarre.

Buyer's Note: Trade paperback.

Suggested Supplements: After the Bomb, also by Erick Wujcik, is the best of a uniformly superb set of supplements. Set on Earth after a catastrophic nuclear war, the book includes new character types, some fascinating locales (such as the Plains of Free Cattle and the Rodent Cartel of Filly), and six adventure scenarios. The *Road Hogs* and *Mutants Down Under* supplements expand on the *After the Bomb* setting, detailing the postapocalyptic regions of the western United States and Australia respectively. Players seeking less-ambitious adventures should investigate *Teenage Mutant Ninja Turtle Adventures* and *Truckin' Turtles,* both of which feature a wealth of outstanding material. The Teenage Mutant Ninja Turtles game is also compatible with Palladium's Heroes Unlimited and Ninjas and Superspies, which can be used as sources for additional material by creative referees.

Teenagers from Outer Space***

Complexity: Low
R. Talsorian Games, Inc., 1988

Teenagers from Outer Space is the nuttiest RPG this side of Toon, a minor classic by designer Michael (Cyberpunk) Pondsmith. Whether a link exists between the game and the 1959 movie of the same name is unclear, but both are based on the idea that adolescents have more in common with alien creatures than normal Homo sapiens. As the game begins, extraterrestrials have landed on Earth and made themselves right at home, enrolling their kids in the local high school, buying lawn furniture at the shopping mall, and stopping at fast-food joints for hamburgers. Players can be Human (the coolest race in the galaxy), Near Human (aliens nearly identical to the coolest race), Not Very Near Human (aliens with only a vaguely humanoid appearance, hence not very cool), or Real Weirdies (scaly, multi-tentacled monstrosities who are definitely not cool, except to other Weirdies). Basic characteristics, determined by dice-rolls, include Smarts, Luck, Looks, and the all-important Relationship With Parents. Because death spoils the mood of the game, a character in Teenagers from Outer Space has a Bonk rating to measure how much damage he can take before he's "bonked" into submission. To round him out, a character is also awarded a few Knacks (skills) such as Talk Sweet to Your Mom, Shoot Big Raygun, Play Air Guitar, and Know About Alien Stuff.

Aside from the character-generation system, there aren't many formal rules. Resolving an action requires rolling a die, adding a difficulty rating decided by the referee, and modifying it by any relevant Knack. Though the appendix includes twenty scenario suggestions with such intriguing titles as "I'm Getting Frozen in the Morning" and "Return of the Patty Duke Show," they're little more than plot summaries; for the most part, it's up to the referee to design and stage adventures. Teenagers from Outer Space is hands-down the all-time funniest RPG, but be forewarned that it takes an experienced referee to realize its potential.

Buyer's Notes: Trade paperback. The revised edition is the one to get, with the picture of a one-eyed alien holding a surfboard on the cover.

Suggested Supplements: Anyone contemplating an extended Teenagers from Outer Space campaign should investigate the *Field Trip* adventure, which details a scholarly excursion by the students of Valleyview High and their Alien Control Officer.

Thieves' Guild**

Complexity: High
Gamelords Ltd., 1984

One of fantasy's most appealing character types is the thief, the scoundrel with a twinkle in his eye who operates outside the confines of the law. Thieves' Guild focuses exclusively on thieves, nearly to the exclusion of everything else. But though the premise is interesting, the execution is so convoluted that it's bound to discourage all but the most dedicated players.

Character creation begins with a series of dice-rolls to randomly determine basic attributes, similar to the system used in Dungeons and Dragons. From there, players are guided through nearly twenty pages of chart-filled, tediously detailed instructions to determine the character's training, family, weapon skills, and sensory abilities in excruciating detail; it took me about two hours to create a minor character. This fascination with numbers also extends to the game systems; picking a lock, for instance, requires that the referee consider the complexity of the lock, the neighborhood in which the lock is located, the skill of the character, the time spent in the attempt, the lock's booby traps, and the influence of the other party members.

That's not to say that Thieves' Guild is devoid of interesting ideas. The combat system features solid rules covering backstabbing, strangulation, and other useful attack options for lawless characters, while a section on the medieval justice system provides thorough guidelines for staging trials, including a dozen different NPC judges. But the lack of magic, monsters, and other elements common to fantasy settings severely limits the game's appeal. Thieves' Guild works better as a source of ideas for other games than a stand-alone RPG.

Buyer's Note: Boxed set.

Suggested Supplements: The Thieves' Guild supplements mix rules expansions, sourcebook material, and adventures. Among the best of them are *Thieves' Guild 3*, which includes a scenario featuring the burglary of a wizard's tower, and *Thieves' Guild 6*, which provides rules for piracy and ship design.

Thieves' World**½

Complexity: Medium
Chaosium Inc., 1981

Thieves' World is not a self-contained role-playing game but a generic supplement detailing the city of Sanctuary, the setting of author Robert Asprin's *Thieves' World* and *Tales from the Vulgar Unicorn*. Just as Asprin invited a number of fantasy authors to contribute to his books, the Thieves' World supplement likewise boasts a veritable Who's Who of game designers, among them Dave Arneson (one of the original Dungeons and Dragons team), Eric Goldberg (DragonQuest), Marc Miller (Traveller), Steve Perrin (RuneQuest), and Ken St. Andre (Tunnels and Trolls). Adaptable to a wide variety of RPG systems, Thieves' World is among the most ambitious projects of its kind and one of the most enjoyable.

The lavish package features three maps, including a detailed layout of the entire city, and three booklets. The first of them, the Players' Guide, provides general background information about Sanctuary and is intended as an overview for first-time visitors to the city. The second, the Game Master's Guide, begins with a series of entertaining essays about life in Sanctuary, such as Lynn Abbey's informative "Palm-Greasing at the Palace," then concludes with detailed encounter tables, floor plans, and location descriptions. The final booklet, Personalities of Sanctuary, profiles all of the major characters from Asprin's books.

Extensive notes are provided for adapting the material to Advanced Dungeons and Dragons, Chivalry and Sorcery, Dragon-Quest, RuneQuest, Traveller, and Tunnels and Trolls. But though it's a terrific idea, converting Thieves' World to all of these systems doesn't always work, owing to the games' diverse approaches to magic, religion, and combat. And in spite of the sheer volume of material, there's only a couple of pages of suggestions for adventures; it's pretty much up to the referee to design scenarios from scratch.

Buyer's Note: Boxed set.

Suggested Supplements: The Thieves' World Companion complements the original package with well-rendered material about the Great Keep, the Beysibs, and other highlights of Sanctuary. FASA has also published a few Thieves' World supplements, the best of which is "Dark Assassin," an adventure concerning the mysterious murder of a local noble by a sneaky demon.

Time and Time Again**

Complexity: Medium
Timeline, Ltd., 1984

An interesting but not wholly successful time travel RPG. Designers H. N. Voss and W. P. Worzel approach the topic from a hard science angle, imagining a twenty-first-century world where time-traveling is under the auspices of the Bureau of Temporal Affairs (an outgrowth, strangely enough, of the French Foreign Legion). As with any science, time travel is governed by strict laws. For instance: (1) it's impossible to visit the future, (2) you can't encounter yourself in the past, (3) the past can't be changed, and (4) only organic material can travel through time.

It's all quite logical, but not much fun, because the game's rigid "science" eliminates every type of what-if scenario (what if the Nazis won World War II? What if Lincoln hadn't been assassinated?), thus limiting adventures to observing past events, capturing renegade time travelers who threaten to tamper with the past, and a few other narrowly focused plots. The game mechanics are adequate, though the character-creation rules are bland and the combat system is far too complicated. There's a lot of general information about science, culture, government, and economics, but there are no specific details about any particular era. If the referee wants to send his players back to ancient Egypt to have them discover who really built the pyramids (a typical Time and Time Again premise), he'll have to go the library and research the era himself. Players who are turned off by the fantasy elements that invariably crop up in other time-traveling RPGs might enjoy the soberminded Time and Time Again, but others should look elsewhere (Timelords, for instance, is a better design and much more fun).

Buyer's Note: Boxed set.

Timelords***

Complexity: Medium/High
Blacksburg Tactical Research Center, First Edition: 1987; Revised Edition: 1990

Timelords is a detailed, intelligent treatment of time travel. The premise is tough to pull off—the RPG graveyard is filled with similar attempts—but designer Greg Porter came up with a winner. Characters flit from era to era by means of the Matrix, a metallic dodecahedron containing massive amounts of complex machinery that allows the PCs to influence the flow of his-

212
....

tory. Historical events are assigned to Event Classes according
to their significance; for instance, the destruction of an insect
swarm is Event Class 0, a presidential assassination is Event
Class 9, and a nuclear war is Event Class 14. However, Event
Classes are relative to the observer; while an assassinated presi-
dent is Event Class 9 to an American citizen, it may only be
Event Class 0 from the perspective of an extraterrestrial. The
discussion of time travel and its ramifications is fascinating, the
most sophisticated analysis ever presented in an RPG.

Players use themselves as characters in the game, and PC
attributes derive from the players' actual characteristics. For instance, if Player A never gets sick, then his PC may have a
Constitution score of 17, whereas Player B, who regularly comes
down with colds and the flu, might only receive a Constitution
score of 5 for his character. PC skills and attributes also derive
from the players' real-life talents. The combat system is extremely complex, excessively so for the genre (time travel
should focus on exploration, discovery, and role-playing, not
combat), and the sample adventure, a routine skirmish in Crete
circa 1500 B.C., doesn't really exploit the best elements of the
game. Still, Timelords contains so many interesting ideas that
it's easily the best-ever time travel RPG.

Buyer's Notes: Trade paperback. The 140-page second edition
is the one to get; the first edition (124 pages with a cover featuring a large red infinity symbol enclosed by a blue ring) is not as
well organized and is a bit more ambiguous.

Suggested Supplements: Not much to recommend. The *Pursuit*
adventure centers around the discovery of an alien artifact, but
it doesn't really go anywhere, though the discussion of time
travel theory is interesting.

Timemaster**½

Complexity: Medium
Pacesetter, Ltd., 1984

What separates Timemaster from other time-traveling RPGs is
its intriguing premise (courtesy of veteran designers Mark
Acres, Carl Smith, and Michael Williams, who at one time or

another all cut their teeth at TSR Inc., the home of Dungeons and Dragons). The PCs belong to an elite seventy-second-century agency called the Time Corps and are sworn to protect the flow of time from interference by the Demoreans, a race of evil aliens bent on altering the events of the past for their own devious purposes. Adventures send the PCs into the past to thwart the efforts of the Demoreans while avoiding any actions of their own that might inadvertently change the course of history.

Each important NPC and event is assigned a Significance Rating, a measure of its relative importance in the flow of time. While a Nazi infantryman might have a low Significance Rating, Hitler himself would have a high one; bumping off the infantryman wouldn't have much historical impact, but assassinating Hitler would have a profound effect. Because the PCs aren't supposed to change history, the referee keeps track of their successes and blunders along the way, translating them into experience points at the end of the adventure. It's a unique approach, as much fun for the referee as it is for the players.

The game's mechanics, unfortunately, mix the elegant with the clumsy, resulting in an awkward set of rules that requires a lot of second-guessing from the referee. Combat includes rules for handling man-to-man engagements, battles between hundreds of men per side, and mass warfare involving thousands of soldiers. It's extremely complicated, forcing players to switch between role-playing and board-gaming; worse, the combat game more or less plays itself, and PC decisions have little effect on the outcome. A single table is used to resolve all actions, but it's not as easy as it sounds, as the referee must consult a myriad of charts scattered throughout the rulebook to interpret the results.

On the other hand, character generation is nicely handled, a smooth blend of randomly determined statistics and allocation of attribute points that creates unique, three-dimensional personalities. Also well done is the colorful skill system, including such intriguing entries as Time Corps Stunner (a weapon skill) and Paranormal Memory (a measure of how well a PC remembers the actual course of historical events before the Demoreans and the Time Corps interfered with them). Like the other

214

Pacesetter games, Timemaster is now out of print. Too bad, because in spite of its flaws, it's a terrific time travel RPG, second only to Timelords.

Buyer's Note: Boxed set.

Suggested Supplements: Each Timemaster adventure is keyed to a particular era. The best of them are *Clash of Kings* (dragons, Merlin, and Demoreans in King Arthur's England) and *Sea Dogs of England* (a humorous mix of piracy and nuclear submarines). *Timetricks* is a superb sourcebook that clarifies many of the original game's fuzzier concepts and adds new Demorean tactics and rules for time-hopping. Timemaster shares the same basic rules as Chill and Star Ace, and many supplements for those games can be adapted to Timemaster with a little work.

Timeship*

Complexity: Low
Yaquinto, 1983

Though Timeship has been out of print for quite a while, it occasionally pops up for sale at conventions, where curious shoppers might be tempted by the intriguing cover art to invest in a copy. Be forewarned that Timeship, an alleged time-travel RPG, is more of an outline than a fully developed game. All of the rules are confined to about ten pages; though the effort to keep things simple is appreciated, anyone with even a casual familiarity with RPGs ought to be suspicious of tackling a subject as complex as time travel in such a short amount of space.

Not surprisingly, the game mechanics are woefully underdeveloped. For instance, players use themselves as characters, which is okay, except that there aren't any comprehensible instructions for doing so. There are no clear distinctions among attributes. (What's the difference between Dexterity and Agility? In the context of the game, it's anybody's guess.) The game's conception of time travel is never made clear. Can past events be changed, or are they unalterable? Who cares? Skip it.

Buyer's Note: Boxed set.

To Challenge Tomorrow**½

Complexity: Medium
Ragnarok Enterprises, 1983

To Challenge Tomorrow is a fairly successful example of a generic role-playing game; that is, an RPG that isn't tied to a particular setting, instead providing a set of general rules that can be adapted to a variety of situations and characters. More precisely, To Challenge Tomorrow stakes out an era extending from the late fifteenth century to somewhere in the distant future. Though designer David Nalle was perhaps a little too ambitious—that's a lot of ground to cover in a relatively few pages of rules—it's a nice effort, with some good ideas and a lot of potential.

The game consists of three booklets, well written but marred by haphazard editing and rough graphics. Book One covers character generation and combat, and includes a simple system for distributing attribute points among four primary characteristics (Physical, Active, Mental, and Social), which in turn generate a number of secondary characteristics (such as Hand Attack Rating, Movement, and Hit Points). An exhaustive skill list allows players to customize their characters with surprising precision. Book Two gives brief guidelines for role-playing in a number of historical settings, ranging from the swashbucklers of the fifteenth century through the intergalactic empires of the year 2000 and beyond; they're fun to read, but frustratingly skimpy. Book Three features four scenarios, including a Romeo and Juliet knock-off (mundane and forgettable) and a hunt for a psionic spy set in the future (unusual and the best of the four). Overall, the scenarios are underdeveloped and graphically weak (the maps, for instance, are tough to read)—problems that plague the entire project.

To Challenge Tomorrow boasts attractively simple rules, an admirable amount of research, and one of the best skill systems I've ever seen. But it suffers from inadequate packaging and too many ideas crammed into too little space, limiting its appeal to enterprising referees.

Buyer's Note: Set of three booklets.

Suggested Supplements: The supplements focus on specific eras, including both sourcebook material and adventures. *Triad* features a twenty-ninth-century setting in a corrupt sector of outer space and is as good a place as any to begin a To Challenge Tomorrow campaign. Players with a taste for the occult should investigate *London By Night*, which includes some fascinating background material on Victorian London and several intriguing scenarios.

Toon***½

Complexity: Low
Steve Jackson Games, 1984

If not the funniest RPG (depending on your sense of humor, that honor may go to Paranoia, Ghostbusters, or Teenagers from Outer Space), Toon is certainly the oddest. Set in the world of Saturday morning cartoons, players take the roles of animated characters in a setting reminiscent of *Who Framed Roger Rabbit?*, which Toon predates. It's a world of utter anarchy, inspired more by the slapstick violence of Warner Brothers cartoons than the relatively benign Walt Disney stuff, and it's a brilliant design by Greg Costikyan.

The character types are virtually unlimited—Talking Dogs, Little Green Men, and Animated Fire Hydrants are among the possibilities—and outrageousness is encouraged. Each character receives attribute ratings in Muscle, Zip, Smarts, and Chutzpah that regulate most of the game's actions; for instance, Smarts determines how well your Animated Fire Hydrant is able to identify Dangerous Things. Special skills called Schticks further individualize a character, while the addition of a Natural Enemy gives him something to worry about; the Animated Fire Hydrant may use his Blow Purple Smoke Rings Schtick to frighten away his Natural Enemy, the Talking Dog.

The referee determines the PCs' successes and failures by a combination of dice-rolls and personal whims. In an ambiguous situation, the referee employs the Fifty Percent Rule by framing the problem as a "yes" or "no" question and rolling a six-sided die; a roll of 1 to 3 means the answer is "yes," 4 to 6 means "no." As anyone knows who's seen Daffy Duck get blown to bits by a shotgun, cartoon characters don't die; when a Toon character loses all of his hit points, he Falls Down, requiring the player to sit out for three minutes, after which his character can rejoin the action, fully recovered.

Any game as freeform as Toon depends heavily on the improvisational skills of the referee, which is the game's major drawback; though the rules burst with ideas for funny situations, it's up to the referee to pull everything together. As adventures screech to a halt after an arbitrary time limit has been reached (one hour is typical), goal-oriented players may feel frustrated. However, in the hands of a witty referee and a group of receptive players, Toon can be hilarious, an excellent introductory game for novices and a delightful change of pace for veterans.

Buyer's Note: Trade paperback.

Suggested Supplements: Both *Son of Toon* and *Toon Silly Stuff* are highly recommended; each contains a variety of bizarre scenarios, rule modifications, and new characters.

Top Secret***

···

Complexity: Medium
TSR, Inc., 1980

The first espionage RPG of any consequence, Top Secret combined Dungeons and Dragons–derived game systems with the larger-than-life heroics of James Bond movies to produce an entertaining game that holds up amazingly well even a decade after its release. Though the game is now out of print, there's still a lot of Top Secret material floating around, and it remains the spy game of choice for a surprising number of die-hard fans.

Admittedly, some of the game mechanics, such as character levels and experience points, show their D&D roots a little too blatantly. Aside from Life Level (hit points) and Offense (which measures success in gun battles), the game doesn't do much with the basic character attributes, leaving the more routine aspects of a spy's life up to the imagination of the referee.

But designer Merle Rasmussen knows exactly what makes the genre so appealing. There are gadgets galore, from thermite bombs and truth serum to silencers and speedboats, a virtual Christmas catalog of high-tech gizmos perfectly suited for the spy trade. Characters are encouraged to pursue careers in Investigation, Confiscation, or Assassination. The first-rate combat system allows for underwater assaults, helicopter battles, and pistol-whippings.

Those tempted to investigate the game are forewarned that Top Secret is officially obsolete, having been replaced by the Top Secret/S.I. revision. Top Secret is good, but Top Secret/S.I. is better. Players are advised to stick with the newer game and use Top Secret and its supplements as sources of supplementary material.

Buyer's Note: Boxed set.

Suggested Supplements: Among the best Top Secret adventures are *Operation: Lady in Distress* (a terrorist hijacking of a ship carrying mutated bacteria), *Operation: Orient Express* (several scenarios taking place on the European railways), and *Operation: Rapidstrike* (industrial espionage involving a Nobel Prize–winning scientist and organized crime).

Top Secret/S.I.****

Complexity: Low/Medium
TSR Inc., 1987

A radical reworking of the old Top Secret game, Top Secret/S.I. is not only an improvement in every respect, it's also the best espionage RPG on the market, a masterful integration of elegant mechanics, evocative atmosphere, and sleek graphics. Well organized and clearly explained, Top Secret/S.I. can be used as a painless introduction to role-playing for novices, yet its systems are sophisticated enough to satisfy hardcore players as well. A top-notch effort from veteran designer Doug Niles.

The game abandons Top Secret's rigid system of character classes in favor of a looser approach that encourages players to customize their own PCs. Following the determination of basic attributes, players can add a varying number of Advantages, such as Acute Vision, Photographic Memory, and Sensuality, all of which must be balanced by Disadvantages, among them Color Blindness, Lechery, and Unattractive Appearance. Players also have the option of creating Tags and Psychological Profiles for their PCs; Tags include distinctive quirks such as Gum Chewing and Ever-Present Pet, while Psychological Profiles are simple ratings for Passion, Loyalty, and other attitudinal characteristics. A wide selection of skills are available, many of them bundled as Career Packages to help steer players into particular specialties; for instance, Military Careers stress Combat skills, such as Basic Firearms and Martial Arts, while Professional Careers stress Educational and Language skills, such as Political Science and Journalism. And to simulate a secret agent's talent for saving his skin at the last minute, each PC receives a varying number of Luck Points that can be spent to dodge bullets, avoid head-on collisions, or execute similarly miraculous last-minute escapes.

The game mechanics seldom require more than a single die-roll, yet they allow for a variety of actions and produce realistic results. Resolving an attack is a simple matter of comparing a die-roll to the appropriate skill. A successful attack also indicates the amount of damage suffered by the opponent. For instance, if a character has a Firearms skill of 70 and rolls a 67, he's shot his opponent in the left hand and has inflicted 6 points of damage. Similar games might require a dozen formulas and tables to resolve an action like this; Top Secret/S.I. accomplishes it in one roll.

There are simple but thorough rules for car chases and explosives, and an entire book devoted to referee tips for designing and staging adventures. The Equipment Inventory booklet details all manner of exotic weaponry, from bug detectors to

220
....

flamethrowers. The Administrator's Guide includes a detailed campaign outline that pits the noble Orion against the Web, a mysterious organization of international criminals bent on world domination. Beautifully packaged, meticulously organized, and thoroughly entertaining, Top Secret/S.I. is a near-flawless balance of playability and realism. This is secret agent role-playing at its streamlined best.

Buyer's Note: Boxed set.

Suggested Supplements: Operation: Starfire (showdowns in Hawaii and the Grand Canyon) and *Doomsday Drop* (nuclear terrorism) are both good introductory adventures. The *Orion Rising* anthology details the Orion bureaus in a dozen cities around the world, and includes a number of interesting scenario outlines.

Two excellent sourcebooks expand the game in radically different directions. *Commando* provides new rules and background information for realistic mercenary and antiterrorist operations in contemporary settings; the *Brushfire Wars* supplement features Commando scenarios set in Libya, Zaire, and other hot spots around the world. *F.R.E.E. Lancers* takes the game into the future, with rules for creating superpowered characters armed with laser guns and wrist rockets.

The two-volume *Covert Operations Source Book* comprises a set of factual essays about the organization and operation of real-life espionage agencies, including the CIA and the KGB; fascinating reading.

Because Top Secret/S.I. includes the appropriate conversion notes, all of the original Top Secret supplements can be used with the newer game.

Traders of the Far Reach*

....

Complexity: Low
Griffen P/L, 1985

Designers who take shortcuts do so at their own risk. The eager-to-please Traders of the Far Reach is an ambitious attempt at combining role-playing with science-fiction board-gaming, but it succeeds at neither. Full of holes, ambiguities, and jarring inconsistencies, it's hard to believe that Traders of the Far Reach received anything remotely resembling a thorough playtesting before it rolled off the presses.

The setting is the fifty-seventh century, where low-cost interstellar travel has spawned a new breed of greedy entrepreneurs, portrayed by the PCs. As newly graduated captains from the Aldeberan Station University, the PCs are given a fixed amount of money to buy and outfit their spaceships, then they're off to roam the galaxy in search of new worlds to explore and new markets to exploit. Discovering planets, selecting cargo, and just about every other important element of the game is determined by random rolls on event tables. The tedious dice-rolling is enlivened by the occasionally ridiculous results from the encounter tables, such as discovering that fish are the dominant life-form on a desert planet.

The role-playing elements seem more like an afterthought than an integral part of the game. Attributes such as Intelligence, Intuition, and Charisma are virtually meaningless, and rules for skills, experience, and other standard role-playing concepts are all but ignored. Whatever role-playing takes place in the game depends on the improvisational skills of the referee—there's not much help from the rules. With its comprehensive cargo lists and hundreds of star types, Traders of the Far Reach has some modest value as a sourcebook for other science-fiction RPGs, but the game itself doesn't amount to much of anything.

Buyer's Note: Booklet.

Traveller****
....

Complexity: High
Game Designers' Workshop, 1977

Traveller is to science-fiction RPGs as Advanced Dungeons and Dragons is to fantasy RPGs; that is, the standard by which all others are measured. It's a brilliant design of remarkable scope (courtesy of Marc Miller and a support team including Frank

Chadwick, John Harshman, Loren Wiseman, and Darryl Hany) and a milestone in the hobby. It's also obsolete, thanks to the publication of Megatraveller in 1987, which expands and revises the original Traveller game and essentially replaces it.

So why is Traveller still worth considering? Two reasons. First, many of the Traveller concepts are so inventive and revolutionary that they continue to ripple through the RPG industry nearly fifteen years after the game's original publication. Second, the sheer volume of Traveller material (forty-plus supplements, multiple editions of the original game, and a multitude of magazine articles) ensures that the game will continue to attract attention, not only from hardcore players who've stayed with the game since its inception but also from curious newcomers.

Set in the far future when interstellar travel is commonplace, the entire universe serves as a background for Traveller. There are new worlds to explore, mysterious aliens to confront, and a host of political, social, and scientific problems to solve. Traveller is by no means simple—starship combat, for instance, involves vector mathematics—but its scope justifies its complexity.

Character creation is almost a game in itself, involving the determination of initial attributes (including Education and Social Standing in addition to the usual Strength, Intelligence, Dexterity, and Endurance) and the selection of a career. By a series of dice-rolls and table consultations, characters gain expertise in their chosen field before the game actually gets underway. Not only does the system give beginning PCs unique and detailed personal histories, it also means that most characters won't embark on their adventuring careers until they've reached midlife. Traveller PCs don't acquire experience as in most other RPGs; on the contrary, their abilities tend to decrease with age. It's a realistic and engaging rule—players aren't only battling hostile aliens, they're also battling against the calendar.

The spacecraft rules allow players to design ships from scratch, choosing weaponry, engines, navigational equipment, and other components from a detailed menu of options. Ships must operate within the laws of physics, but the rules are so clearly explained that even scientific illiterates can navigate them. Economics are also considered in depth, including how much cargo and crew a ship can transport, how much fuel is needed for a given space trip, and how much money must be set aside for maintenance.

The most fascinating rules are those pertaining to world building. Step-by-step instructions guide the referee through the creation of an entire planet, complete with terrain characteristics, native life-forms, and technological and cultural backgrounds. It's an elegant, logical system; animal life, for instance, derives from natural habitats (such as rain forests, bogs, and badlands) and ecological roles (such as grazing, gathering, and carrion-eating).

Over the years, nitpickers have questioned a number of the Traveller design decisions—wondering why, for instance, swords and other anachronistic weapons are included in the combat system, and why characters don't seem to grow or change much over the course of an extended campaign—but the objections are mostly trivial. A more pertinent question might be whether it's advisable to invest in Traveller material in the wake of Megatraveller. I'd reluctantly recommend that players new to both games forgo Traveller in favor of Megatraveller—the latter game is the one that will continue to receive official support from the publisher. But it's nearly impossible to go wrong with either; in the hands of a skilled referee, material from one game can be adapted to the other.

Buyer's Notes: Traveller has appeared in a number of formats. Basic Traveller is a boxed set of Books 1 to 3 (*Characters and Combat, Starships,* and *Worlds and Adventure*). Deluxe Traveller includes the three Basic Traveller books, along with Book 0 (*Introduction to Traveller*), a good introductory adventure, and a large star map. The hardback *Traveller Book* is the best buy, containing revised versions of Books 1 to 3 and the essential material from Book 0.

Suggested Supplements: There are a mountain of expansions, sourcebooks, and adventures available for Traveller. Here's a rundown of the best:

Expansions: Book 4, *Mercenary*, features advanced rules for character generation, combat, and military operations. Book 5, *High Guard*, details the Space Navy, including rules for advanced starship construction and space combat. Both are recommended.

Supplements: *1001 Characters* features pregenerated characters based on the Book 1 systems, and *Animal Encounters* lists pregenerated creatures derived from the Book 3 rules; considering the time required to create characters and creatures from scratch, referees will find both quite helpful. The Alien module series features detailed background information on a particular extraterrestrial race; all are terrific, but especially recommended are *Solomani* (fierce advocates of racial supremacy) and *Hivers* (starfish creatures who abhor physical violence).

Adventures: *Tarsus* is an ambitious boxed set that includes voluminous sourcebook material about the planet Tarsus along with a series of linked scenarios; it's an excellent introduction for newcomers and an exciting package for veterans. Other recommended adventures: *Murder on Arcturus Station* (a tense murder mystery), *Research Station Gamma* (a rescue mission at a biology station), *Prison Planet* (survival in an oppressive prison facility), and *Argon Gambit/Death Station* (two scenarios involving an unusual burglary and a deadly research ship). Ambitious referees should check out *The Traveller Adventure*, a 150-plus-page campaign involving a devious interstellar smuggling operation and a memorable villain.

Traveller: 2300**½

Complexity: Medium
Game Designers' Workshop, 1986

Set in the twenty-fourth century when exploration of other planets is just getting underway, Traveller: 2300 wedges itself between the postapocalyptic nightmare of Twilight: 2000 and the intergalactic intrigue of Megatraveller, two other science-fiction games by GDW. While technically set in a universe of its own, comparisons are inevitable, and Traveller: 2300 is a distant third, lacking both the focus of Twilight: 2000 and the rich texture of Megatraveller.

Following a nuclear war that caused the collapse of numerous Earth governments, a handful of countries are now engaged in fierce competition to establish colonies throughout the galaxy. Currently there are twenty-nine planets hosting fifty-five human colonies, three of which have won independence. China and France have taken a firm lead in the space race, while the United States struggles to hold third place, with Canada and Latin America nipping at her heels. The Player's Book presents the history, political geography, and technological breakthroughs of the setting in great detail, and while it's fun to read, there's also a lot of it, a burdensome amount of background to digest before players can get started.

Character creation is the game's most interesting feature, with basic attributes derived from a PC's homeworld. Characters from Core worlds are more cultured and civilized than their counterparts from the Frontier planets. While Frontier characters tend to be less educated, they're also stronger and tougher. Homeworld gravity levels also affect a character's physical build, resulting in the sturdy and able-bodied Mesomorphs, the towering and wiry Ectomorphs, and the short and solid Endomorphs. Skills, occupations, life levels, nationalities, and bank accounts round out the PCs, who then receive supplies from an imaginative catalog of weapons and equipment, ranging from Solar Powered Personal Fuel Processors to Quinn-Darlan MK 2-A2 Man-Portable Plasma Guns. Oddly, there's no procedure for awarding experience points, meaning that characters can't grow as they complete adventures; it's an annoying flaw in an otherwise solid set of rules.

The game mechanics are nowhere near as elegant as the character-creation rules, involving a task-resolution system that's both awkward and ambiguous. For each attempted action, the referee must determine its difficulty level, the applicable skills and attributes, the time required to complete the task, and any relevant modifiers, all of which require extensive number juggling. If the task fails, the referee consults yet another table to check for mishaps. The results are logical, but they take far too long to calculate and slow the game down to a crawl. The game suggests that referees build a "task library" in a notebook or computer file to help them navigate the system, but the designers should've provided something like this themselves or, better yet, some easier rules.

The combat rules are likewise complicated, less so for space battles than ground skirmishes, meaning that frazzled referees may be tempted to steer potential confrontations into outer space rather than struggle with the rules for man-to-man encounters. Well-written but convoluted rules for planet creation and spaceship design complete the game, and a brief scenario entitled "Tricolor's Shadow" introduces the players to the game universe in an adequate if perfunctory fashion.

Experienced players won't have any trouble handling all this, but those familiar with GDW's other science-fiction games may wonder why the game exists in the first place. All of the Traveller: 2300 material could've been covered in a Megatraveller sourcebook or even as an expansion to the Twilight: 2000 universe. The systems are adequate but nothing special, the premise is interesting but not spectacularly so. Traveller: 2300 isn't a bad game, it's just an unnecessary one. (Traveller: 2300 was revised and reissued as 2300 A.D., a superior effort in every way.)

Buyer's Note: Boxed set.

Suggested Supplements: There are no supplements specifically intended for Traveller: 2300, but all of the 2300 A.D. supplements are compatible with both games.

Tunnels and Trolls***

Complexity: Low
Flying Buffalo Inc., 1975

One of the earliest and most enduring fantasy RPGs, Tunnels and Trolls was introduced in 1975 as a simple alternative to Dungeons and Dragons. Though the game has received numerous refinements over the years (the fifth edition was published in 1979), designer Ken St. Andre has kept T&T charmingly straightforward, resisting the temptation to add more detail in order to win the favor of players used to Advanced Dungeons and Dragons, RuneQuest, and other sophisticated games. With its streamlined systems, T&T is the perfect choice for players who react to charts and tables like vampires react to crosses.

Most T&T mechanics are similar to those of Dungeons and Dragons. Players randomly determine six basic attributes for their characters; Strength, Intelligence, Dexterity, Constitution, and Charisma are not unlike their D&D counterparts, with the Luck attribute being the only significant departure. Experience points (here called Adventure Points), advancement levels, and other basic concepts will also be familiar to D&D players. Character classes are restricted to Warriors, Wizards, and Rogues (with Warrior-Wizards an option in rare instances). Most important, the tone of the game is the same as D&D; players roll up their characters, outfit them with weapons and armor, and send them into a medieval fantasy setting to battle monsters and scrounge for treasure.

The most notable difference between T&T and D&D are the magic and combat systems. To cast spells, a wizard expends Strength points; when all of his points have been spent, he can't cast spells again until he recovers his Strength. Not only are low-level wizards a bit more versatile than their D&D counterparts, they have easier access to high-level magic. Though hardly realistic, the combat system gives acceptable results; basically, opponents compare modified die-rolls, with the difference taken as damage by the low roller. Monsters have only one significant attribute, a "Monster Rating" that determines their ferocity and their combat strength; with only one rating, the monsters aren't particular interesting, but they're easy to run.

Of course, nitpickers will have a field day looking for holes, and there are plenty to find. Combat is painfully abstract; there's no meaningful difference between battling a giant spider and a proficient warrior. Strength, Intelligence, and other attributes can increase to absurdly high levels, as they grow with each new level and there are no apparent limits. Spell effects are imprecise, open to wide interpretation from the referee. But for those intimidated by more difficult fantasy RPGs (which includes everything from Dungeons and Dragons on up), and for those who can handle the amount of improvisation demanded by a game this loose, Tunnels and Trolls is an excellent choice.

Buyer's Note: Boxed set.

Suggested Supplements: With its simple rules, Tunnels and Trolls is a natural for solo play, and the solitaire T&T supplements are among the best of their kind. Best adventures: *Arena of Khazan* (gladiator combat), *Sea of Mystery* (ocean adventures), and *Catacombs of the Bear Cult* (bizarre lycanthropes).

2300 A.D.***

Complexity: Medium
Game Designers' Workshop, 1988

Understandably, many players assumed that Traveller: 2300 was a spin-off of the Traveller game. But it wasn't; Traveller: 2300 existed in its own universe with its own background and its own rules. To clear up the confusion, GDW withdrew Traveller: 2300, gave it a new name, and while they were at it, added some new material and refined the old. It's a dramatic improvement; 2300 A.D. can now hold its own against GDW's other science-fiction RPGs, including Megatraveller and Twilight: 2000.

All of the basics of Traveller: 2300 are intact. The Chinese, French, and American governments remain in tense competition for interstellar colonization, the history of which is explained in entertaining background notes. Character creation is still the game's highlight, which is slightly more flexible than in the original game. It's also been expanded to include a desperately needed experience system, allowing characters to improve their old skills as well as learning new ones. A nice touch is the addition of Renown, which rates the PCs for public service and notoriety, and affects the ways in which they interact with NPCs.

Unfortunately, 2300 A.D. carries over some of the problems of the original game, most notably the clunky task-resolution system. Though it's been streamlined somewhat, it's still convoluted and far too chart-heavy, requiring the referee to navigate a river of charts and formulas and second-guess the ambiguous results. Combat is likewise number-heavy, reducing combat encounters to slow-motion math contests where frustrated players twiddle their thumbs while the referee gropes for the applicable modifiers.

Still, the strong points far outweigh the deficiencies. It's a sharp-looking product, attractively illustrated and lucidly written. Helpful sections on running and designing adventures support the significantly expanded sourcebook material, and the improved organization makes 2300 A.D. a lot easier to learn than Traveller: 2300. Designers Marc Miller, Frank Chadwick, Timothy Brown, and Lester Smith turned a fair game into a great one, an impressive accomplishment.

Buyer's Note: Boxed set.

Suggested Supplements: The definitive 2300 A.D. sourcebook, *Colonial Atlas*, covers the history, cultures, personalities, and governments of twenty-nine space colonies. Unmatched in its vivid presentation of alien worlds, *Colonial Atlas* makes an excellent source of ideas for other science-fiction games. The *Aurore Sourcebook* and *Nyotekundu Sourcebook* examine specific worlds in detail; both are recommended. Also excellent is the *Kafer Sourcebook*, which explores the culture, physiology, and philosophy of the evil Kafer aliens, the primary villains of 2300 A.D. The best adventures: *Mission Arcturus* (a battle against the Kafers in a dangerous research station) and *Ranger* (a war of the nomadic Eber aliens involving the Texas Rangers).

Twerps**½

Complexity: Low
Reindeer Games, 1987

Maybe "the world's easiest role-playing system" was intended as a joke, but not only does it work as a game (albeit on its own modest terms), it cleverly introduces the fundamentals of role-playing in a couple of pages. PCs are rated for one characteristic only—Strength—which is determined by a roll of a ten-sided die. The action takes place on a hex map where one hex equals 10 feet and one round of combat equals 10 seconds; players move their character counters a number of hexes equal to their Strength. To resolve an attack, opponents roll a die and add their Strength scores; if the attacker wins, the defender subtracts a variable number of points from his Strength. The referee assigns a Difficulty Level from 1 to 10 for all other actions; if the player's roll exceeds the Difficulty Level, the action succeeds. Players can try out the system in an introductory adventure entitled "Watery Depths" (map and counters included). Obviously, Twerps isn't going to hold anyone's attention for more than a few minutes, but those few minutes are actually kind of fun.

Buyer's Notes: Plastic bag, containing the rulebook and play aids. (If you can't find it locally, try writing for information to Gamescience, 1512 30th Avenue, Gulfport, Mississippi 39501.)

Suggested Supplements: "Twerps Magic" adds a magic system; as silly and fun as the original game. Other supplements are available, but after "Twerps Magic" the joke gets old pretty quick.

Twilight: 2000***

Complexity: Medium
Game Designers' Workshop, 1984

Skillfully combining military role-playing and an after-the-holocaust setting, Twilight: 2000 is a rare example of a game that's satisfying for both role-players and tactical wargamers. The game takes place a few years after the onset of World War III, casting the players in the roles of NATO soldiers lost in Poland. Isolated from friendly troops and presumed dead, the PCs must fight their way through enemy territory and find their way back to the United States. With nary a laser beam or bug-eyed monster in sight, Twilight: 2000 is realism in the extreme, with survival the order of the day.

The character-generation system is the game's weakest feature. Though it produces realistic, usable characters, the procedure takes forever, involving innumerable modifiers and convoluted formulas, even when determining statistics as trivial as a PC's age (the formula goes something like [Number of Months In Combat/12] + Result of Education Roll + Some Modifier + 8). A simple character can take two hours to create, time that would've been better spent trekking across Poland. The skill system is much more streamlined, with PCs assigned a number of Skill Points to be spent on various military, educational, and background specialties. Generally, the more points spent, the higher the level of skill in a particular area. Percentile rolls determine if skills are used successfully, and levels can be improved as the PC acquires experience.

Twilight: 2000 features an exceptionally clean combat system that strikes a nice balance between realism and playability. Essentially, players make skill rolls to see if an attack is successful, modified by such factors as weapon type, range, and rate of fire. Secondary rolls determine hit locations and the amount of damage inflicted. To simulate the possibility of soldiers panicking under fire, each character is rated for Coolness Under Pressure. The higher the rating, the longer he'll freeze before reacting. The lethality of certain weapons is fudged somewhat, and characters seem to be able to take an excessive amount of damage before dropping dead, but these compromises with reality enhance the game's excitement level and are therefore forgivable. Add slick, cohesive rules for vehicles, chemical warfare, and minefields, and you've got a first-rate set of mechanics, one of the most realistic and exciting combat systems ever to grace an RPG.

Military operations usually take a backseat to the problems of day-to-day survival, a situation that accounts for much of the game's appeal. Twilight: 2000 paints a gloomy picture of the future, where water is in short supply, radiation-crazed looters roam the streets, and a tank of gas is more precious than a bag of diamonds. With an excellent premise supported by well-drawn rules from designer Frank Chadwick, Twilight: 2000 is easily the best of the postapocalyptic RPGs.

Buyer's Note: Boxed set. Watch for a 1990 revision.

Suggested Supplements: Twilight: 2000 supplements tend to feature general guidelines for adventures rather than detailed scenarios, meaning that the referee must do a fair amount of work to develop the encounters and storylines himself. Still, the supplements supply plenty of material to work with, including colorful backgrounds, engaging NPCs, and beautifully rendered maps. The best of them: *Ruins of Warsaw* (an urban battle with cutthroat marauders), *Free City of Krakow* (recovery of secret documents), and *Going Home* (a chance to return to the U.S.). The ambitious Last Sub series (including the *Last Submarine, Mediterranean Cruise,* and *Boomer* adventures) forms the basis of an involving campaign concerning the journeys of the last American submarine.

Valley of the Pharaohs*½

Complexity: Low/Medium
Palladium Books, 1983

Ancient Egypt seems like a good setting for a role-playing game, but you couldn't tell it from Valley of the Pharaohs, an unattractive, underdeveloped effort that barely qualifies as a nice try.

Players roll on a Caste Chart to determine if their characters belong to the Nobility, Clergy, or Bureaucracy, or if they're ordinary Commoners. They then determine their PCs' occupations (Soldier, Priest, Scholar, Merchant, or Thief); the occupation indicates the number of skills a PC can learn. It's an unsatisfying system, producing characters that are colorless (there's no meaningful difference between the occupations aside from their skills), unbalanced (it's possible for a Nobleman to have as few as four skills, while a lowly Commoner could have eight), and puzzling (why does a Bureaucrat have an Intellect bonus?).

Worse, Valley of the Pharaohs doesn't begin to exploit its setting. Though the game provides reasonably extensive sections on Egyptian culture and history, all of it could be found in an afternoon at a library, and there's not a clue as to how it should be organized into a cohesive adventure. The Encounter Tables offer only dull, skimpy suggestions on the order of "man falling off boat" and "party member gets pickpocketed." The skill choices are run-of-the-mill, and the weapon lists feature nothing more exotic than spears and swords. And out of all the occupations possible in an Egyptian setting, what's a Thief doing here? With minor exceptions, Valley of the Pharaohs could be describing a medieval fantasy world or, for that matter, any ancient era with a little magic tossed in.

The combat rules fill less than two pages and, like the other game systems, are woefully inadequate for a game with such lofty ambitions. There are some interesting magic items, especially the ushabti figures (animated statues that can perform manual labor), but they hardly compensate for this mundane treatment of a fascinating topic.

Buyer's Note: Boxed set.

Villains and Vigilantes***

Complexity: Medium
Fantasy Games Unlimited, First Edition: 1979; Revised
Edition: 1983

The appearance of Villains and Vigilantes in 1979 introduced a brand-new RPG concept—comic-book superheroes. In spite of its clunky systems and less than stellar graphics, Villains and Vigilantes met with unreserved enthusiasm—until the appearance of more sophisticated superhero games like Champions made it seem crude by comparison.

But V&V came back with a vengeance in 1983, with a completely revised edition by designers Jeff Dee and Jack Herman that cleaned up the ambiguities of the original while losing not a whit of its charm. Though a flood of superhero games have appeared since then, V&V continues to hold its own, thanks to its tongue-in-cheek approach and some genuinely inspired concepts.

The most notable V&V concept—and certainly the most no-torious—is the character-generation system. Instead of basing characters exclusively on die-rolls or point allocation, Villains and Vigilantes characters are based on the players themselves. If Rick Swan is playing the game, Rick assigns himself ratings for Strength, Intelligence, Charisma, and other basic attributes based on his real-life characteristics. The referee also has a say in these determinations, which can make for some interesting negotiations; if Rick believes he has an Intelligence of 18, the referee may be obliged in the interests of fair play (and common sense) to lower it to a more realistic level of 3 or 4.

Superpowers are determined more or less at random by roll-ing on various tables; in addition to such commonplace abilities (for comics, that is) as Wings and Size Change, there are also a good number of oddball choices, like Dimension Travel (com-parable to time traveling, except that parallel Earths are in-voked, so characters can't actually change the past) and Cosmic Awareness (which gives the PC access to the referee's informa-tion). Though some players object to this system, because it inhibits the creation of customized characters, it strikes me as appropriate to the source material, as Spider-Man, Superman, and a host of other memorable characters were essentially flukes of nature (although it's true that this system doesn't account for self-created types like Batman and Iron Man).

The rest of the game, sadly, lacks the elegance of the charac-ter-creation rules. Combat is heavy on dice-rolling and number-juggling. The vehicle rules are interesting but incomplete. The effects of Charisma are unclear, as are the rules for reaction modifiers and loyalty.

But though they're frustrating, V&V's problems are relatively minor and are unlikely to prevent determined players from en-joying one of the best superhero games on the market. V&V is easier than Champions, more frivolous than Superworld, and less rigid than Heroes Unlimited. For those with a little role-playing experience under their belts, Villains and Vigilantes is a terrific introduction to superhero games.

Buyer's Notes: The game is available both as a paperback rulebook and as a boxed set that contains the rulebook along with a referee's screen and an introductory adventure. As the price difference is only a few dollars, take the plunge and go for the box.

Suggested Supplements: The adventure supplements are a mixed bag, frequently suffering from underdevelopment and weak plots; proceed with caution. The best of the bunch: *Death Duel with the Destroyers* and its sequel, *The Island of Dr. Apocalypse; For the Greater Good* (a surprisingly serious treatment of prejudice), and *Enter the Dragon's Claw* (a well-paced Oriental scenario).

Warhammer****
....

    Complexity: Medium/High
    Games Workshop, 1986

A grim, richly textured fantasy RPG, Warhammer is a triumph of design, brilliantly written and beautifully packaged by British authors Richard Halliwell, Rick Priestley, Graeme Davis, Jim Bambra, and Phil Gallagher. Set in the Old World, a vast area of several continents based on Middle Age Europe, a corrupt humanity struggles against the Gods of Chaos and their degenerate minions for control of all creation. Should Chaos prevail, then "all life will decay into a seething mass of protoplasm in which lost and screaming souls float helplessly. . . ." Yechh.

Players begin by creating Character Profiles for their PCs, a collection of fourteen basic attributes including Weapon Skill, Will Power, and Dexterity. Though only four races are available (human, elf, dwarf, and halfling), players can select from nearly seventy careers, ranging from the mundane (Herdsman and Servant) to the exotic (Herbalist and Troll Slayer) to the bizarre (Pit Fighter and Rat Catcher). Each career modifies the PC's attributes (Rat Catchers add 10 to their Weapon Skill, Pit Fighters add 10 to their Dexterity) and suggests appropriate skills (Arcane Language and Herb Lore for the Herbalist, Dodge Blow and Street Fighter for the Troll Slayer). Additionally, each PC receives a certain number of Fate Points that can be spent during the game to bail him out of otherwise fatal situations. It's a terrific system; the sheer number of careers ensures variety, and their vivid descriptions make them easy to play.

Most game mechanics involve the concept of "tests," a simple procedure where the referee decides which skill applies to a particular action, the player rolls percentile dice, and the referee adjudicates the outcome by comparing the die-roll to the skill level. Combat is complicated, but not excessively so; the referee determines which characters strike first, players declare their actions and roll dice, and the referee assesses damage for all the participants. The magic system combines spells levels (similar to the ones used in Advanced Dungeons and Dragons) with magic points (not unlike those of RuneQuest). Casting a spell requires the expenditure of magic points; the higher the level, the more points that must be spent. There are dozens of interesting spells, augmented by an imaginative selection of magic items that includes dawnstones, runes, and wands. The rulebook concludes with an inspired section on religions, a thorough history of the Old World, and an exciting introductory adventure.

Barely five years old, Warhammer is already a certified fantasy classic, a status shared only by Advanced Dungeons and Dragons and RuneQuest. But where AD&D and RuneQuest are hopeful and majestic, Warhammer is dark and cynical. This is a game where PCs can become alcoholics and manic depressives, swords rip muscles and splinter bones, Bloodsedges and Snotlings lurk in the shadows, and bad guys worship the Lord of Murder. If this sounds appealing, you're in for the time of your life—in its treatment of dark fantasy, Warhammer is without peer.

Buyer's Note: Warhammer is available in both hardback and paperback versions. As both include the same material, thrifty shoppers can opt for the paperback.

Suggested Supplements: "The Enemy Within" and "Shadows Over Bogenhafen," available together in the *Warhammer Campaign* hardback, form the basis for an exciting, exquisitely detailed campaign. Better yet is *Something Rotten in Kislev*, a brilliant series of linked adventures that blends humor, high adventure, and interpersonal relationships; a state-of-the-art fantasy supplement.

Wild West**

....

Complexity: Medium
Fantasy Games Unlimited, 1981

Wild West attempts to simulate adventures set in the American Old West circa 1850, but it's only a nice try. Though the rules are basically sound, poor production and a baffling lack of background material leaves would-be cowboys with only a vague idea of how to put together a satisfying Western campaign.

The game's best feature is its clever character-generation system. Players can take the roles of a wide variety of Western characters, including cattle barons, gamblers, and lawmen, each with his own goals and motivations. Players select skills for their characters from a menu of about fifty choices, ranging from the all-important Marksmanship to the relatively useless but colorful Weather Forecasting and Mule Skinning. Because characters earn Experience Points for achieving their individual goals, the stage is set for some decidedly bizarre adventures; a frontier dentist, for instance, earns points for extracting teeth, while a shepherd earns points for keeping his flock intact. Also nice is the task-resolution system, which essentially boils all actions down to a single chart; by cross-referencing a character's skill rating (for instance, his Locksmithing ability) with the difficulty rating of an attempted action (such as picking an especially formidable iron lock), you're shown the chance of success (the character has an 80 percent chance of successfully picking the lock).

Unfortunately, the rest of the game is a hodge-podge of underdeveloped ideas. The combat system is pointlessly complicated, the equipment lists are colorless and inadequately detailed. Barroom brawls and main street showdowns are standard fare in Western scenarios, but they're handled here like an afterthought. Worst of all, there's virtually no background mate-

rial—nothing about Doc Holiday, Jesse James, or other Western stars; no descriptions of Dodge City, Little Big Horn, or
any other notable locales; and only a few skimpy paragraphs
about Indians.

The awkward organization (combat rules are scattered all over
the book) and hand-drawn maps don't do much to enhance the
game's appeal. Western aficionados might be able to dig out a
few interesting character generation ideas, but casual players
will find Wild West to be more frustrating than fun.

Buyer's Note: Boxed set.

Suggested Supplements: Trouble at Widow's Peak, a generic
shoot-'em-up that's reasonably exciting, is as good as it gets.

Witch Hunt***

....

Complexity: Medium
Statcom Simulations Inc., 1983

A forgotten gem, Witch Hunt is a fascinating concept, superbly
executed, that has fallen out of print, unfortunately. Set during
the Salem witch trials circa 1692, the game re-creates the super-
stitious hysteria of the era with impressive historical detail and
some extremely clever rules.

Unlike most RPGs, where cooperation is the name of the
game, Witch Hunt players are divided into two teams. Some
assume the roles of Witches, while the rest become the law-
and-order obsessed Magistrates. The Witches have access to a
variety of spells, including Withering, Tanglefoot, and Pole
Riding (interestingly, these are the same spells that actual
"witches" of the era were accused of using). With the Witches
operating in secret, it's up to the Magistrates to gather enough
evidence to take them to trial. The Magistrates interview suspects, search for incriminating evidence, and employ a special
witch-finding device called the Staff of Law that detects the
magical aura radiated by those corrupted by evil forces. A set of
ingenious rules handles the legal showdown with suspected
Witches. Broken down into Search, Arrest, Interrogation, and

Trial segments, the legal rules give the Magistrates ample opportunity to prove their accusations and the Witches plenty of chances to squirm out of them. Victory points are awarded to individual players for such activities as discovering evidence and issuing arrests (for Magistrates) and eluding arrest and causing trouble (for Witches).

The game is laced with humor, which prevents the proceedings from becoming too grim, and even though there's virtually no combat, the referee, in the guise of the Town Crier, keeps the players on their toes with a continual stream of rumors, announcements, and startling proclamations. ("The wife of Edwin Luce was sighted conversing with black crows on the evening of the Sabbath!") Unfortunately, Witch Hunt never found an audience and soon faded from sight. Until designers Paul Baader and Roger Buckelew find a new publisher, the original edition is worth seeking out.

Buyer's Note: Boxed set.

Suggested Supplement: Look for *A Tyme of Darkness*, an interesting adventure that expands the scope of the game and clarifies some of its murkier concepts.

Worlds of Wonder***

Complexity: Low
Chaosium, Inc., 1982

Out of print and tough to find, Worlds of Wonder may be worth the search for beginners, as it's not only one of the best introductory RPGs ever published, but it also introduces concepts pertinent to three distinct genres. The box includes four books, the first of which, *Basic Role Playing*, features general rules for character creation and other basic mechanics. The remaining three books each detail a specific environment and add rules for skills, combat techniques, and background material appropriate to each setting. *Magic World* is a fantasy environment comparable to basic Dungeons and Dragons; enough spells, monsters, and treasure items are included to get an introductory campaign off to a rea-

240

....

sonably good start. *Future World* is a poor man's Traveller, a superficial treatment of a high-tech future that's heavy on planetary exploration but skimps on space travel. *Super World* is the best of the three, an entertaining and exciting introduction to comic-book-hero role-playing (this material, revised and expanded, later became the basis for the Superworld game). There are better introductory games available in every genre covered here (Dungeons and Dragons for fantasy, Marvel Super Heroes for comic books, and—though both are more demanding than Future World—Star Wars or Star Trek), but as a user-friendly overview, Worlds of Wonder is an excellent package.

Buyer's Note: Boxed set.

Year of the Phoenix**½

Complexity: Medium
Fantasy Games Unlimited Inc., 1987

This is a difficult game to discuss, because much of its appeal depends on keeping the players in the dark about the details of the game world. But without giving too much away, it's safe to say that Year of the Phoenix takes place in the future with players assuming the roles of elite space soldiers charged with protecting the extraterrestrial interests of the United States. The character system includes rules for generating detailed histories and personalities, producing well-rounded PCs that are as fun to create as they are to play. Skill Spheres suggest appropriate talents and specialties, and the background notes are sufficient to help the referee set up a modest campaign.

Though the basic mechanics are simple, they're smothered in an avalanche of charts, tables, and numbers that makes the game difficult to master, especially for the referee who has to keep track of it all. And the big surprises aren't all that surprising—they're actually sort of silly. Still, Year of the Phoenix contains enough good ideas to make the effort worthwhile for science-fiction role-players looking for an offbeat alternative.

Buyer's Note: Boxed set.

Ysgarth***

....

Complexity: High
Ragnarok Enterprises, 1982

Excessive complexity in RPGs usually means tons of rules, not more depth. Ysgarth is a pleasant exception. Though it's as complicated as, say, Chivalry and Sorcery or Rolemaster, Ysgarth uses its dense rules to create a rich background with vivid characters. Designed by David Nalle and published by the relatively obscure Ragnarok Enterprises, Ysgarth may not be the "revolution in role-playing" as claimed on the cover, but it's certainly one of the hobby's best-kept secrets.

The heart of the system is the first rulebook, *Rolecraft*, which details character creation and combat. Players distribute attribute points to a dozen primary characteristics; along with the typical Strength, Dexterity, and Intelligence, there are some unusual additions, including Zeal, which measures the intensity of a character's moral principles and devotion to his religion. Nearly twenty secondary characteristics, among them Size Class, Attack Rating, and Hit Points, are derived from the primary characteristics by complicated formulas; for example, the formula for Attack Rating is $[2 \times \text{Intelligence}] + [2 \times \text{Dexterity}] + \text{Strength} + \text{Agility} - \text{Size Class}/10$. The rules for skills and training are no less complicated, but they're quite inventive. Skills are purchased according to fixed costs, and the number of skills available to a character is limited only by the number of Skill Points he's willing to invest. Previously purchased skills can modify the costs of new skills, as can the character's social and cultural background; characters from Kernwyk are exceptional Tinsmiths and Net Fishers, while those from Marmar excel at Logistics and Geography. The skill lists include a staggering number of choices, ranging from Cartography and Storytelling to Gymnastics and Clam Digging, all concisely explained and neatly integrated into a smooth system of task resolution.

Admittedly, there's a lot of record-keeping. Combat requires the spending of Activity Points to execute an attack, modified by the target's Defense Rating points. Characters receive Karma Points for good deeds and Dharma Points for bad ones. Renown Points measure a character's fame, Influence Points reflect his clout. Deity Influence Points can be spent to gain favors from his church and his gods. Spellcasting—detailed in the *Spellcraft* book—involves the expenditure of Mana Points, Activity Points, and Fatigue Points. But in spite of the mountain of information, it's all clearly presented and it works very well.

The third rulebook, *Worldcraft*, ties the game together with lucid explanations of customs, races, economics, and other background material. Ysgarth is not a game for beginners in any sense—even experienced players will have their hands full with rules as dense as these—but the diligent will be rewarded with a tremendously satisfying game.

Buyer's Notes: Trade paperback. The *Rolecraft*, *Spellcraft*, and *Worldcraft* books are available separately, but all are needed to play the game.

Suggested Supplements: The Wine of the Moon is a good place to start a Ysgarth campaign, as it features some helpful rules clarifications and expansions, along with a top-notch introductory scenario.

Appendixes

. . . .

Recommendations
. . . .

My favorite games are listed below. The choices for best adventures and supplements are intentionally eclectic, with no RPG system represented more than once on each list. All lists are alphabetical; rank on each list has no significance.

THE AUTHOR'S TEN FAVORITE GAMES
 1. Advanced Dungeons and Dragons, TSR Inc.
 2. Call of Cthulhu, Chaosium Inc.
 3. GURPS, Steve Jackson Games
 4. Megatraveller, Game Designers' Workshop
 5. Oriental Adventures, TSR Inc.
 6. Paranoia, West End Games
 7. Pendragon, Chaosium Inc.
 8. RuneQuest, The Avalon Hill Game Company
 9. Talislanta, Bard Games
10. Warhammer, Games Workshop Ltd.

THE TEN BEST GAMES FOR BEGINNERS
1. Bullwinkle and Rocky, TSR Inc.
2. DC Heroes, Mayfair Games
3. Dungeons and Dragons, TSR Inc.
4. Ghostbusters, West End Games
5. Marvel Super Heroes, TSR Inc.
6. Prince Valiant, Chaosium Inc.
7. Space: 1889, Game Designers' Workshop
8. Toon, Steve Jackson Games
9. Top Secret/S.I., TSR Inc.
10. Tunnels and Trolls, Flying Buffalo Inc.

THE TEN BEST ROLE-PLAYING ADVENTURES
1. *Five Coins for a Kingdom* by Allen Varney (for Dungeons and Dragons, TSR Inc.)
2. *Griffin Island* by Rudy Kraft, Paul Jacquays, Greg Stafford, and Sandy Petersen (for RuneQuest, The Avalon Hill Game Company)
3. *Live and Let Die* by Gerald Klug (for James Bond 007, Victory Games/The Avalon Hill Game Company)
4. *Masks of Nyarlathotep* by Larry DiTillio (for Call of Cthulhu, Chaosium Inc.)
5. *Ravenloft* by Tracy and Laura Hickman (for Advanced Dungeons and Dragons, TSR Inc.)
6. *Scavenger Hunt* by Brad Freeman (for Star Wars, West End Games)
7. *Something Rotten in Kislev* by Ken Rolston (for Warhammer, Games Workshop Ltd.)
8. *Tournament of Dreams* by Les Brooks, Sam Shirley, and Greg Stafford (for Pendragon, Chaosium Inc.)
9. *The Traveller Adventure* by Frank Chadwick, John Harshman, J. Andrew Keith, Marc Miller, and Loren Wiseman (for Traveller, Game Designers' Workshop)
10. *The Yellow Clearance Black Box Blues* by John M. Ford (for Paranoia, West End Games Inc.)

THE TEN BEST ROLE-PLAYING SUPPLEMENTS

1. *Covert Operations Source Book, Volumes 1 and 2* by John Prados (for Top Secret/S.I., TSR Inc.)
2. *Cthulhu by Gaslight* by William Barton (for Call of Cthulhu, Chaosium Inc.)
3. The Gazetteer Series; in particular, *The Principalities of Glantri* by Bruce Heard, *The Northern Reaches* by Ken Rolston, and *The Five Shires* by Ed Greenwood (for Dungeons and Dragons, TSR Inc.)
4. *Gods of Glorantha* by Sandy Petersen, Greg Stafford, Steve Perrin, and Charlie Krank (for RuneQuest, The Avalon Hill Game Company)
5. *GURPS Space* by Steve Jackson and William Barton (for GURPS, Steve Jackson Games)
6. *Kafer Sourcebook* by William H. Keith Jr. (for 2300 A.D., Game Designers' Workshop)
7. *Lands of Mystery* by Aaron Allston (for Justice Inc., Hero Games)
8. *Manual of the Planes* by Jeff Grubb (for Advanced Dungeons and Dragons, TSR Inc.)
9. *Q Manual* by Greg Gorden (for James Bond 007, Victory Games/The Avalon Hill Game Company)
10. *Star Wars Sourcebook* by Bill Slavicsek and Curtis Smith (for Star Wars, West End Games)

Addresses

....

Following is a partial list of game publisher addresses, including most of the majors along with many of the smaller ones. The inclusion of any publisher on this list is not meant to be an implied or implicit endorsement, or a guarantee of the quality of either the product sold or the services rendered; they're provided as possible resources to the reader.

Adventurers' Guild
401 New Castle Road
Marshalltown, IA 50158

The Avalon Hill Game
   Company
4517 Harford Road
Baltimore, MD 21214

Bard Games
PO Box 7729
Greenwich, CT 06836

Blacksburg Tactical Research
   Center
1925 Airy Circle
Richmond, VA 23233

Chaosium Inc.
950-A 56th Street
Oakland, CA 94608

Columbia Games Inc.
PO Box 8006
Blaine, WA 98230

Creative Encounters
1314 South York Road
Gastonia, NC 28052

Dream Park Corporation
4251 Ponderosa Court
Boulder, CO 80301

Empire Wargames
PO Box 94
Marne, MI 49435

Escape Ventures
PO Box 4330
Virginia Beach, VA 23454

Fantasy Games Unlimited,
    Inc.
PO Box 1082
Gilbert, AZ 85234

FASA Corporation
PO Box 6930
Chicago, IL 60680

Flying Buffalo
PO Box 1467
Scottsdale, AZ 85252

Games Designers Workshop
PO Box 1646
Bloomington, IL 61702

Godiva Productions
1003 Springside Way
Louisville, KY 40223

Iron Crown Enterprises
PO Box 1605
Charlottesville, VA 22902

Steve Jackson Games
PO Box 18957
Austin, TX 78760

Kingslayer Publications
PO Box 441
Lathrup Village, MI 48076

Leading Edge Games
PO Box 70669
Pasadena, CA 91107

Lion Rampant
3264 Nature's Walk
Suwanee, GA 30174

Mayfair Games Inc.
PO Box 48539
Niles, IL 60648

Palladium Books
5926 Lonyo
Detroit, MI 48210

Ragnarok Enterprises
1402 21st St. NW
Washington, D.C. 20036

Rapport Games
1031 E. Battlefield, Suite
    114B
Springfield, MO 65807

Star Childe Publications
44567 Pinetree Dr.
Plymouth, MI 48170

Stellar Games
PO Box 156
Swanton, OH 43558

Stellar Gaming Workshop
105 Great Oak Drive
Annapolis, MD 21403

R. Talsorian Games Inc.
PO Box 7356
Berkeley, CA 94707

Task Force Games
14922 Calvert Street
Van Nuys, CA 91411

T.C. International
4005 West River Dr. N.E.,
PO Box 188
Comstock Park, MI 49321

Thoughts and Images
PO Box 15168
Portland, OR 97215

TSR Inc.
PO Box 756
Lake Geneva, WI 53147

21st Century Games
587-F North Ventu Park Rd.
#806
Newbury Park, CA 91320

Waterford Publishing House
  Ltd.
Box 3742, Main Post Office
Vancouver, B.C., Canada V6B
  3Z1

West End Games
RD 3, Box 2345
Honesdale, PA 18431

Whit Productions Inc.
PO Box 1397
Murray, KY 42071

Glossary

. . . .

Like many hobbies, role-playing has its own language. The definitions of some of the most commonly used terms follow. This is by no means a complete list, nor are the terms used in the same way in all games.

Adventure: The story in which the PCs are participating. Published adventures are available for most games. Creative referees can also write their own.

Alignment: A general indication of a PC's moral outlook. The most basic alignments are Good, Evil, and Neutral. If a PC is of Good alignment, the controlling player knows the PC is supposed to behave like a hero.

Attributes: A PC's basic characteristics, such as Strength, Intelligence, and Dexterity. Unlike skills, attributes are considered to be inherent rather than acquired; these are the characteristics a PC is "born" with.

Campaign: A series of linked adventures. Like a soap opera, a campaign can continue indefinitely.

Character Generation: The process of creating a PC or NPC.

Class: A PC's career or occupation. It can also refer to a PC's race.

252
....

Components: The physical parts of a role-playing game, including books, dice, and maps.

Damage: The amount of injury taken by a successfully attacked victim, usually expressed as a number of lost hit points.

Designer: The author of a game.

Encounter: A single scene of an adventure, typically involving a meeting with an NPC, a battle with an adversary, or the exploration of a new locale.

Expansion: A supplement featuring advanced rules for a particular RPG.

Experience: A numerical rating of a PC's success in an adventure, usually expressed in terms of points. Experience points are awarded for finding treasure, destroying monsters, and completing quests. They can be exchanged for better skills and higher levels.

Game Universe: See *game world*.

Game World: The setting of an RPG. The game world of Marvel Super Heroes is described in Marvel Comics; the game world of Call of Cthulhu is described in the writings of H. P. Lovecraft.

Grid Map: A type of game map divided into squares or hexes to facilitate the movement of playing pieces.

Hit Points: A numerical rating that indicates a PC's health. A PC with 20 hit points is harder to kill than one with 5 hit points. A PC reduced to zero hit points is usually considered to be dead.

Initiative: Who goes first in a combat round. A PC who's won the initiative (usually the result of a die-roll) decides what action he'll take before any of the other PCs get to decide theirs.

Level: A general rating of a PC's abilities. A PC of level 2 is stronger, has more hit points, and has a wider range of talents than a PC of level 1. Typically, PCs advance in levels by acquiring experience points.

Mechanics: Another name for the rules. See *system*.

Miniatures: A type of wargame using toy soldiers and miniature vehicles for playing pieces. Role-players sometimes use miniature figures to represent their PCs. Miniatures are usually made of lead or plastic.

Modifier: A number added to or subtracted from a dice-roll.

Module: See *supplement.*

Nonplayer Character: NPC. An imaginary character controlled by the referee.

NPC: See *nonplayer character.*

Referee: The impartial judge of a role-playing game.

Party: A group of player-characters.

PC: See *player-character.*

Percentile Dice: Dice that generate random numbers between 1 and 100. Usually, two ten-sided dice function as percentile dice. One of the dice provides the first digit of a two-digit number, the other supplies the second digit.

Playability: How easily a game plays. A game that is slow and sluggish is said to have low playability.

Player-Character: PC. The imaginary character controlled by a player. The flesh-and-blood person sitting in the chair is the player; the player-character exists only on paper and in the player's head.

Pregenerated Character: A ready-to-play PC or NPC, complete with skills, attributes, and statistics. Pregenerated characters are often provided in sourcebooks and published adventures.

Prerolled Character: See *pregenerated character.*

RPG: Role-playing game.

Saving Throw: A dice-roll made by a player to prevent or reduce damage to his PC. For instance, if the PC accidentally eats a poison cookie, the referee may require the player to make a saving throw. If the right number comes up, the PC suffers no damage.

Scenario: See *adventure.*

Skills: A PC's special talents or areas of expertise, such as Archery, Swimming, and Occult Knowledge. Unlike attributes, skills aren't considered to be inherent; instead, they're acquired through study and practice.

Sourcebook: A supplement containing background material relevant to a particular game or particular genre of games. Animals, weapons, personalities, locations, and cultures are typical sourcebook subjects.

Supplement: A general category of books containing support material for a specific game. Expansions, sourcebooks, and adventures are among the types of RPG supplements.

Staging: Refers to how a referee explains an encounter to the players; it's similar to the way a director presents the scene of a play.

Statistics: The numerical ratings that define a PC, NPC, or monster.

System: A collection of rules, usually concerning one particular element of the game, such as the combat system or the character-generation system.

Tactical Wargame: One of three general categories of wargames, based on the scale of play. In a tactical wargame, a single playing piece usually represents a single soldier or vehicle. In an operational wargame, a single piece represents an entire battalion or division. In a strategic wargame, a piece represents a unit as large as an army group. Role-playing games are almost exclusively tactical; when playing pieces (or miniatures) are used, each piece represents a single character.

Wargame: A military board game, usually based on a specific historical battle.

Subject Index
··················

For quick reference and purposes of comparison, all of the games included in this book have been sorted according to subject and are listed below. Most of the subjects are self-explanatory, but a few should be clarified: *Anthropomorphic* games feature humanoid animals in a futuristic setting. *Universal* games can be adapted to any genre or setting. *Cyberpunk* is a school of science-fiction featuring high-tech vigilantes, cybernetic implants, and monolithic corporations. The *postapocalyptic* category includes games set in a future world devastated by nuclear war or some other disaster. Many of the games defy categorization, so please consider the following to be a general guide only.

ANTHROPOMORPHICS
    Albedo
    Teenage Mutant Ninja Turtles

COPS AND ROBBERS
    Crimefighter
    Gangbusters
    Gangster

CYBERPUNK
Cyberpunk
Cyberspace
Shadowrun

ESPIONAGE
Danger International
Espionage
James Bond 007
Mercenaries, Spies, and Private Eyes
Top Secret
Top Secret/S.I.

FANTASY
Advanced Dungeons and Dragons
Arcanum
Arduin Adventure
Ars Magica
Chivalry and Sorcery
Conan
Darksword Adventures
DragonQuest
Dungeons and Dragons
Elfquest
Empire of the Petal Throne
Fantasy Hero
Fantasy Wargaming
Hawkmoon
High Fantasy
Ironhedge
Kabal
Lands of Adventure
Lords of Creation
Man, Myth, and Magic
The Mega Role-Playing System
Middle Earth Role Playing
Palladium Role-Playing Game
Pendragon

Powers and Perils
Prince Valiant
Rolemaster
RuneQuest
Sandman
Stormbringer
Swordbearer
Talislanta
Thieves' Guild
Tunnels and Trolls
Valley of the Pharaohs
Warhammer
Witch Hunt
Ysgarth

GENERIC SETTINGS
City State of the Invincible Overlord
Harn
Haven
Role Aids
Shadow World
Thieves' World

GIANT ROBOTS
MechWarrior
Mekton II
Robotech
Robot Warriors
Sentinels

HORROR
Beyond the Supernatural
Call of Cthulhu
Chill
Stalking the Night Fantastic

HUMOR
Bullwinkle and Rocky

Critter Commandos
Ghostbusters
Ghostbusters International
It Came from the Late Late Late Show
Macho Women with Guns
Paranoia
Teenagers from Outer Space
Toon
Twerps

LIVE ACTION
IFGS Fantasy Rules
Swordtag

MILITARY
Behind Enemy Lines
Delta Force
Freedom Fighters
Merc
Phoenix Command
Price of Freedom
Recon

ORIENTAL
Bushido
Land of the Rising Sun
Oriental Adventures

POSTAPOCALYPTIC
Aftermath
Deepsleep
Gamma World
The Morrow Project
Twilight: 2000

PULP HEROES
Daredevils
Indiana Jones

Justice Inc.

SCIENCE FICTION
Book of Mars
Cyborg Commando
Doctor Who
Domination
Element Masters
Expendables
Fringeworthy
FTL: 2448
Future Worlds
High Colonies
Judge Dredd
Justifiers
Living Steel
Mach
Manhunter
Mechanoids
Megatraveller
Metamorphosis Alpha
Midnight at the Well of Souls
Morpheus
Mutazoids
Ninjas and Superspies
Other Suns
Psi World
Reich Star
Ringworld
Skyrealms of Jorune
Space: 1889
Space Master
Space Opera
Star Ace
Star Frontiers
Star Hero
Star Trek
Star Wars

Traders of the Far Reach
Traveller
Traveller: 2300
2300 A.D.
Year of the Phoenix

SUPERHEROES
Batman
Champions
DC Heroes
Enforcers
Golden Heroes
Heroes Unlimited
Marvel Super Heroes
Masters of the Universe
Super Squadron
Supervillains
Superworld
Villains and Vigilantes

SWASHBUCKLERS
En Garde
Flashing Blades
Muskateers
Pirates and Plunder
Privateers and Gentlemen
Skull and Crossbones

TIME TRAVEL
Time and Time Again
Timelords
Timemaster
Timeship

UNIVERSAL
Eternal Soldier
GURPS
Multiverse

To Challenge Tomorrow
Worlds of Wonder

WESTERN
Boot Hill
Wild West